Cream Teas, Traffic Jams and Sunburn

Cream Teas, Traffic Jams and Sunburn

The Great British Holiday

BRIAN VINER

SIMON &
SCHUSTER

London · New York · Sydney · Toronto

A CBS COMPANY

First published in Great Britain by Simon & Schuster UK Ltd, 2011
A CBS COMPANY

1 3 5 7 9 10 8 6 4 2

Simon & Schuster UK Ltd
1st Floor
222 Gray's Inn Road
London
WC1X 8HB

www.simonandschuster.co.uk

Simon & Schuster Australia
Sydney

A CIP catalogue for this book
is available from the British Library.

ISBN: 978-1-84737-726-5

Typeset by M Rules
Printed in the UK by CPI Mackays, Chatham ME5 8TD

For my parents-in-law
Anne and Bob Sanderson
sandwich queen and sandcastle king

Contents

Prologue

The British on holiday: how can four simple words evoke so many vivid images, images of raw sunburn and relentless rain, of John Bull's Pub (in Lanzarote) and Antonio's Tapas Bar (in Torquay), of endless queues to get through security at Manchester Airport, or Gatwick, or Glasgow, or Luton, and endless tailbacks on the M5, or M6, or M25, but also images of carefree sploshing in Portuguese swimming-pools and lazy lunches in the Provençal sun?

This book celebrates the holidaying British, with their quirks and their quinine tablets, and their blithe assumption that the elderly man selling oranges at the roadside in Corfu, so photogenic with his walnut face and three teeth, must surely understand just a few, uncomplicated English sentences. It examines the fortnight-long cruise at one end of the holiday spectrum, and a day's rambling in the Lake District at the other. It looks at how the holidaying British evolved into the big-spending, many-headed beast we know today, by recalling not only the holidays that we took as children, but the holidays our grandparents, and their grandparents, took. It is a story that connects Thomas Cook, a devout Baptist from Derbyshire, born in 1808, with the South African-born Sir William Heygate Edmund Colborne Butlin, mercifully known as Billy. It is a story that connects Blackpool with Barcelona, Mauritius with Margate. It is a story, indeed, that connects you with me.

The first half of this book addresses the phenomenon of the British holidaying in Britain. It is a growing phenomenon, while the holiday abroad, perhaps surprisingly in this age of low-budget airlines, is on the decline. Meanwhile, there are more than 20 million of us who holiday only in Britain, which seems remarkable, given the proximity of countries such as France and Spain, and the comparative cheapness of getting there. Are there any other people anywhere in the world who spend their precious holidays within 100 miles or so of home, among their own kind, speaking their own language, yet rendered as wide-eyed and flummoxed by local customs or accents as if they were in the foothills of the Andes?

I have some insight into this because we have two small holiday cottages attached to our home in rural Herefordshire, and it is not unusual for visitors from Birmingham, scarcely fifty miles away, to return to their cottage from a trip into nearby Leominster in a state of wonder, rather as you might expect folk to return to their hotels on the banks of the Zambezi River having just seen the Victoria Falls for the first time, except that what has astounded these Brummies is Leominster's policy of half-day closing.

Needless to add, one shouldn't generalize. Some Brits take half-day closing in Leominster, or indeed their first sight of the Victoria Falls, perfectly in their stride. One shouldn't write about the British on holiday as if they are a single coach-party writ large, which is why this book is divided into so many chapters, but in some of them, I hope, you will find some truths about yourself, your family, or at the very least Mr and Mrs Perkins from across the road, inveterate caravan enthusiasts, or Mr and Mrs Babcock from the sub-post office, seasoned naturists.

PART ONE

The British in Britain

1

Bandstands, bastards and Barnstaple

I grew up beside the seaside, although not beside the sea. Southport, located in Lancashire when I was a small boy but rudely shifted into Merseyside by the 1974 municipal boundary changes, is a handsome, genteel Victorian resort on the southern banks of the Ribble estuary, seventeen miles north of Liverpool and fifteen miles south-west of Preston. In his 1983 book *The Kingdom by the Sea*, the American travel writer Paul Theroux described Southport as condescendingly as only a man from Massachusetts in round tortoiseshell glasses can, as a place containing 'gritty northern splendour' but also a great number of elderly people, adding 'to Southport's atmosphere of feebleness and senility'. This is monstrously unfair, a calumny for which any self-respecting, ablebodied Sandgrounder should feel entitled, even now, to bop him on the nose.

Sandgrounder is the marvellous name for natives of Southport,

3

which regrettably I am not, quite, having moved there (with a bit of help) when I was just over a fortnight old. The name is decidedly apt, because the place has a great deal of sand. The incoming tide invariably has a half-hearted, almost apologetic air about it, as if it lost all its confidence on the journey over from Ireland; indeed the beach often seems to meet the horizon without any intervening water, causing local wags, of whom there are a great many, to quip that Southport inspired the saying 'Long time no sea'.

Paul Theroux typically laced his assessment of Southport's sealessness with a sneer. 'When the tide was down, the beach was a long ludicrous desert,' he wrote, 'but flatter than any desert I had seen. Cars drove across it. The pier was high and dry. The sun at 9.30pm seemed to be setting at the far end of Egypt.' In fairness, he had a point, and by now you probably get the picture. To enjoy a worthwhile paddle in Southport you either need to be unusually short, or possessed of unusual stamina.

But that didn't stop the town's steady growth as a holiday resort in the nineteenth century, and although Southport's golden age was emphatically over by the time I was growing up there, in the 1960s and 1970s, I still had to get used to sharing its broad pavements with day-trippers and sometimes dedicated holidaymakers from Liverpool, Manchester and beyond. Some of them even knew what I knew: that Woolworths on Chapel Street was the best place for a spot of casual shoplifting. The comedian Jenny Eclair, formerly plain Jenny Hargreaves and eighteen months older than me, told me many years later that she used to travel all the way to Southport from her home in posh Lytham St Annes, on the opposite bank of the Ribble estuary, such were the easy pickings in the Chapel Street branch of Woolies. But let's not get sidetracked by lax security around the pick 'n' mix. The fact is that my Southport childhood afforded me a regular and vivid glimpse into the myriad traditions and conventions of the English seaside holiday, some of them truly strange, such as the Punch and Judy show, at which children were expected to laugh their socks off while a hook-nosed hunchback beat up his wife.

Another that springs arbitrarily but pleasingly to mind is the knickerbocker glory. For much of my childhood, no two words in tandem excited me quite as much as knickerbocker and glory, at least not until I was old enough to appreciate the image conjured by the words Raquel and Welch. There are conflicting theories as to the origins of the name knickerbocker glory. That impressively authoritative but frequently inaccurate source Wikipedia boringly suggests that it derives its name from knickerbockers, 'a type of long trouser traditionally worn by young children (but particularly young boys)', with the word glory reflecting 'the typical reaction of a child presented with such a dessert'.

This, just to introduce another kind of food to the equation, is quite clearly baloney. How many children, even in the early decades of the last century, would ever have instinctively cried 'Glory!' on being given a dish of ice-cream, fruit and jelly? I am reminded of the explanation given in my dictionary for the word 'ha-ha', which pops up in several of Jane Austen's novels meaning a kind of walled ditch, sunken into the ground so that it can act as a fence without breaking the flow of the landscape, and which apparently owes its name to 'the typical exclamation of surprise on coming across such an unexpected obstacle'. Yet if that were really true, a ha-ha would more likely be called a 'bugger me', and by the same logic a knickerbocker glory would surely be a 'knickerbocker wow', or a 'knickerbocker yum'? And in any case, why name a dessert after an item of clothing?

Whatever, the first recorded mention of what was then a plain knickerbocker appears to have been in the recipe book of a New York soda dispenser, in 1915. The original recipe rather exotically combined ice-cream with chocolate syrup, crushed raspberries, whipped cream, rose essence and brandied cherries, all of which were layered in a tall sundae glass. By the time I had my first knickerbocker glory, *circa* 1967 at Rossi's ice-cream parlour in Nevill Street, Southport, it had become a considerably more prosaic affair, heavily reliant on the tinned fruit cocktail. That didn't mean it wasn't a big treat, but it wasn't quite the treat it was for my wife Jane, when she was a little girl holidaying with her sister and parents at Flamborough on the Yorkshire coast.

Growing up in Southport meant being indulged with classic seaside-holiday treats, like a trip to the beach or the funfair, or to the amusement arcades on the pier, or indeed a knickerbocker glory, once every two or three months, rather than once a year. But for Jane these were annual treats, with an accordingly revered status in her memories of childhood.

She grew up near Barnsley in the South Yorkshire coalfields, and so the once-a-year family trip to the seaside assumed momentous significance. On their last day at Flamborough, where every year they stayed in a caravan until their parents were affluent enough to afford lodgings at a pub called the North Star, Jane and her older sister Jackie would be allowed the knicker-bocker glory they had craved since the day of arrival. Then, when every last drop of melted ice-cream and tinned fruit-cocktail syrup had been drained, when every last hundred and thousand had been dabbed from the inside of the sundae dish with a wet finger, they were allowed across the road to a gift shop, where they pooled their spending-money to buy their mum and dad a meaningful souvenir of the holiday. And so it was every year that a small owl encrusted in winkle shells, or something similarly tasteful, would inexorably find its way to the mantelpiece above the glass-fronted solid-fuel fire back in Hoyland Common. Incidentally, it was only by prodding Jane's memories of the Flamborough knickerbocker glories that I unlocked her memory of the winkle-encrusted owl. Marcel Proust would have been proud of me.

Of course, there is no law decreeing that knickerbocker glories can only be consumed at the seaside. But it is to the seaside that they unequivocally belong. Moreover, to the buttoned-up British, that most extravagant-looking of ice-cream sundaes has always carried the whiff of decadence that we all need, occasionally, on our holidays. In 1937 one was even cited in a court case, when a Mr Devlin sued a Mr Cooper for enticing his wife away from him, and the prosecution produced an incriminating letter from Mrs Devlin to Mr Cooper, saying 'Do you remember when we went there together and had a knickerbocker glory?'

In 1938, a year after the cuckolded Mr Devlin cut up rough, mandatory holiday pay was introduced in Britain via the nobly intentioned Holiday With Pay Act. Holiday-savings clubs were promptly set up in factories all over the country, while the Labour Party grandees Clement Attlee and Harold Laski even organized a committee to subsidize holidays for the jobless 'to get away from the misery and drabness of their everyday lives'. For those in work, some enlightened employers had done the decent thing already. Workers at the Rowntree's factory in York first enjoyed a week's annual holiday on full pay as far back as 1918, albeit eight full years after the company's more urgent introduction of the Walnut Whip. But once the entire country was entitled to paid leave, seaside holidays proliferated. By the end of the 1930s, 15 million people a year were spending at least a week at the seaside, and I should think it almost certain that it was the seaside where Mrs Devlin and Mr Cooper enjoyed their illicit liaison.

If so, we can be sure that there was also some canoodling by a bandstand. All English seaside resorts worth their salt air have at least one bandstand. Southport's was shaped like a giant version of those Iced Gem biscuits the origins of which, I might just tell you as an aside, can be traced all the way back to 1850, when the biscuit barons Thomas Huntley and George Palmer gave the thumbs-up to a batch of biscuits that inexplicably emerged from the oven somewhat on the tiny side. In 1910, somebody in the factory had the bright idea of piping a little swirl of coloured icing on to them.

Anyway, around the time that Huntley and Palmer were first marketing their accidentally tiny biscuits, the railway reached Southport from Liverpool, and five years later, from Manchester. The town was suddenly accessible to Lancashire's congested industrial heartland and it needed to offer all those mill workers something in the way of entertainment. A bandstand was built to accommodate another new-fangled invention, the brass band.

An enthusiasm for brass bands was at first confined to the north of England, the cradle of the Industrial Revolution, and within the north of England, specifically to the working classes. More refined northerners did not care for it, and the factory-owning classes in Lancashire and Yorkshire could be positively withering about the musical tastes of their workers. Thomas Beecham, born in St Helens in 1879 into the Beecham's pills fortune, and later to found the London Philharmonic Orchestra, loftily observed that 'brass bands are all very well in their place . . . outdoors and several miles away'. And that from a man who owed his comfortable start in life to a laxative. Still, he was only trying to be witty, and since he also splendidly said that everyone should try everything once except folk dancing and incest, we can forgive him. He also tends to be cited in dictionaries of quotations as the conductor who supposedly stopped a lady cellist in rehearsal with the memorable reproach: 'Madam, you have between your legs a magnificent instrument, capable of bringing pleasure to thousands, and all you can do is scratch it.' But his biographer loyally ascribes that to the more vulgar Henry Wood, founder of the promenade concerts.

Gradually, brass bands began to grow in popularity even outside the north of England, and by the mid-1930s many British seaside resorts had second-generation bandstands, streamlined art deco replacing ornate Victoriana. Like the knickerbocker glory, bandstands were not restricted to the seaside, but it is to the seaside that they too spiritually belonged, harbouring the rosy-cheeked worthies of the Salvation Army band enthusiastically puffing their way through 'A Nightingale Sang in Berkeley Square', accompanied by more raucous songbirds in the form of screeching, wheeling seagulls, while elderly holidaymakers in sensible hats and mackintoshes dozed in deckchairs.

The deckchair is linked almost umbilically to the bandstand, and reclined contentedly in one of them, when I turn my mind's eye to my seaside childhood, is my late grandmother. My grandma lived in Southgate, north London, and having been widowed since the early 1960s she used to come to stay with us in Southport for four or five weeks every year. I was an only child, and with both my parents working every day in Liverpool – where my mum re-packed ladies' underwear that my dad had bought direct from the manufacturers, with a view to selling it on to small department stores and market traders – my welfare was very often her responsibility until I became old enough to look after myself during the school holidays. I suppose my memory might be wrong-footing me, but between the ages of about five and nine, as I recall it, I went with my grandma every summer's day for a walk on the promenade and a sit by the bandstand, before catching the number 17 bus home together.

I can't remember ever doing anything more fun with her, like playing pitch-and-putt, or renting a motor boat on Marine Lake (at the time the largest man-made lake in Europe, so every

9

Southport schoolchild was told). But at least these regular excursions to the bandstand offered me an early understanding of Britain's holiday culture, for my grandma would almost always fall into conversation with other old people who were spending a week at the seaside, and I came to see Southport through their rheumy eyes, as an annual tonic from their unexciting lives in landlocked Levenshulme or Llangollen. I didn't, like that bastard Paul Theroux, conclude dyspeptically that Southport was perforce full of the elderly, the feeble and the senile. On the contrary, the pleasure my grandmother's superannuated acquaintances drew from my town all but made my little white chest burst with proprietorial pride.

Living at the seaside, however, did not stop my parents from taking me on holiday to places that represented, in that curious phrase, a home away from home. I have never quite understood why the discovery of 'a home away from home' on a holiday should be interpreted as a positive thing, when surely the whole point is to leave home well behind. But one summer we went to Largs in Ayrshire, which was more or less to Glasgow what Southport was to Liverpool and Manchester, and for Whitsun half-term in 1968 we went to Barnstaple in Devon, another resort redolent of home (and 'a slightly frumpish, down-at-heel town', according to the ever-critical Theroux).

It is a holiday I can confidently date because at the end of it, on the interminable drive north in our gold (in truth a rather muted yellow) Vauxhall Viva, some news suddenly broke over the car radio that was deemed important enough for the BBC to interrupt Cliff Richard merrily singing 'Congratulations', the UK's entry for that year's Eurovision Song Contest. Abruptly cutting into Cliff's message that he wanted the world to know he was as happy as could be came the news that the US Democratic Party's likely presidential candidate Robert F. Kennedy had been shot, possibly fatally (as it duly proved), in the Ambassador Hotel in Los Angeles. Even if Cliff was as happy as could be, the world manifestly wasn't, and the news flash had a bewilderingly dramatic effect on my mother and father. My dad pulled the car into a lay-by where they listened in grave and I think even tearful disbelief.

Hushed into silence on the back seat, I was aware, aged six, that something terrible had happened. I also knew that the bad news from the distant United States about this Kennedy fellow put the tin lid, or however I might have framed that thought at the age of six, on a really miserable week. It had rained relentlessly in Barnstaple, falling not even in a steady drizzle, but in merciless sheets. In the hotel bedroom I shared with my parents, I actually attempted to relieve the desperate boredom one afternoon by cutting off clumps of my own hair, for which I received a sharp smack from my mother, adding physical pain to the uncomfortable sudden realization that on one side of my head I had rendered myself almost completely bald.

I'm pretty sure that anyone who has grown up holidaying at the English seaside has at least one place that is enduringly synonymous with abject monotony and misery. For my friend Becky, for example, that place is Ottery St Mary which, may the county's tourist board forgive me, is also in Devon. She remembers going there for a week in the 1970s and her dad repeatedly saying, 'If it rains once more, we're going home'. On the Wednesday, half-way through the holiday, it rained once more, and off they went. Becky has never returned to Ottery St Mary. For me, though, Barnstaple is the name that conjures up that image of rain hammering the window pane when you go to bed at night, and still hammering it when you wake up in the morning. It was a demon I tried to slay in the summer of 2009 when I went back to Barnstaple for the first time in forty-one years, but guess what? It pissed down.

2

Sun, sandcastles and surf dudes

The epic unreliability of the British weather means that only repeated annual visits to a seaside resort can be sure to yield at least some memories of fun-filled, sunny days, which is why my wife Jane has grown up with so many fond recollections of those holidays in Flamborough, and why, once we were parents ourselves, we took our children to Constantine Bay near Padstow on the north coast of Cornwall, staying in the same room in the same hotel for the same ten days every summer for ten successive years, and pitching the same windbreak in the same spot on the same beach every morning at the same time. Creatures of habit? Not at all. Sometimes we paid someone at the hotel to make our sandwiches, sometimes we made them ourselves.

What is it, incidentally, with the British and windbreaks? Bill Bryson, another American travel writer, has observed with his trademark acerbic wit that if you need to shelter from the wind, maybe it's not such a great idea to be on the beach in the first place. But then the Iowa-raised Bryson, by his own admission, doesn't even begin to understand the British attachment to the seaside. In a column in the *Independent* in 1999, he presented a very funny, very sarcastic account of how, before they moved from old England to New England, his wife might enthusiastically suggest a visit to the coast. This was how he cruelly paraphrased her suggestion.

'We'll get sand in our hair. We'll get sand in our shoes. We'll get sand in our sandwiches and then in our mouths. We'll get sunburned and windburned. And when we get tired of sitting, we can have a paddle in water so cold it actually hurts. At the end of the day, we'll set off at the same time as 37,000 other people and get in such a traffic jam that we won't get home till midnight. I can make trenchant observations about your driving, and the children can pass the time sticking each other with sharp objects. It will be such fun.'

The tragic thing is that because my wife is English, and therefore beyond the reach of reason where saltwater is concerned, she really will think it's fun.

I'm firmly on Mrs Bryson's side, but I can see how we must look to incomers. I suppose it's something to do with us being an island nation that the seaside appeals to us so. In the United States and even larger European countries such as France there must be plenty of people who have never set foot on a beach, but in Britain paddling in the sea is practically a birthright. Not that this was so before the invention of the railway and subsequently the motorcar. When the novelist Charlotte Brontë first set eyes on the sea in the mid-nineteenth century she was described by a companion as 'quite over-powered, she could not speak till she had shed some tears . . . she made stern efforts to subdue her emotions . . . for the remainder of the day she was very quiet, subdued and exhausted.'

Which sounds more like the reaction of a person who has been flashed at than one who has seen the sea for the first time, but then the Brontës were sensitive creatures, and it was understandably a big day for her.

At around the same time that Charlotte Brontë was making stern efforts to subdue her emotions, a canny entrepreneur called Thomas Cook was chartering a train for his first commercial excursion, from Leicester to Loughborough, just eleven miles away. It was 5 July 1841, and though even Thomas Cook can hardly have suspected such a thing, the very dawn of the era of mass tourism. Not that, if he had known it, he would have raised a celebratory glass of frothing ale. Cook was a fierce campaigner on behalf of the Temperance Society, and even found time to edit the *Children's Temperance Magazine*, a high-minded publication for 'the instruction and amusement of little teetotallers', some of whom accompanied him to Loughborough that day.

Loughborough was the perfect destination for Cook's pioneering day-trippers – almost 600 of them – because they, like him, were signatories of the temperance pledge and Loughborough was dry, so entire families could go without fear of meeting drunkards. Which is not, it has to be said, a guaranteed prospect on Britain's railways today. And let it not be whispered anywhere near Thomas Cook's grave in Welford Road cemetery, Leicester, but modern Loughborough houses all those sports-science students, drinking Guinness and crème-de-menthe cocktails strained through the rugby captain's jockstrap.

Anyway, Cook quickly realized that he had to strike out beyond pious Loughborough, and started organizing trips to the seaside, which was already a popular destination among the gentry and aristocracy, and had been so since the mid-seventeenth century, when a Lewes doctor called Richard Russell wrote a pamphlet with the catchy title, 'A Dissertation on the use of Sea Water in the Diseases of the Glands, particularly the Scurvy, Jaundice, King's-Evil, Leprosy and the Glandular Consumption'. The transformation of Brighton from a sleepy fishing-village to a cosmopolitan resort favoured by royalty owed a great deal, if not everything, to Dr Russell's endorsement of seawater, and in 1817, in her unfinished novel *Sanditon*, Jane Austen gently mocked those who believed that a seaside visit could cure any ill.

'The sea air and sea bathing together were nearly infallible,' she wrote, 'one or other of them being a match for every disorder of the stomach, the lungs or the blood. They were anti-spasmodic, anti-pulmonary, anti-septic, anti-bilious and anti-rheumatic. Nobody could catch cold by the sea; nobody wanted [for] appetite by the sea; nobody wanted spirits; nobody wanted strength.'

Not until the railways came along, though, did ordinary folk from inland Britain get a regular taste of that bracing sea air, and it took Thomas Cook to organize them properly. His first trip to the seaside was from Leicester to New Brighton, on the Wirral peninsula, in 1845. The following year he took his rail-trippers to Fleetwood in Lancashire, then on a steamer to Ardrossan on the Firth of Clyde, where they got back on a train and chuffed into Glasgow, to be greeted, such was the significance of the occasion, by the city's brass band. Soon enough, tourists were a regular sight around Britain, no longer considered a sufficiently big deal for the local brass band to turn out. Once the Bank Holidays Act of 1871 (of which more later in these pages) had enshrined full public holidays at Whitsun and over the first weekend in August, organized excursions to the seaside in particular were commonplace. By the turn of the twentieth century most working-class folk in even the most landlocked towns knew what it felt like to feel cool seaside sand between their toes.

And so back to sand. It might get into every nook and cranny, as the beach heretic Bill Bryson points out, but beaches, in my humble opinion, are greatly diminished without it. Maybe it's because I grew up in Southport that I cleave unapologetically to the view that a beach made of pebbles is not a proper beach. That obligatory newspaper photograph of tens of thousands of trippers packed on to Brighton beach every August bank-holiday weekend (English weather permitting) is an annual source of puzzled wonder to me.

Obviously, the proximity of Brighton to London and the conurbations of the south-east is one explanation for the bank-holiday madness, but as a general rule of thumb, applicable pretty much all over the world, the less accessible beaches are also the best beaches. Take the beach at Constantine Bay in Cornwall, which at the height of summer is a three-hour drive or there-abouts even from Bristol, the nearest large city. It is just about the finest beach I know, the kind of beach that belongs on the front of one of Enid Blyton's Famous Five books, forever stuck in the 1950s, a beach of kite-flying and French cricket and sandcastles and rock-pooling, separated by a range of weather-beaten dunes from Trevose, one of England's classic golf links, fashioned as much by the prevailing wind as by the great golf-course architect Harry Colt.

I should add that Constantine Bay in the summer also has a thriving teen culture, which is not very 1950s, although we stopped going to Cornwall when our eldest child, our daughter Eleanor, was fourteen, not yet old enough to join the surf dudes holding debauched beach parties after dark. And debauched they plainly were. There was one summer when all the local beaches were closed at ten p.m. on account of the detritus found on the sand the following morning. Flotsam, jetsam and Litesomes. Enid Blyton would have been horrified.

For us, the beach meant more wholesome family activities, like watching other families' wholesome family activities. The British on holiday are great, if covert, people-watchers, and Constantine Bay is marvellous for people-watching. I suppose all popular British beaches are on a sunny summer's day, but the presence of those surf dudes lends an extra dimension; lithe, toned, tanned youngsters striding purposefully to the shore past acres of sunburnt blubber; humanity in its many and varied forms. And of course, while it's unacceptably sizeist to make muttered asides about elephantine women laboriously changing into frilly blue sundresses, it is also irresistible. I can remember us all watching in silence one summer as this particular spectacle unfolded fifty yards or so away, and then my father-in-law, Bob, quietly informed us what his late mother Nellie, born and bred in Hoyland Common, would have remarked had she been with us. 'She'll tek some britchin'.'

My parents-in-law went with us to Cornwall every August, throughout the years when, just as every beach holiday needed buckets and spades and factor-50 suncream, so it also needed a grandma and a granddad. Even when they are grandparents themselves my kids will remember Bob's sandcastles: enormous yet intricate, with forbidding dungeons and slate staircases and windows framed with empty mussel shells. To their painstaking construction he brought all the skills he had acquired in nigh on fifty years as a mining engineer, although his castles were not classic English crenellated jobs but more like Saracen fortresses, invulnerable to all infidels but not, alas, to the incoming tide.

As it happens I had never given much thought to the design of sandcastles until we had a beach holiday in the New England state of Maine the summer before we started going to Cornwall. That was when we realized that American children, and their fathers and grandfathers (for there as here it is principally a male undertaking), build sandcastles wholly inspired by Disney. They have a different technique entirely, fashioning tall, improbable towers by carefully drizzling wet sand, until they have created a structure which might conceivably, in a young imagination, house Sleeping Beauty.

The European sandcastle tradition is more historically and architecturally accurate, clearly based on the fact that, unlike the Americans, we never needed Uncle Walt to show us what castles look like. Not that Bob has ever visited any Saracen fortresses, but had there been any passing Saracens in Constantine Bay I'm sure they would have vouched for the authenticity of his constructions. And after he'd applied the finishing touches, usually with a preter-naturally steady hand, a keen eye for geometry and a lolly stick, our children were able to put on proprietorial airs just as, in different circumstances, I had as a child, alongside the pensioners by the bandstand in Southport.

The completion of one of Bob's sandcastles was always an event on Constantine Bay beach, with other children bringing their parents and grandparents over to look, admire, and indeed envy. Envy is an emotion often harboured by the British on holiday. I have encountered muscle envy, flat-tummy envy, swimsuit envy, tan envy, Ray-Ban envy, picnic envy, bucket-and-spade envy, kite envy, even flip-flop envy, and while I can't honestly claim to have been the object of any of the above, that's not so of sandcastle envy. I preened no less than the children as strangers crowded round Bob's monoliths, even though I'd had only a junior role as assistant turret engineer.

In our ten consecutive summers at Constantine Bay I also saw a burgeoning encampment envy, as people, including ourselves, became more and more sophisticated in the ways they set up for the day. Where simple windbreaks had once been enough, the tent-and-windbreak combo gradually gathered in popularity, and by the time we spent our last holiday there in August 2007, the tent-windbreak-brick-built-barbecue combo seemed to be catching on. If we ever go back, then I fully expect to find the tent-windbreak-barbecue-Portaloo combo. It can only be a matter of time.

And yet for all the growing sophistication of the encampments, the beauty of the beach at Constantine Bay, of any great beach, lies in its simplicity. Ultimately, what the British are after on holiday are simple pleasures, the more so for those who have left complicated, stress-filled lives behind, which frankly is most of us.

At Constantine Bay the most effective antidotes to stress come in the form of a £2.95 fishing net and a £3.50 bucket. Every summer its rock pools are full of lawyers, stockbrokers and captains of industry, metaphorical big fish in literal small ponds, carefully parting fronds of seaweed in search of those ever-elusive Cornish crabs. You sometimes see them muttering to themselves, all their cares and worries condensed into the quest for a crab bigger than the one they caught the day before. Usually they have kids with them, but quite often not. After all, the measure of a good beach is one on which we can all regress to childhood. One sunny day during the sporadically warm summer of 2004 I quite lost myself with my sons Joe and Jacob playing a game of cowboys and Indians in the dunes, to the extent that I spent an hour shuffling on my belly through spiky grass, cradling a piece of driftwood that, in my head, had become a Model 1873 Winchester rifle, only, suddenly and embarrassingly, to spot my boys, who had got bored but hadn't bothered to let me know, back on the beach playing Frisbee.

Still, I made a virtue of the spectacle by hauling myself upright in the dunes, insouciantly shrugging off the concern that I was making myself an unmissable target for any passing Apache brave, and watching them from afar, marvelling at the way in which my sons were inextricably part of, and yet completely insulated from, everything else happening on the beach. I was reminded that what I love most about a fine, versatile English beach on a warm summer's day is the extraordinary variety of unfolding activities: the games of Frisbee, cricket, football, paddle-tennis, catch, piggy-in-the-middle, children burying their dads up to their heads in sand, dads making sand racing cars and rowing-boats for their kids; the kite-flying, rock-pooling, sandcastle-building and paddling; the windbreak-erecting, sandwich-making and barbecuing; the walks back and forth to the car, the loo, the ice-cream van; the arguments, the tears, the laughter. Not to mention the people wriggling into swimsuits under towels only just big enough to cover their private parts, a triumph of modesty over flexibility at which the British excel. If climbing into a swimsuit under a towel were an Olympic sport, we'd be guaranteed a gold medal every four years. Anyway, the point is that I have stood on beaches all over the world and never seen a comparable kaleidoscope of activity.

And I haven't even mentioned the water sports, which brings me to the lifeguards, who increasingly on English beaches seem to be Australasian. At Constantine one year I got chatting to an Antipodean Adonis, and I can recall being grateful that my daughter alongside me was only ten at the time. Eight or nine years later and I might have had to talk sternly to him about his future prospects. As it was, as it is, he and his ilk are an immensely reassuring presence at Constantine and lots of other English beaches, muscular young men, and occasionally women, standing knee-high in the surf good-naturedly directing people away from the deadly riptides. In August 2006 I even saw two of them leap impressively into action, when a distraught mother wailed that she had lost five-year-old Oliver.

The distraught mother is another staple of the English seaside holiday, no less than buckets, spades, and the family from Runcorn with matching doses of boiled-lobster sunburn. I put my own mother through it, aged four, going AWOL for two hours on the beach at Mudeford in Dorset. And whenever I see a lost-child drama unfolding, I am always reminded of the scene in *Jaws*, when a woman goes tearing along the beach, frantically calling her son's name. When a similar scene occurs in real life, unless it is happening to us, I am unfailingly struck by the positively filmic counterpoint that I suppose also appealed to the *Jaws* director Steven Spielberg – 99.9 per cent of people on the beach having a perfectly lovely time, 0.1 per cent having a total nightmare. Happily, as in almost every instance, and like me in Mudeford, Oliver was found that day, safe and sound.

Yet it's worth noting that we suffer a proportionately higher number of lost-children crises, accidents and mishaps, when we are on holiday than when we were are at home. The novelist Louise Doughty, a former colleague of mine, has written evocatively about being lost for hours during a caravan holiday in Devon when she was eleven, in 1974. She'd had a blazing row with her older brother and stormed off the caravan site, only to find herself befuddled by those country lanes with their towering hedgerows. At home in the Midlands she'd have trudged round the neighbourhood for a while, sulking, then returned to the bosom of the family. But holidays are different. In Devon she walked on and on, at one point accepting a lift from a couple in 'a large silver car' – an innocuous enough description yet one that sounds so sinister in the context of a lost child.

Thankfully, like the vast majority of strangers even now, an era in which we are sometimes encouraged to think that paedophiles stalk every country lane, every beach, every municipal swimming-pool, the couple had only good intentions. They dropped her in the village nearest the caravan site, but she still didn't find her way back there until long after dark. Her parents were searching frantically for her, but, it being 1974, hadn't yet called the police.

Nonetheless, her disappearance left them traumatized. For decades afterwards, any reference to the incident made Louise's parents blanch and give one another 'the sort of looks war veterans might exchange in the company of civilians'.

Then as now, almost all children who go missing on holiday are found. Anecdotally, of course, it seems otherwise, because the found-safe-and-sound stories are nowhere near as dramatic as tales such as that of Ben Needham, who was not yet two when he went missing during a family holiday on the Greek island of Kos, in 1991, and at the time of writing has never been found.

As for poor Madeleine McCann and her stricken family, I'll mention them only once in this book, but it might as well be here. Had they been at home in Leicestershire, the McCanns would never have left their children in the house alone. Many people have self-righteously said that they shouldn't have done so on holiday, either. Yet it makes a certain kind of grim sense that when we are at our most relaxed, we are also at our most vulnerable. My heart went out to the McCanns not least because in 2000, also on the Iberian peninsula, we had suffered what might easily have been a similarly devastating family tragedy, when Jane and I took our eyes off two-year-old Jacob just long enough for him to topple headfirst out of an open restaurant window, 40ft above rocks.

But that's a story for the second half of this book. For now we're staying beside the English seaside, and I can scarcely believe that it has taken me two chapters to get to the *sine qua non* of any book featuring English seaside resorts; the place, indeed, that puts the 'sin' into *sine qua non*. Come with me to Blackpool.

3

Blackpool, big dippers and boarding-houses

In 1937, an organization called Mass Observation was founded by a group of cosmopolitan, leftish intellectuals. They fancied themselves as a kind of new social movement, but at the top of their manifesto was an undertaking to document everyday behaviour in Britain in as much detail as possible, which bizarrely included pretending to be drunk and 'accidentally' tripping over amorous couples doing their heavy petting outdoors, to find out exactly where they were putting their fingers. Where better to do that than Blackpool, visited that year alone by 7 million people, which in 1937 amounted to almost a sixth of Britain's population?

Blackpool, it was felt, would yield valuable anthropological material about the working classes on holiday, so that is where

Mass Observation conducted its first and most ambitious survey. It is thanks to this splendid initiative that we know that, on Blackpool beach in the half-hour before midnight on one perfectly standard evening in 1937, twenty-three official observers found 120 couples embracing while sitting down, 46 embracing while lying down, and 42 while standing up. There were 25 recorded cases of sitting and kissing, 3 cases of standing and kissing, 9 cases of necking in cars, and 7 cases of girls sitting on men's knees.

Among these randy couples, quite possibly, were our old friends Mrs Devlin and Mr Cooper, for it was in that same year of 1937 that the court case citing a shared knickerbocker glory was brought by Mrs Devlin's angry husband. But Blackpool was not quite the Sodom or Gomorrah that the Mass Observation operatives imagined. One of the observers later remarked, with what we can only hope was an air of disappointment, that 'when we began work in Blackpool we expected to find copulation everywhere. What we found was petting and feeling ... with only three cases of full penetration.' Shame.

Oddly, the Mass Observation team was helped by a culture of what we know now as dogging. According to their report: 'Watchers are not youths only. For older men of scoptophilic tendencies, the sands at night are a happy hunting ground. Whenever a couple get down on the sands in the dark shadows of the Central Pier, they very quickly have a ring of silent staring individuals around them less than two yards away, apparently immune from rebuke. This tolerance naturally helped observers in their study.'

I think it's probably fair to assume that one if not two or three or even more of the Mass Observation chappies were almost as excited as the scoptophiles (a Greek word, unsurprisingly enough, meaning those who gain pleasure from watching others have sex). At any rate it is solemnly recorded that one of them ended up boosting his own statistics, catching the eye of a saucy young woman on the promenade and putting his clipboard aside for a quick knee-trembler.

Already the seaside was considered a place of lax morals, thanks largely to the saucy postcards drawn by the great Donald McGill, whose innuendo-laden humour – 'Do you like Kipling?' 'I don't know, you naughty boy, I've never kippled' – anticipated and perhaps even paved the way for the *Carry On* films. By 1937 the alfresco smooch or fumble was a Blackpool speciality no less than McGill's postcards and sticks of rock (first fashioned by Ben Bullock, a Dewsbury sugar-boiler, following a holiday in Blackpool in 1887). And like the rock, it was something less readily available at home. The Mass Observation report concluded that: 'Both men and women go to Blackpool for the things they cannot get at home – oysters, sleep, sea air, the Big Dipper, (George) Formby in person, a first-rate dance band, variety, and no factory. The tension of sex, often as severe as the tensions of time, money and work, is a thing from which for one week you try to get away. The random pick-up, a new one each day, and the surface satisfaction it provides, apparently keeps the tension under control.'

This reminds me, incidentally, of a lad I was at school with across the Ribble estuary in Southport in the late 1970s, who when we reached the sixth form sometimes used to give me a lift to school in his battered old van, at least until the day that he fixed a green plastic strip across the top of the windscreen, bearing in large white lettering the bold message 'Sex relieves tension'. I took the bus after that.

Still, all credit to him for sticking to his guns, and quite possibly his sheets. He was teased mercilessly but kept the sign on his windscreen for months, ever hopeful of losing his virginity, which by now I suppose he has done. Forty years earlier he might have sought satisfaction in nearby Blackpool. A hundred years before that, however, Southport was still Lancashire's premier seaside resort. Even after the railway reached Blackpool in 1846 it took another twenty years or so for the town to surpass Southport and then Morecambe, becoming not only the most popular resort in Lancashire, but in the whole of the north of England, and in due course the entire country.

By 1865, with rail-excursion numbers up to 285,000 a year, wealthy Mancunians in particular were falling over themselves to invest in Blackpool. Not one, not two, but three piers were built. And in 1891 the forward-thinking mayor, a well-to-do hotelier called John Bickerstaffe, commissioned a pair of Manchester architects to build a replica of a structure he had seen and been instantly smitten by on a recent family holiday, very possibly organized by Thomas Cook's increasingly dynamic company, to Paris.

In May 1894 Gustav Eiffel's fabulous tower got a Blackpool lookalike, equally fabulous in its own way. One can only imagine how incongruous it must have looked at first, rising more than 500ft out of the flat townscape, not least to the crew of the *Abana*, a passing Norwegian ship heading, in December 1894, from Liverpool to Florida. Rather substantially short of their destination they unfortunately mistook the new tower for a lighthouse and duly ran aground just up the coast at Little Bispham, where the wreck of the *Abana* is stuck to this day. Happily, the crew of sixteen were all saved and taken straight to a pub called the Red Lion, where they and the lifeboatmen who saved them got epically drunk together. There's proper Lancashire hospitality for you: save their lives and then get 'em pissed.

It has to be added, however, that the fabulousness of Blackpool represented by the handsome tower and its huge ornate ballroom became less pronounced, the town's Golden Mile conspicuously less golden, as the twentieth century wore on. Following the

Labour Party Conference that took place there in 1949, an unnamed contributor to the *New Statesman* decided that Blackpool, 'with its ugliness and high prices, is the supreme example of the commercial exploitation of working-class limitations'. Paul Theroux, visiting in 1982, was predictably even ruder, although at least in rubbishing the home of proud Blackpudlians he placated offended Sandgrounders.

'And now I began to reassess Southport – it is only hindsight that gives travel any meaning – and, looking back, I realised that Southport had been modestly elegant. I had called it cluttered, but Blackpool was real clutter: the buildings that were not only ugly but also foolish and flimsy, the vacationers sitting under a dark sky with their mouths open, emitting hog whimpers. They were waiting for the sun to shine, but the forecast was rain for the next five months.'

As ever, Theroux's compatriot Bill Bryson was funnier, if not notably kinder. In his enduringly delightful 1995 book *Notes from a Small Island*, Bryson noted the 'amazing' facts and figures about Blackpool; for instance that it attracts more visitors every year than the whole of Greece, and consumes more chips per capita than anywhere else on the planet (forty acres worth of potatoes a day, apparently). That it was raking in a quarter of a billion a year from tourism was no small achievement, he added, considering that 'Blackpool is ugly, dirty and a long way from anywhere, the sea is an open toilet, and its attractions nearly all cheap, provincial and dire'. He even skewered the reputation of the famous illuminations, a fixture on the promenade since 1902. 'I suppose if you had never seen electricity in action, it would be pretty breathtaking,' he wrote, 'but I'm not even sure of that.'

On that score he was right, though it pains me to admit it. When I was a small boy, the trip to what my friends and I all knew as 'Blackpool Lights' was an annual ritual. In fact, since my birthday fell at the end of October when the nights were drawing in, it was very often my birthday treat to choose a couple of favoured friends and for us all to be driven by my dad to Blackpool, where we joined the bumper-to-bumper motorcade creeping along the prom, oohing and ahhing or perhaps even hog-whimpering at little coloured bulbs festooned along wires in the shape of stars and elephants and ice-cream cornets, before stopping somewhere to make our own contribution to Blackpool's daily chip consumption.

My memories of these trips are wholly affectionate, yet on my most recent trip to Blackpool, as a birthday treat for my own daughter, Eleanor, in 2008, I saw the illuminations afresh through young and decidedly unimpressed eyes. Eleanor and her friends, standard-bearers for the Facebook and iPod generation, actually chortled at the very notion that I might once have been dazzled by so unutterably mundane a spectacle.

For this reason it's always dangerous to expose your children to your own childhood treats, not that we were there for the lacklustre illuminations. We went for the thrill of the funfair, and there at least the generation gap shrank back from a chasm to a crevice, Blackpool's vast, 44-acre Pleasure Beach affording Elly and her mates no less fun than it had me and my mates at the same age. And just as bloody well given the modern-day price of admission, I might add, yet of course the place was packed. Not for the first time I marvelled at the mighty spending power of the British on holiday, although the anonymous columnist in that 1949 issue of the *New Statesman* had put it another way, quoting a contemporary radio philosopher called Cyril Joad, who had noted the 'drainage system which preserves the quiet of our countryside by canalising working-class holidaymakers into places like Blackpool ... where their year's savings are painlessly removed from their pockets in a few days'.

This rather ungenerous verdict cast those working-class holidaymakers as hapless victims of a heist or confidence trick, but, then as now, if they went home refreshed after a successful, happy week beside the seaside, then if it was some sort of con, surely they were cheerfully complicit. J. B. Priestley, in *English Journey*, his timelessly fascinating chronicle of a trip round England, in his trusty Daimler, in 1933, was not the slightest bit mystified by Blackpool's appeal.

Compared with this huge mad place, with its miles and miles of promenades, its three piers, its gigantic dance-halls, its variety shows, its switch-backs and helter-skelters, its array of wine bars and oyster saloons and cheap restaurants and tea houses and shops piled high and glittering with trash; its army of pierrots, bandsmen, clowns, fortune-tellers, auctioneers, dancing partners, animal trainers, itinerant singers, hawkers; its 70 special trains a day; its hundreds and hundreds of thousands of trippers; places like Brighton and Margate and Yarmouth are merely playing at being popular holiday resorts,

he wrote, a tad wordily, but with proper reverence.

Old Cyril Joad might have had a point, but never had so many savings been removed from so many pockets in such an exciting variety of ways. And variety was the word. According to *Family Britain 1951–1957*, David Kynaston's marvellously formidable doorstop of a book, Blackpool in just one random week in the summer of 1951 offered a choice of no fewer than six shows: Vera Lynn at the Opera House, Elsie and Doris Waters at the Palace Variety, Wilfred Pickles in *Hobson's Choice* at the Grand, Ted Heath and his Music at the Empress Ballroom, Dave Morris, a comedian, at the South Pier, and Al Read, another comedian, at the Central Pier. By the way, Al Read's highly popular catchphrase was 'right monkey!' but what can I say, it was another era.

As alternative entertainment, there was also the perennial Blackpool favourite Reginald Dixon hammering his Wurlitzer organ at the Tower Ballroom, Madame Tussaud's waxworks, boxing, wrestling, greyhound racing and, during the few weeks when the holiday season overlapped with the football season, the great Stanley Matthews jinking down the wing at Bloomfield Road. It's not hard to see why the working classes flocked to Blackpool for their holidays.

Moreover, the column in the *New Statesman* was plainly informed, whether the writer knew it or not, by arrant snobbery. There were clear distinctions sixty-odd years ago between Britain's upper, middle and working classes, and all kinds of more subtle sub-divisions. There was an easily defined upper-middle and lower-middle class, and even, for keen observers of these things, an upper lower-middle class and a lower upper-middle class.

In the twenty-first century those precise distinctions have become irretrievably blurred, thank heavens, yet our society is still, to a greater or lesser degree, governed by class. It was Alan Ayckbourn who wrote that if you put three Englishmen on a desert island, within an hour they'll have invented a class system. And it wouldn't be wrong to say that Blackpool at high season is still a predominantly blue-collar resort, pandering to blue-collar expectations.

All of which brings me to that great English institution, the Blackpool boarding-house or small private hotel, and indeed the Blackpool landlady. I had my first taste of it, and her, when in October 1999 I was sent by the *Independent* to cover the Conservative Party Conference. In truth, I was there as an afterthought. All the paper's political correspondents and sketch writers were in town, but at the last minute someone decided to despatch me to write a mickey-taking article about the Young Conservatives, the journalistic equivalent of shooting fish in a barrel.

After a maddeningly long train journey from London, almost certainly slower than it would have been in 1846, I arrived at my hotel in a side-street off the north promenade just after six p.m. I was hungry and weary, in that order, and after checking in I asked the proprietress, a gaunt, lugubrious woman who looked as though she had last enjoyed herself in 1964, whether she served evening meals. She eyed me with the suspicion that English hoteliers so often reserve for that most vexatious of animals, a customer. 'We do, yes,' she said, shortly. 'Oh good,' I said, 'then could I possibly have a table for one this evening?' She bared four or five brown teeth, whether amused by my politeness or my presumption I wasn't sure. 'We stopped serving at 'alf past five, love.' Rarely had I been made to feel less like somebody's love.

That the least hospitable of people so often work in Britain's hospitality industry is an enduring paradox most famously seized upon by John Cleese, who was not fantasizing when he created *Fawlty Towers*. That benighted establishment was modelled on the Hotel Gleneagles in Torquay, and Basil on the irascible proprietor of the Gleneagles, an ex-naval commander called Donald Sinclair. In 2000, with the twenty-fifth anniversary of *Fawlty Towers* fast approaching, I went down to Torquay on the *Independent*'s behalf to talk to people who had worked for Sinclair. From them I learnt that, if anything, Cleese's barking Basil had been a rather understated version of dreadful Donald. A woman called Trixie, who had worked as a waitress and chambermaid for Donald and his formidable wife Betty, just as Connie Booth's Polly did for Basil and Sybil Fawlty, told me that on days when

Donald seriously upset the staff, Betty used to lock him in their flat.

'If he went into the kitchens in the morning,' she recalled, 'Betty would sometimes be three staff short by the evening. She'd lock him in, and say to us, "If Donald starts knocking, girls, don't let him out." The funny thing is that he didn't like the guests being unpleasant to the staff – that was his job. I remember a humungous woman checking in one evening, with a weedy little husband, and they complained that we were giving them nasty looks, which we were, because we had to stay on to give them a late supper. Mr Sinclair said, "How dare you criticize my staff! Get out of my hotel!" He actually threw them into the street, poor things.'

It could only have happened in Britain. But *Fawlty Towers*, even with its resident rat, was a model of hygiene compared with my hotel in Blackpool. In a corner of my en-suite bathroom I found a toilet-brush that – how can I put this? – bore distinct traces of historic blockages. If I'd wanted a record of how other guests had passed their time in the same room, a comments book would have sufficed. But would the comments have noted the bedroom's gossamer-thin curtains, the threadbare towels, the worn carpets? Probably not. None of those features were unique to that establishment, or to Blackpool; indeed the place was all too typical of thousands of such places all over Britain, yet oddly the British go on accepting them.

The following morning, after a dismal breakfast served by my cadaverous landlady about as graciously as you might expect to be served with an eviction notice, I walked along the street, noting that every single property was a hotel, and wondering whether any of them might be more welcoming than mine. I concluded not, although I did find one with a newspaper cutting proudly displayed outside. I laughed out loud at the headline, which was 'Muesli for breakfast puts B&B ahead of the pack'. It was 1999, not 1979, or 1959, yet in Blackpool this was evidently what passed for visionary thinking.

A couple of years later, Blackpool copped a whole lot more visionary thinking, when the multi-millionaire Trevor Hemmings unveiled his plan to turn the town into the 'Las Vegas of the North'. When I heard about this I informed my Blackpudlian friend, Derek. 'Bloody hell,' he said, 'how much is this fella worth?' I told him that Hemmings was reportedly worth over £500 million. 'Not for long,' said Derek.

It was certainly a hell of a gamble. Those celebrated Las Vegas illusionists Siegfried and Roy might have turned camels into elephants, and elephants into aeroplanes, but turning Blackpool, home of Syd Little, into Vegas, home of Gladys Knight, was always going to be a much harder proposition. And Hemmings was duly stymied when in 2007 the government rejected Blackpool's application to house Britain's first super-casino development, awarding the opportunity to Manchester instead.

But even with the endorsement of government, could Blackpool ever really turn into an English Las Vegas? In May 2010 the improbable promotion to the Premier League of the town's football club represented a welcome boost in fortunes, but even then you didn't have to be the palm-reader on the Golden Mile, Gypsy Petulengro (real name Langton), to visualize problems in turning Blackpool into Vegas, problems embodied by my unwelcoming landlady. It would be quite unfair to tar all Blackpool landladies with the same toilet-brush – I have since encountered a couple of others possessed of almost overwhelming kindness and warmth – but the point is that 150 years of dealing with the British on holiday in such vast numbers have imbued Blackpool with a culture all of its own, a culture not easily compatible with a slick, American-style, service-orientated approach to tourism.

For example, Blackpool's two main casinos were, for many years, the Castle and the Grosvenor, and in neither of them would you ever have expected to find Omar Sharif playing blackjack. However, you might once have found me chancing my arm at the roulette table, and watching in amusement as three dinner-suited security men delivered a birthday cake to a valued punter, a woman of indeterminate years and indeterminate hair colour. 'Happy birthday to you/ happy birthday to you/ happy birthday, dear madam/ happy birthday to you,' they droned, as joyful as pallbearers. You can't imagine that happening in the Nevada Desert.

What Blackpool does is take American culture and customize it. Consider the custom of celebrities owning restaurants. Vegas has a restaurant called Ago, co-owned by Robert de Niro; Blackpool's equivalent for many years was a burger joint on the prom, co-owned by the comedian Lennie Bennett, and called Fat B'stards. There are further parallels. Vegas gave the world a one-name star: Liberace. Blackpool gave the world a one-name star: Sooty. I won't lower myself by making a vulgar, counter-intuitive joke about one being a squeaky-voiced entertainer never more animated than with a fist up his backside ... and the other a flamboyant American pianist. Besides, it's true; the late Harry Corbett was strolling along North Pier when he spotted a cute little glove puppet staring out from a toy stall. He bought it and the rest is showbiz history.

I'm not being sarcastic; as a child I was very fond of Sooty. Besides, Blackpool itself occupies a bona-fide place in showbiz history. Jayne Mansfield switched on the illuminations in 1959; Kermit the Frog, in 1979. And there are plenty of acts that have headlined at both Caesar's Palace, Las Vegas, and the North Pier, Blackpool. I can't think of any off the top of my head, but I know there must have been some. Besides, Lennie Bennett, Tony

Bennett, Frank Sinatra, Frank Carson . . . a headline act's a head-line act. At any rate, if Blackpool really is to metamorphose into England's Las Vegas, it needs to stay true to itself. After all, the best of Blackpool and the best of Vegas could yield something incredible. Siegfried and Roy 'Chubby' Brown. What a show that would be.

4

Lakes, lochs and Lopez

Looking north from Southport promenade on a clear day, beyond Blackpool Tower and the mother of all rollercoasters, the Pepsi Max Big One, which are plainly visible in the middle distance, you can easily see the dramatic silhouette of the Lake District. And looking south, if the day is really clear, you can almost as easily see the craggy outline of Snowdonia. Apart from the 235ft-high, 5497ft-long Pepsi Max Big One, which opened in 1994, this was the 180-degree view that I grew up with, a view that encompassed sea and mountains, and also, in the foreground, some particularly smelly public lavatories, but we'll forget about those.

The point is that I feel blessed to have grown up in such proximity to some of Britain's loveliest regions. And yet we are all similarly blessed, to a greater or lesser extent. Everyone raised in this extraordinary little country, even in the grimmest urban wasteland, has a glorious stretch of countryside or seascape if not on the doorstep, then within little more than an hour's car, bus or train journey. That, I should add, is assuming no road works, signalling problems or cows on the track, which in Britain is the Pepsi Max Big One of all assumptions, but the general point remains; that none of us living in these idiosyncratic islands live too far from scenery to gladden the stoniest heart.

Having it there, though, and making the most of it, are two separate things. I was raised among kids in Southport who'd never been to the Lakes, or to Snowdonia, or in one or two really puzzling cases even to the beach. Their antithesis, to be found in Southport and across the entire north-west of England, is a breed of person I call a Lakes snob. This is a person who will listen with faintly contemptuous impatience when you tell them that your favourite lake is Windermere, or Ullswater, or even Coniston, and then tell you that theirs is Bogglethwaite Tarn, or Cockswater, or somewhere else so far off the beaten track that not even the chaps at Ordnance Survey have stumbled across it.

A similar phenomenon applies to Cornwall. Tell a Cornwall snob that you holidayed near Padstow for ten consecutive summers and they will say 'How lovely, so you're familiar with Tregobonit Bay?' and of course you're not. But at least you have to credit these annoying people with getting to know the country they inhabit. There is another breed of Brit who knows the Algarve or the Costa del Sol intimately, yet has never been to the Lake District, or Cornwall, or Scotland, or the Yorkshire Dales. I would wager that more of my countrymen have seen the inside of Faro Airport than have seen the inside of York Minster or Lincoln Cathedral, and without wanting to be a holiday-snob myself, that seems like a crying shame.

But before air travel revolutionized the possibilities for the British on holiday, and for those unwilling to get on a boat, the choice was fairly stark: seaside or countryside. And before the railways opened up the seaside, and encouraged the development of seaside resorts, the choice was even starker: countryside or nowt.

More significantly then than now, the Lake District represented countryside *in excelsis*. No other part of Britain, not even the more spectacular parts of Scotland, kindled so much artistic creativity, above all from the so-called Lakeland poets, notably William Wordsworth, Samuel Taylor Coleridge and Robert Southey. And even before they came wandering along lonely as clouds, the Lakes had inspired generations of sensitive-spirited men and women to reach for their quills. *Journal in the Lakes*, written in 1769 by Thomas Gray of 'elegy' fame, is one of the earliest examples of what was an emerging genre in the eighteenth century, travel-writing. 'To the left,' he wrote, of standing on Walla Crag near Keswick, 'the jaws of Borrowdale, with that turbulent chaos of mountain behind mountain rolled in confusion; beneath you, and stretching far away to the right, the shining purity of the lake, just ruffled by the breeze to show it is alive.' He was the Judith Chalmers of his day.

It is hard to be unimpressed by the Lake District. That unfailingly waspish, unfailingly readable journalist A. A. Gill calls it 'a mimsy, lyric clotted tea' of a place, and prefers neighbouring Northumberland, 'set in stone and heather and hoarfrost and rhyme, dug out of blasted moor', but if he knew the Lakes better he'd know that the wildness he so admires in Northumberland is there in the Lakes too. However you want your natural beauty, whether chocolate-boxy or rugged, the Lake District has it in spades.

Even Paul Theroux knew that, which is probably why, in *The Kingdom by the Sea*, he didn't go there. Instead, he skirted it, sticking to the coastal railway line, which took him past the nuclear power station at Windscale and gave him something else to be catty about. 'I had expected something different, greener, higher, fresher, perhaps Wordsworthian,' he wrote. 'That was the trouble with England – it was imaginary. "The West Cumbria Line" called up images of deserted woodland and steep fells and pikes, not a nuclear time-bomb of incomparable ugliness on a black coast.' I mean, really. Why didn't he just stay in Massachusetts?

There is nothing imaginary about the loveliness of the Lakes, as extolled by Wordsworth and friends, and later, Arthur Ransome. In *Swallows and Amazons*, published in 1930, Ransome evoked the kind of holiday that we all either had or wish we had as children, with the Lakes as the perfect, shimmering backdrop. I would have read *Swallows and Amazons* to my own three children if he hadn't given one of his main characters the name Titty, which would without doubt have reduced either them, or me, or all of us, to fits of helpless giggles. What was he thinking of? The others are John, Susan, Nancy, Roger and Peggy, for heaven's sake. Why Titty? Even in 1930 it must have elicited laughter.

The Lake District of *Swallows and Amazons* is still very much there, of course, but with infinitely more cars and people in it. It would be disingenuous of me not to point out that there aren't many more depressing places to be on a drizzly summer's day than Bowness or Ambleside, part of a great mooching multitude of folk, shuffling in and out of gift shops with one or two irreverent souls feeling that the sight of one more Beatrix Potter teapot, paperweight, alarm clock or duvet cover might just tip them over the edge and make them run into the street screaming 'Fuck Jemima Puddleduck'. Even my friend Hunter Davies, a Lake District devotee, gently suggests in his excellent book *A Walk around the Lakes* that Windermere and Derwent Water are best avoided on bank holidays.

And this brings me to the curse of the British on holiday in Britain, namely other British people holidaying in Britain. If it is something of a topographical miracle that such a small island has so much diversity of landscape, it is also an unusually crowded island, with lots of people wanting to do the same things at the same time.

Very often this involves them being in their cars on the same stretch of tarmac at the same time, a situation for which the narrow roads of the Lake District, and in particular the wretched A591 between Kendal and Windermere, are almost risibly ill-equipped. And not even the bigger roads to the Lake District can cope when the Great British Public decides *en masse* that it wants to see those daffodils about which Wordsworth wrote so fetchingly. In the twenty-first century we could, indubitably, substitute motor vehicles for daffodils as the subject of his most famous poem. 'Continuous as the stars that shine/ And twinkle on the milky way/ They stretched in never-ending line . . .' Well, they certainly stretched in never-ending line on 17 April 1987, when the worst traffic jam in the history of British traffic jams crippled the M6 between Charnock Richard and Carnforth, involving around 200,000 people in 50,000 vehicles.

Sitting in a seemingly endless jam on the way to the countryside feels far more depressing than it does on the way to the seaside. At the seaside you know there are going to be lots of people – it's practically part of the fun – and they've got to get there somehow. But the very word 'countryside' implies tranquillity, which in turn implies a scarcity of humanity. Between April and September it's not at all easy to wander lonely as a cloud in the Lake District, unless it's a cloud in a very busy sky, and at the height of summer the only place anywhere near Grasmere that you will find Wordsworth's 'bliss of solitude' is on a tea-towel. Which I suppose is why those Lakes snobs find refuge sitting on the ferny banks of Bogglethwaite Tarn, or skimming stones across the gentle surface of Cockswater. They are paragons of that peculiarly

British strain of hypocrisy, whereby we look disdainfully down our noses at day-trippers and out-of-towners when we are, ourselves, on a day trip out of town.

How many times have we all heard or articulated the sentiment 'It was a nice place, but it was ruined by far too many tourists'? We overlook the incontrovertible truth that, had we too not been in the nice place, there would have been slightly fewer tourists to ruin it. Yet few of us look at ourselves in a mirror, even with a camera around our neck – heck, even with a panama hat on – and see a tourist. A traveller, yes. An explorer, even. The Americans and the Japanese, above all nationalities, suffer from no such delusions. And we silently despise them for it, or at least mock them. But maybe we're the ones who deserve to be mocked, for not wanting to unfold a map – certainly not in our own country – in case we get mistaken for that most gauche and well-travelled yet paradoxically unworldly of creatures, a tourist.

There is, however, a breed of Briton that is never happier than when unfolding a map, and then refolding it carefully along the creases. I refer, of course, to the rambler. And let me lay my cards on the table: I love ramblers. To me they represent the essence of Britishness, a little bit like morris dancers and train-spotters, which might seem like being damned with faint praise but really there is no greater praise. These are all folk who pursue their enthusiasms without self-consciousness, in open view of people who almost ritually scoff at them. Is there a more pleasing sight than a group of cagouled ramblers on a country lane, clambering over a stile? Well, actually, I can think of a few. Jennifer Lopez with hardly any clothes on, England winning the Ashes, my stingy mate Mick getting a round in, that sort of thing. But to me the spectacle of ramblers rambling offers a kind of reassurance that all is basically well with the world, which can't honestly be said of a near-naked J-Lo.

Moreover, anyone who cherishes days out in rural Britain owes more than they probably know to ramblers, or at least to the Ramblers' Association. Its roots, like those of so many British institutions, lie in the Industrial Revolution, in the big dirty wake of which more and more people looked to the countryside for rest and recreation, and sought to protect their rights – and, ultimately, our rights – to walk along country footpaths. The Association for the Protection of Ancient Footpaths in the Vicinity of York, formed in 1824, was an early forerunner of the Ramblers' Association, and in Glasgow in 1892 the first formal federation of groups of ramblers was established. Forty years later, in April 1932, it became clear just how emotive the issue of access to open land had become, when disagreements between landowners and ramblers over rights of way through the Duke of Devonshire's grouse moors in Derbyshire led to the famous and altogether splendid mass trespass on the Peak District's highest plateau, Kinder Scout.

In truth the trespass was politically motivated; it was orchestrated by the Manchester-based and Communist-inclined British Workers' Sports Federation and, according to a contemporary report in the Manchester *Guardian*, the 400 or so trespassers sang 'The Red Flag' as they marched up the hill. But that doesn't mean they weren't right to fight for the freedom to roam. And fight they did. The report added that as a result of a scuffle between the ramblers and the Duke's stick-wielding gamekeepers, there 'will be plenty of bruises carefully nursed in Gorton and other parts of Manchester tonight, but no-one was at all seriously hurt except one keeper, Mr E Beaver, who was knocked unconscious and damaged his ankle'. There is no surviving record of Mr E. Beaver's first name, incidentally. We can only pray that it was Eager.

Whatever, the episode ended with five ramblers jailed for between two and six months, which in turn generated a torrent of public sympathy. Three years later the Ramblers' Association itself was formed, and was highly influential in the drafting, and passing into law, of the National Parks and Access to the Countryside Act of December 1949. We are all beneficiaries. So next time you feel tempted to speak dismissively of ramblers or rambling, think on.

Maybe the fact that people do is somehow connected with the very word 'rambling', which in a verbal context has a slightly pejorative meaning. We none of us like to listen to someone rambling, and even in a physical sense it suggests a vagueness of purpose, whereas in fact there is hardly anything more purposeful than a group of ramblers striding towards the next symbol on their OS map. And due credit to them, too, for experiencing the countryside properly. In the Lake District, how many visitors restrict themselves to an amble round Ambleside and perhaps a Windermere Lake Cruise (by a country mile the most popular attraction in the region) without ever venturing even a bit of a way up a proper Lakeland fell? Thousands upon thousands is the answer, but not the ramblers, who in the Lakes even have a patron saint: the late Wainwright.

If there is something uniquely and reassuringly British about rambling, so there was about Wainwright, who, rather like Inspector Morse, energetically avoided using his first name. It wasn't as if, like Morse's name Endeavour, it was anything truly embarrassing. It was Alfred. But he didn't like it, and he was clearly a man of fixed likes and loathings. Among the latter was giving interviews, so it was quite a coup for Hunter Davies when he cajoled his way into Wainwright's modern house in a Kendal cul-de-sac for a chat, although even that was on condition that no account of their conversation would end up in a newspaper.

Instead, Hunter ended up writing the old boy's biography – a few respectful years after Wainwright had hopped over the celestial stile, of course – and also devoted a chapter to him in *A Walk around the Lakes*. Every line of it makes the heart sing. Wainwright's Lakeland guides have sold well over half a million copies, yet he was unsociable almost to the point of misanthropy. I think that's wonderful. For years hardly anyone knew who he was, rather like the high-class call girl Belle de Jour, except, on reflection, not at all like the high-class call girl Belle de Jour. For one thing, he opened his legs more than she did. He climbed and chronicled all 214 Lake District fells, which took him thirteen years, but he also found time to devise a 192-mile coast-to-coast walk from St Bees Head in Cumbria to Robin Hood's Bay in Yorkshire. Almost more remarkably than anything, though, he only ever got from A to B by walking or, when he absolutely had to, on the bus. God knows what he'd have managed to write if he'd had to rely on rural bus services today. The definitive guide to Lake District bus stops, I suppose.

But if he could do without any kind of internal combustion engine, so much the better. 'It's a natural function of the body to walk,' he told Hunter. 'It isn't to drive a car.' Tell that to the poor sods stuck, perhaps even as I write, on the A591. Actually, from a fell way above them, and through the clenched teeth with which he gripped his pipe, Wainwright probably did.

Could anywhere other than Britain produce someone like Wainwright? I don't think so. But that doesn't mean he was a one-off, for we are a nation that rather specializes in the nature-loving grump. At the end of a long walk I once ambled into a white-washed little inn beside a loch in the Scottish Highlands. Sitting at the bar with some fishing tackle next to him was an old Scotsman, who looked as though he had stepped out of the picture on the lid of a tin of shortbread. He had a bushy ginger beard, through which a sturdy brown pipe emerged, and he was wearing a kilt. Other than me and the barmaid, he was the only person in the bar.

I ventured a cheery hello. He gave a grunt. 'Will ye have another, Hamish?' trilled the barmaid. I now felt as though I had stepped inside the shortbread tin, or perhaps into a 1960s film starring Virginia McKenna and Andrew Cruikshank, such was the slightly other-worldly Scottishness of the situation. 'Aye,' said Hamish. She poured a double Scotch and set it before him. I tried again to make conversation, asking if he lived locally, which admittedly was a pretty brainless question, since he clearly wasn't a stockbroker in the area for a couple of days' rest and recreation.

'Aye,' he said.

'Have you always lived round here?' I chirped.

Slowly, he turned to make eye contact, and with great deliberation removed his pipe. 'No,' he said, testily. 'I lived abroad for six years.'

'Oh really,' I said. 'Whereabouts was that?'

He held my gaze, but his eyes narrowed. There was no sign of his mouth under the enormous beard, but I could sense that it was fixed in a sneer. 'Have ye ever heard,' he grunted, 'o' a place called High Wycombe?'

5

Camping, canoes and cordage

It was in Scotland, not far from where I was put in my sassenach place by Hamish, that I enjoyed my first British camping holiday. It was May 1983 and I was an undergaduate at St Andrews University on the east coast of Scotland. My friends Chris, Doug and I had just seen the charming film *Local Hero*, which featured a dazzling display of the northern lights and made us want to witness this remarkable natural phenomenon for ourselves. When we learnt that the beach scenes in the film were filmed at Morar on the west coast, on the fabled 'Road to the Isles', we hitchhiked across Scotland and set up camp there.

We never did see the northern lights, but we had a marvellous time, almost *Swallows and Amazons*-esque if with a regrettable absence of Titty, at least until we realized that in the sun and the wind all three of us had acquired a positively crippling case of sunburn. I hitched gingerly back to St Andrews with the worst sunburn I had ever had, or have ever suffered since. It was so bad that the sight of my face, when I went into a pharmacy to get something to soothe the pain, made a little boy cry.

Further musings on sunburn must wait until this book ventures, with due respect to Hamish, properly abroad. After all, sunburn is part of the story of the British on holiday no less than buckets and spades. But actually it's not uncommon for Brits to get more badly sunburnt in Britain than overseas, where we're far more alert to the dangers.

The other lesson I learnt on that camping trip long ago, is that a campfire, like the sun, generates serious heat. Chris, Doug and I collected armfuls of driftwood and felt very much like Robinson Crusoe, Man Friday, and I suppose Man Thursday, as we arranged the wood into an appealingly picturesque pile and set it alight. The plan was to cook baked potatoes on the fire, for which we had various sumptuous fillings ready. The potatoes were duly wrapped in foil, and tucked into the fire for twenty minutes or so. Then we took them out, using another piece of wood we had carefully fashioned into a long fork, and carefully unwrapped them. To our astonishment and horror the potatoes were completely cremated. It would be misleading to say they were inedible, because they simply weren't there any more.

This brings me to my contention that the British, as far as one can generalize, are not nearly as outdoorsy as we think we are. The Saxons might have been pretty terrific when it came to cooking over fires in forest clearings but, sometime during the last millennium or so, the skill was either lost, or exported to the dominions. The Australians, Americans and Canadians are naturals but, for the British, the back-garden barbecue tends to stretch us to the limits of our potential as backwoodsmen. In short, when we go camping, we are really not playing to our strengths.

Nevertheless, we go camping in increasing numbers. In 2009, a remarkable 30 per cent of Britons had a camping or caravanning holiday, compared with 17 per cent the year before, and at the time even that had been considered an unusually high percentage. The astonishing surge had a good deal to do with the biting economic recession and the performance of the ever-more muscular euro against the ever-more feeble pound, but it also owed something to a steady improvement in campsites, as well as a burgeoning middle-class embrace of camping culture.

Camping, in fact, might even be the new taramasalata, in the sense that the middle classes have discovered it and made it their own, scarcely aware that it was there before them. The rapidly growing middle-class interest in camping has also given rise to the phenomenon of 'glamping', a contraction of 'glamorous camping', by which you sleep in a canvas structure that has more in common with Claridges than a two-man nylon bivouac, and of course has already been erected by some other poor sod. To me this seems contrary to the whole spirit of camping. Isn't putting up the tent, struggling with the guy-ropes and swearing at the tent pegs, an essential and possibly even rewarding part of the experience?

Maybe, maybe not. For my money, if camping doesn't involve at least a little bit of hardship, it's not proper camping. But perhaps I'd change my tune if I had a holiday in a yurt, which are all the rage among seasoned glampers. Yurts are round, portable dwellings traditionally used by nomads in the steppes of Central Asia, and now used by Jonty and Jocasta until it's time for them to go home to Chiswick. How bemused would our great-grandparents be, even if they could get their heads round the notion of www.yurtsdirect.com, to see us borrowing ideas from Mongolian nomads in pursuit of a lovely family holiday in, say, Dorset?

I still haven't tried glamping, but in the early summer of 2004 I took my first camping trip since that elusive search for the northern lights twenty-one years earlier. We went as a group of six adults and nine children – I can't remember when we and our friends started to be so emphatically outnumbered by children; it seems to have happened by stealth – and we stayed at the Pencelli Castle Caravan and Camping Park in the Brecon Beacons, where there resounded the merry sound of the bourgeoisie enjoying themselves, clinking champagne flutes in celebration of the altogether splendid idea to rough it under canvas for a few nights.

It was the musical clink of real glass, too, not the dull thwock of plastic. If you can drive right up to your pitch, then why not take real, breakable glassware? We even, on occasion, drove from the tent to the toilet block, which was entirely contrary to the spirit of camping but seemed expedient given that the loo was roughly quarter of a mile away. As for those words 'toilet block', they have a slightly penal ring and also evoke childhood memories of evil-smelling cesspits, but the toilet block at Pencelli Castle was a pleasure to visit. It would have been a bit weird to eat off the floor, but we certainly could have done.

I asserted earlier that a proper camping experience requires at least some hardship. On the other hand, roughing it can be good for the soul. Where we live in Herefordshire there are a proliferating number of companies resourcefully offering short holidays designed to address the average Brit's cluelessness in open-air survival techniques. Obviously, not many of us are likely to be pitched into a situation where we have to snare and skin a rabbit to stay alive, but there is certainly a growing willingness to learn. I blame that Ray Mears.

In April 2007, my wife and two sons went on just such a trip, to a forest in the Brecon Beacons not far from Pencelli Castle Caravan and Camping Park, yet a world apart. Jane wanted to get in touch with her inner Ray Mears, but unfortunately found that her inner Ray Mears and her outer Naomi Campbell were incompatible, there being nowhere to plug in her hairdryer for two days.

Still, she coped doughtily, made a particularly fine fish-hook out of a hawthorn bush, and drew further comfort from the fact that eleven-year-old Joseph and eight-year-old Jacob had gone feral and were having the time of their lives. That our daughter Eleanor and I were at home eating hot meals, enjoying warm showers and watching *Coronation Street*, she tried not to think about.

The 48-hour trip was organized and led by a former SAS man called Dugald, and needless to say I omit the SAS from my generalization that the Brits are innately not all that resourceful in the wild. Living in Herefordshire I know quite a few ex-SAS soldiers, and any one of them could make a serviceable sleeping-bag out of three dock leaves and a sheep.

As for Dugald, he had designed this particular trip especially for parents and children, which, in every case bar that of Jane and her friend Diana, meant father and son. 'Right, listen up, lads and dads . . . erm, and mums,' Dugald kept saying. But by the end of the trip he'd stopped adding 'and mums'. By then, Jane and Diana were honorary dads. Of course, there's no reason in the world why mums shouldn't do survival courses with their kids. It had been Diana's idea, because her son Nick desperately wanted to go, but only if a friend could go, too. So Diana mentioned it to Jane and suddenly, no sooner were we back from a skiing holiday in Austria, where we stayed in a very comfortable hotel, than she was standing under the shower giving herself the Last Hairwash.

The bathroom facilities in the forest were predictably basic. When they arrived, Dugald directed them to the rudimentary latrine, a kind of shallow trench. Jacob took one look at it and declared that he wouldn't be doing a poo for the duration of his stay, which he didn't. Jane didn't set foot in the camp latrine, either. 'I made other arrangements,' she later reported, gnomically.

On the first night they slept in tents, but on the second night they had to make their own shelters out of wood, leaves, bracken and moss. Dugald told them that children always make the best shelters, driven by the impulse to have a better den than anyone else, so maybe, even in the Facebook age, the spirit of *Swallows and Amazons* endures. To her amazement, Jane found that her night in the shelter was the highlight of the trip, a rather blissful communion with nature. It helped that the weather was glorious: sunny days and clear, starry nights. And Dugald lived up to his SAS billing; my boys came home with their sleeping-bags tied to their rucksacks with cordage they had made themselves, from reeds.

They also prepared meals for themselves, which was a less successful enterprise. On the first night they had hot water weakly flavoured with carrot, optimistically described by Dugald as vegetable broth, and for lunch the following day they gutted some trout he provided, having failed dismally to catch any themselves.

'Don't worry about the smell of fish guts on your hands, I've got something for that,' said Dugald, cheerfully.

'What's that?' asked Jane.

'The smell of rabbit,' said Dugald. And sure enough, that night they skinned a rabbit and cooked it in what was left of the first night's 'broth'. 'It was disgusting,' Joe told me later.

Dugald and his assistant, Norry, left the camp at dinner time, taking a pan of the rabbit stew to eat at the bottom of the next field by their Land Rover, but later that evening, while they were learning trapping techniques in the forest, Diana reckoned that she could smell some telltale garlic on Norry's breath. The next day, just before they climbed into the Volvo to drive back to home comforts, Jane confronted Dugald.

'You didn't eat that rabbit stew last night, did you?' she said.

Dugald conceded that he and Norry had enjoyed a ready meal, beef in chianti, in the back of their Land Rover, where they even had a microwave. It appeared that even hardened SAS men preferred Tesco's Finest over a rabbit stew made in a forest clearing, which brings me back to the bourgeois scenes at Pencelli Castle, where scarcely any concessions were made to the fact that we were eating out of doors, using portable stoves and gas cylinders. We ate magnificently. Nor did it hurt that on a moderately clear day the Brecon Beacons are visible from our house. In getting there, we weren't exactly invoking the spirit of Shackleton, yet it was comforting to know that if persistent rain set in, we could dismantle the tent and be home in just twelve hours, allowing for an hour's driving time on top of the eleven hours required to dismantle the tent.

We had recently bought a Khyam Galaxy 600, which could, I realize, be just about anything – a type of razor, a make of car, a brand of vibrator – but was in fact a tent, and, for the unitiated, not a particularly easy tent to erect. Moreover, I wasn't able to join Jane and the children until several hours after they had arrived, so they had to get it up on their own, which effectively meant Jane getting it up on her own. On the day we left, this made the tent pegs fiendishly hard to pull out of the ground; it was clear that they had been hammered in with attitude.

Still, little tiffs and grudges are part of the camping experience, indeed part of the holiday experience. A holiday is, perversely, a hugely stressful undertaking. And much of the stress derives from the fact that it's meant to be the precise opposite. Many people work hard all year so that they can take an annual holiday. In their fortnight in Spain, or Cornwall, or the Maldives, or wherever, there is hope and expectation invested, no less than money. And a commensurate amount of dread, lest it rains, or the travellers cheques are stolen, or the mosquitoes attack, or a child falls ill, or the money runs out, or the journey home goes wrong, or any of the thousand other things that can blight a much-needed holiday, and duly whip up stress.

In August 2010, 7200 jokes told by performers at the Edinburgh Fringe were whittled down to 24, which the public then voted on to determine the best one, and it was comedian Tim Vine's one-liner: 'I've just been on a once-in-a-lifetime holiday ... I'll tell you what – never again.' Obviously it was just a gag, and no doubt the comedy was all in the delivery, but in a paradoxical way the sentiment makes sense; why would anyone want to go on a once-in-a-lifetime holiday more than once? All that hope, all that money, all that potential for expectations to go unmet.

I wouldn't go quite as far as the novelist Arnold Bennett, who once said, possibly because he was feeling peevish knowing that posterity would remember him less for his fine novels than for the omelette named after him, that 'no holiday is ever anything but a disappointment ... there is nothing like an unsatisfactory holiday for reconciling us to a life of toil'. All the same, most of us can probably think of moments on holidays down the years when we felt 100 times more stressed than we ever do in the familiarity and security of our homes. I remember once waking up in a small hotel in northern Portugal, before Jane and I had children, and opening the shutters to find a low blanket of grey cloud and a steady drizzle. It was June, and this was the third day of our holiday and the third day without sun. Jane, not a woman anyone would describe as highly strung, burst into tears.

Camping holidays can intensify this misery and stress by adding discomfort to the equation. So why do we do it? Because it's cheap, of course, which for the hard-up British is increasingly a consideration, but also because, when everything goes right, it can be more invigorating than almost any other kind of holiday.

That w-word 'when' is a huge one, though, and first, you have to overcome the challenges of living under canvas. For example, until those few days at Pencelli Castle I had never faced the interesting challenge of letting a nine-year-old desperate for a piddle out of a tent in the middle of the night. Which would have been a sight easier but for the fact that our Khyam Galaxy 600 had an absolutely bewildering array of zips, so you'd think you'd let him out of the tent to pee only to find that you'd sent him into the pod where his sister was sleeping.

By the time we next went on a family camping holiday, at the end of August 2009, we no longer had a nine-year-old with a demanding bladder and even more significantly we had bought a far more sensible tent, a large bell tent, a truly splendid thing, a tent like tents used to be before they became over-complicated with pods and compartments and zips and stuff. But this trip had an extra dimension, something else to start apprehension rising in the breast of a middle-aged British male who was never even a boy scout: canoes.

The leader of the expedition was our friend Simon, who was not only a scout but retains a scout leader's zest for the outdoor life. He had suggested that along with his family and two other families we should canoe a 25-mile stretch of the River Wye, with an overnight stay under canvas in a field belonging to his Uncle Chuff, who farms 400 acres not far from Hay.

We started one Sunday morning at Glasbury-on-Wye, seven adults and eleven children in six canoes, only two of which capsized, happily into water that was only knee-deep. One was a tiny purple kayak, more like a big kazoo, into which our friend Patrick had squeezed. The other was the canoe containing four sixteen-year-old girls, who dealt with their predicament with dignified, resourceful calm. Or rather, didn't.

At around five p.m. Simon identified what he thought was a stretch of riverbank in the lee of Uncle Chuff's field, so we hoicked the canoes up a steep bank of mud and nettles, with at least one of us remembering Ratty's comment about there being nothing half as much fun as messing about in boats and silently resolving to burn his copy of *Wind in the Willows*.

When eventually we made it through the mud and nettles, we found ourselves on the edge of a vast cornfield, and began to set up camp. This was the bit where we Viners finally came into our own, erecting our accommodation with something approaching panache. Jane had bought the bell tent six months earlier so the children could have sleepovers in the garden with their mates, consigning the Khyam Galaxy 600 to a box in the cellar, where it remains to this day, unlikely ever to emerge. Unlike the Galaxy 600, the bell tent is easy to put up, and once up, it has an elegant, faintly eastern aura, slightly reminiscent, I shouldn't wonder, of a Mongolian yurt. In the field next to the Wye this eastern look was compounded by a kilim rug, which for some reason best known to herself Jane had chucked into the car along with wellies and sleeping-bags. With the kilim placed just inside the entrance, our bell tent could have passed for the home of Suleiman the Magnificent. Or at the very least that of his son, Suleiman the So-So. And our tent quickly became the focal point of our little temporary community. I felt as though I was finally earning my spurs as a camper.

As afternoon turned into evening, a general state of nirvana descended, even upon the child feeling deprived of his games console, who had earlier got excited when he overheard his father's intention to 'go for a wee', fleetingly thinking that he might be going for a Wii. The only thing interfering with the wholesome outdoorsiness of the occasion was Simon's *sotto voce* admission to Jane and me, repeated several times, that he wasn't certain we were actually on Uncle Chuff's land. So when we saw a Land Rover trundling purposefully across the field towards us, we feared the worst. And sure enough, it was a farmer and his wife, incandescently angry that we had pitched camp in their field and ordering us to leave.

The angry farmer is a stock British character with an impressive lineage, from *The Mayor of Casterbridge*, through *The Tales of Peter Rabbit*, through the hopping-mad cartoon farmer in the 1971 public-information film about the Countryside Code, to this fellow, with his beetroot-red face. I tried to calm him down, offering to pay, and promising that we wouldn't build a fire, which seemed to be his main concern, but he would not be placated. He'd never heard of anyone called Chuff and didn't want our money, he just wanted us to 'bugger off'. Yet we knew it would take us hours to dismantle all the tents and find somewhere else. In fact a more sensible option was to drive home, and the children were close to tears at the prospect, but the farmer was pitilessly unyielding. And his wife just sat there in the Land Rover, looking daggers at us. The trip was turning sour before our eyes.

It was at this miserable point that Simon stepped forward and introduced the beetroot-faced fellow as his Uncle Chuff, while the woman looking daggers at us from the Land Rover was his Auntie Candia. He had conspired with them to hoodwink Jane and me. Simon's uncertainty about whether it was the right field was entirely faked, and all the other adults were in on the joke, which, it has to be said, was brilliantly executed. Moreover, far from being the mean-spirited, hatchet-faced pair they had seemed, Uncle Chuff and Auntie Candia turned out to be utterly delightful, pulling flasks of tea and a wicker hamper full of lemon drizzle cake from the Land Rover's boot. Not that it's easy to warm instantly to people who moments earlier have appeared to be ruining your day; it took Jane two mugs of strong tea to stop shaking.

The rest of the trip, happily, passed without incident. The

night under canvas was as comfortable as any night spent sliding slowly but inexorably downhill in a sleeping-bag can be, and the rest of the majestic Wye was safely negotiated the following day. We even saw a kingfisher. In more ways than one, Jane and I got home feeling well and truly Chuffed. And also aware that one of the key requisites for full enjoyment of a British camping holiday is a fully formed British sense of humour.

6

Cottages, caravans and comments books

In November 2009, having written extensively in the *Independent* about the travails of a holiday-cottage owner, I was invited by an organization called Farm Stay UK to be the guest speaker at their annual dinner-dance, which was held in a modern hotel close to a motorway junction, about as far removed from a characterful farmhouse as could be imagined, near Scunthorpe. In my speech I praised the members – owners of farmhouse B&Bs and self-catering cottages – for being bulwarks of the British tourism industry. This was partly in the hope of getting a nice round of applause, but also because I believe it to be true – throwing open your homes to strangers is the very definition of hospitality, even when there's a bill presented on the morning of departure.

It's an excellent idea for B&B and holiday-cottage owners to have some kind of federation, because dealing with the Great British Public can be unnerving, and it helps to be able to share experiences. Until I stood up to make my speech I spent much of that evening swapping stories with the woman next to me, a doughty character called Maggie who was Farm Stay UK's chairman ('not chairwoman, and certainly not chair, I've no time for all that nonsense, it's chairman').

I told Maggie about some of the oddballs we'd had staying in our two self-catering cottages in Herefordshire, but she trumped me by describing the platoon of middle-aged Englishmen into Second World War re-enactment weekends, who descend every year on her huge, 24-bed converted barn in Kent. Coincidentally, she was expecting them the following Friday.

'They're very polite and keep themselves to themselves,' she said, 'but the strange thing about them is that they're a German re-enactment group.' Apparently, they spend the entire weekend in German uniforms, acting out high-level meetings. I suggested that they might be neo-Nazis, but she said she was sure they weren't. All the same, I had this unsettling image of an ersatz Wannsee Conference – the meeting in January 1942 at which Nazi top-brass agreed on how the 'Final Solution of the Jewish Question' was to be carried out – unfolding every November in a barn near Folkestone. Maybe it is as well that these Wannsee wannabes keep a low profile; there must be more than a few elderly people in Kent whose hearts wouldn't be robust enough to cope with seeing two dozen Gestapo officers walking into a pub, in full uniform.

My conversation with Maggie, which I enthusiastically relayed to Jane when I got home the following day, was positively therapeutic. I shared with her a statistic I'd once been given by someone who attended a conference on British tourism, to the effect that 95 per cent of the holidaying public are perfectly nice, 4 per cent can have niceness forced upon them, and 1 per cent are impossible to please. Maggie agreed wholeheartedly.

Everyone in the hospitality business has encountered that 1 per cent. A few months earlier we'd had a couple from Derbyshire and their young, disabled daughter staying in one of our cottages. Every time I saw them in our garden I asked how they were getting on, and whether they wanted any produce from our vegetable garden, and every time they politely declined my cabbages and lettuces but assured me that they were having a nice time and that everything was fine. 'Job's a good 'un,' the man said at the conclusion of every exchange, which I interpreted as some sort of East Midlands expression of approval.

After they'd gone, however, we found a rather brusque line in the comments book, referring us to a separate piece of paper. And on that paper they had meticulously listed a dozen reasons why they had felt dissatisfied with their accommodation, including the bizarre claim that the stairs, a flight of stairs notable for the ordinariness of its gradient, were too steep. For them, clearly, job hadn't really been a good 'un, in fact it had been a crap 'un, yet they hadn't been brave enough to register their dissatisfaction directly with us, despite numerous opportunities. It is a curiously British trait – don't complain, don't make a fuss, don't provoke a confrontation – but it does no favours either to the would-be complainants or to those who might be able to improve the experience for them, but can do nothing after they have gone.

Whether as holiday-cottage proprietors you think that such complaints are unwarranted is not really the issue. If you can do something to improve a guest's stay you should do it. But at the same time, it's hard not to feel affronted in the face of such biting criticism, even though it was hard in this instance not to feel as though the problems were theirs, not ours. Our comments book was full of notes and sometimes mini-essays from previous customers who'd loved the cottage, the garden, the view, the area, everything. Where this couple had shown themselves to be downright odd, we felt, was in doggedly listing so many areas of dissatisfaction. Not all their points were unreasonable. They complained that there were no child locks on the upstairs windows, an oversight on our part that we'd kept meaning to address but hadn't. But the steep stairs? They devalued the valid complaints by adding others that were transparently ridiculous.

Still, you can't ignore pieces of paper like that, and Jane duly e-mailed them to apologize for what we conceded might have been flawed, but also to ask why they hadn't raised these matters with us directly, and to stand up for a holiday cottage that we knew – not least because other people kept telling us so – was comfortable and charming. Unsurprisingly, there was no reply. Even over the internet, with the safety-buffer of cyberspace, very British rules of non-engagement applied. But it would be hypocritical of me to pretend that they had not also applied to me at various times in my life. That grim hotel in Blackpool in 1999 was a prime example. I could have confronted the lugubrious hostess, the hostess with the leastest, with complaints about the bed, curtains, towels, toilet-brush and absurdly early evening meals, but I didn't. I didn't even leave a note. And if I had, maybe she too would have dismissed me as histrionic, thinking 'he might have a point about the towels, but there's nowt wrong with the curtains, and who wants their tea any later than 'alf five?'

As for our own unhappy guests, Mr and Mrs 'Job's a good 'un', they had at least done us the small kindness of not adding their litany of complaints directly to the comments book. For the proprietor, the placing of a comments book is a calculated gamble, on the basis that comments can be good, indifferent or bad, and nobody wants to arrive in a hotel room or self-catering property and leaf through the remarks made by previous guests, to find 'Shame about the daily alarm call from the bloody cockerel' or 'We'd have had a nicer time if little Nigel hadn't been bitten by Winston, the owners' Staffordshire bull terrier'.

Happily, at least from a host's perspective, there seems to be an inherent decency among the British, a code of good manners which dictates that the comments book is respected as a forum for positive or, when absolutely necessary, only slightly negative observations. If you don't think much of the accommodation, then just say how convenient it is for nearby National Trust houses or good local pubs, seems to be the unwritten convention. The British are masters at damning with faint praise, an exercise in subtlety that tends to be recognized only by other Brits.

We are also very good at leaving comments that teeter on the gnomic, of which my all-time favourite is one already recorded in my book *Tales of the Country*, so I apologize for repeating myself, but it's a cracker. It was left by someone who had stayed in a very upmarket self-catering cottage in Cornwall. 'Thanks very much,' they wrote. 'We've had a wonderful holiday and the cottage is beautiful. Only one disappointment. Not enough cake tins!!!'

Not enough cake tins; isn't that a fantastic complaint? There was clearly at least one cake tin, maybe even two, but that wasn't enough, and it shows the difficulty facing the holiday-cottage proprietor – you simply cannot provide for all the varied needs of the Great, and sometimes endearingly bonkers, British Public. Not that everyone who stays in a holiday cottage in Britain is British, of course, but I wouldn't mind betting that over 95 per cent of them are. There are still battalions of Brits determined to explore their own back yard, so to speak, before striking out down the street. God bless 'em.

Increasingly, they rent self-catering properties, hence the growth of what really does deserve to be called a cottage industry. Companies such as English Country Cottages and Rural Retreats have very astutely fed the secret yearning of metropolitans in particular to have a little place in the country. Or on the coast, of course, although, if the knickerbocker glory belongs spiritually to the seaside, the holiday cottage surely belongs in a country lane, beside a dingly dell, with a thatched roof and a charming but overgrown garden. Not that images of thatched cottages with overgrown gardens exactly leap out from the expensively produced brochures of Rural Retreats and their ilk. And when they do, the thatched cottage invariably comes with an up-to-the-minute Poggenpohl kitchen, Farrow & Ball colours throughout, and not so much growth in the garden that there isn't room for a hot tub. These days, the metropolitan yearning for a little place in the country carries certain preconceptions. Leafing through a brochure for one of these upmarket cottage-rental companies I find a 'Grade II-listed thatched threshing barn' in East Anglia, with a small indoor swimming-pool and a sauna. There was a time when folk would have been quite happy to stay in a Grade II-listed thatched threshing barn without the provision of swimming and sauna facilities.

Of course, the cost of such places – in this instance £1195 for three nights at the height of the season – is prohibitive for many of us. But there is another, cheaper way for townies or city folk to enjoy a retreat in the country, or at the seaside, and that is to take it there themselves. I refer to the touring caravan.

There are caravans and caravans, of course, and like any other possession the caravan is often subject to that very British impulse to keep up with the Joneses, whereby yours has to be at least as good as, and preferably better, than your neighbour's. I say British, yet the phrase 'keeping up with the Joneses' is American: it was the title of a comic strip, which began in the New York *World* newspaper in 1916. On the other hand, that wonderful word 'one-upmanship' was coined by the ineffably British Stephen Potter (Westminster School, Oxford and the Coldstream Guards), and Potter would have enjoyed an exchange my father-in-law had with his next-door neighbour a few years ago.

'All right,' said Bob, by way of greeting over the garden fence.

'All right,' said his neighbour, adding, apropos of nothing, 'wife's up at £32,000 caravan at Ingermells.'

'Oh, it's a small 'un then,' replied Bob, quick as a flash.

The word 'caravan' is foreign in origin – it derives from the ancient Persian word 'Karwan', meaning groups of travelling traders – and it was Romany gypsies in the nineteenth century who introduced the notion of portable homes to the British, but it was a Scotsman, William Gordon Stables, a former naval surgeon and author of adventure books for boys, who turned the concept into a leisure activity.

In 1885 Stables commissioned a 'gentleman's caravan' from the Bristol Carriage Company and travelled through the country in it, to great popular acclaim. It was called the Wanderer, accommodated Stables, his coachman, his valet, his dog and his cockatoo, and was pulled by two horses, which doubtless enabled it to go more quickly than my friend Tony's Uncle Stefan's caravan, towed by his elderly and inappropriately named Triumph Dolomite Sprint. Tony tells me that whenever Uncle Stefan arrives at his destination – having eschewed all motorways, which he loathes – he always comments on how jolly quiet the roads were. This of course is because there was a twenty-mile build-up of traffic behind him, to which, every time, he remains cheerfully oblivious.

If you've been in that tailback behind Uncle Stefan's caravan, or any tailback like it, you might not wish to celebrate the memory of William Gordon Stables. But he is owed an eternal debt of gratitude by caravan-lovers, and happily he lived just long enough to see his idea catch on. He died in 1910 but the Caravan Club was founded in 1907, and is still going strong, with no fewer than 375,000 family memberships. I might as well also tell you that a friend of mine once went to a London hospital a few weeks after having a vasectomy, to see whether the operation had worked. Invited to provide a sample of sperm he was shown into a small room, where the nurse assured him, with a conspiratorial smile, that he would find 'some magazines' to help him ejaculate. He was understandably taken aback to find *Motorhome Monthly* on top of the pile, but maybe that just shows what a devoted, and excitable, fan base there is in this country for caravans and motorhomes.

Moreover, the humble caravan actually occupies a rather noble footnote in British military history: in the First World War several were used on the Western Front by the Red Cross, and in the Second World War, Field-Marshal Montgomery famously planned the El Alamein campaign from his caravan, gazing at a picture of his German counterpart, Field-Marshal Rommel, as he tried to second-guess the enemy. All of which brings me to the Volkswagen camper can, which evolved out of Adolf Hitler's plan to deliver affordable cars to the masses; even those of us who owe what very little German we speak mostly to 1970s episodes of *Secret Army* know that the very word Volkswagen means 'people's car'.

I am loath to connect any enduring icon of design with Hitler, yet the VW camper van is undoubtedly iconic, and indeed is the star of the show at an annual event called Vanfest, which takes place at the Three Counties Showground near Malvern, not half an hour from where I live, right in the heart of Elgar country, for heaven's sake. Not even the need to research this book would tempt me to Vanfest, but I suspect the event is full of people who would not have been at all surprised to find *Motorhome Monthly* as a masturbatory aide. I found posted on the internet the following blog, relating to Vanfest 2009. 'The vans on display in the "Show and Shine" competition were truly inspiring. I think my favourite had to be the incredibly low rat style Split Screen. However, the "Pool Bay Hooker" Bay Window was also very cool as was the immaculate Komet T25 with hard side pop top.' I'm glad he had a nice time – it can only have been a he – but I think his blog alone justifies my resolution to stay well away from Vanfest.

Yet it is not quite as strange as it seems to find in the middle of Middle England a communal genuflection before a vehicle with Nazi connections. Reassuringly, the VW camper van owed a great deal to British expertise, and in particular a Sidmouth-based firm of cabinet-makers, J. P. White. By the 1960s J. P. White, in partnership with the VW dealers Lisburne Garages, were producing a range of customized vans with oak fittings, electric lighting, Formica surfaces, an 'Easicool' food-storage cabinet, and an eighteen-litre water container. These were given names such as Caravette, Eurovette and the memorably racy Moonraker, while the no-frills models were called Torvettes and, in homage to J. P. White's Sidmouth base, Devonettes.

By the mid-1960s VW camper vans were commonplace on the sleek, newly built motorways of Britain, an exciting alternative to staying in boarding-houses. Twenty years later they looked *passé*, but now the 'Vee-Dub' is right back in fashion; indeed I know of a company, Snail Trail, that does very nicely renting them out, and anthropomorphizes them even to the point of giving them old-fashioned girls' names. At the time of writing it costs £825 per week to rent Betty, Pearl, Flo, Elsie, Matilda, Nell, Maud, Dot, Daphne or Ruby, and I know a captain of industry whose summer holiday in 2010 was a week in Pearl, an experience of which he, his wife and kids talk very fondly. Pearl wasn't a 1960s original but a replica, imported from Brazil, with all the classic features right down to the gearstick that vibrated at speeds over 40mph, and needed careful coaxing to shift from second gear into third.

It's altogether bizarre when you think about it, but then my own children, without ever having set foot inside one, think that an old VW camper van is at least as cool as the latest Aston

Martin. Each of them even has a porcelain VW camper-van egg cup, which is not an item you're likely to find in the home of our friend Jane, for whom the 1960s camper van evokes miserable memories of going on holiday with endlessly squabbling parents. It was all very well having a Torvette or even a racy Moonraker, but if you were spending that much time together in a confined space, it was vital that everyone got on. And the brutal truth of the matter is that holidays, for as long as people have been taking them, have provoked arguments and tears no less than fun and laughter. As I write, Jane's parents, now in their eighties, are still very much together. Yet Jane remembers most family holidays in the camper van ending up with her and her brother being asked to decide which parent they were going to live with.

Still, for the increasing numbers of people looking to take their accommodation with them on holiday, looking to join the merry waltz from collective to individual leisure, the mid-1960s was an exciting period. In 1965 a man called Sam Alper launched the Sprite Alpine caravan, and it duly became the best-selling touring caravan of all time. It is the one most of us still think of when we picture a caravan.

Alper, in fact, is one of the heroes of this book, like Thomas Cook. He made his first touring caravan in 1947, using brakes from a Spitfire fighter plane, and fashioning the roof from the material used in barrage balloons. That led to his Sprite caravan, which was made from tempered hardboard and sold for less than £200. He was determined to make caravans affordable, but no less determined to prove their reliability. In 1952 he drove 10,000 miles around Europe and North Africa towing one behind his Jaguar, and despite a little bit of local bother when tribesmen in the Sahara had to dig his vehicles out of the sand, the trip made the charismatic Alper a media star, and established the company's reputation for excellence.

Thanks largely to Alper, membership of the Caravan Club doubled between 1960 and 1970, by which time the club operated no fewer than 200 sites, mostly around the coast. By 1970, according to Dominic Sandbrook's meticulously researched book *White Heat: A History of Britain in the Swinging Sixties*, caravans accounted for almost a fifth of all holiday accommodation. And the versatility of the caravan opened up parts of the country as yet hardly touched by mass tourism. Which didn't do much for the aesthetics of our green and pleasant land, but certainly gave the local economies a boost in backwaters such as Norfolk and Cornwall. In 1969 *The Times* thundered that the far south-west of England was blighted by 'perennial summer traffic chaos'. Just a decade earlier there had been no such thing.

Old Sam Alper died in 2002, aged seventy-eight, having also found time in his remarkably busy and accomplished life to make and champion English wine, invent a successful table-football game called Soccerette (I suppose all those -ette suffixes in the 1950s and 1960s were thought to imbue a product with a sleek, American-style glamour) and, even more significantly, to found a chain of roadside restaurants. He got the idea from eating at classic diners while in the United States promoting his caravans, came home and called his chain Little Chef. And while you might think that the man who invented Little Chefs deserves no kind of posthumous credit at all, while you might even think that the inventor of Soccerette might have called his roadside restaurant chain Sickette, I'm not ashamed to admit that when I was a child being lugged round Britain in my parents' Vauxhall Viva, a stop at a Little Chef represented a treat of Olympian proportions. So hats off to Sam Alper.

Regrettably, we never had a caravan behind the Vauxhall Viva on those journeys round Britain; I think my mother and father would have considered it a little *infra dig.*, as they say in Southport.

Nor did we ever stay on fixed-caravan sites and, listening to my good friend Ian's memories of childhood holidays, I can't say I'm sorry. Every summer Ian's parents used to take him and his two brothers from Richard's Castle, a small village on the Herefordshire/Shropshire border, to stay in a caravan at Borth on the Welsh coast.

'You know how you're supposed to remember childhood holidays with affection,' Ian says now. 'Not me. To this day if I was offered the choice between a caravan holiday or staying at home, I'd stay at home. We had no privacy, we had to trudge through a muddy field to the shower block, but worst of all was the journey there. My dad drove a Morris 1000 van, so the three of us boys sat in the back, where there were no windows, and no seats. One of my brothers used to start spewing up pretty much as soon as we left home. My mum gave him a bucket even before we got in the van.'

By happy contrast, I didn't enjoy my first caravan holiday until I was eighteen, when I went to the Lake District with my friends Mike, Pete and Kevin, to stay in Kevin's family caravan. Pretty much all I can remember from that trip is Kevin assuring us that he intended to prise a girl called Alison away from her long-term boyfriend Neil, and Mike, Pete and I very unsupportively ridiculing the idea. It's peculiar that I can remember a conversation from a holiday more than thirty years ago, but then I can also remember what books I read on certain holidays going back decades. And I'm sure I'm not alone: the most mundane holiday experiences are somehow seared into the memory in a way that similar experiences at home simply aren't. Incidentally, I don't know what happened to Neil, but Kevin and Alison have long since celebrated their silver wedding anniversary. Our ridicule was shamefully misplaced. Maybe she had fancied Kevin all along. Or maybe she couldn't resist marrying into a family with a caravan in the Lakes.

7

'Closed' signs, congestion charges and Clint Eastwood

While Britain's A-roads and motorways disgorge people out of the towns and cities, pointing them towards the coast or the countryside as they seek some respite from urban life, the same A-roads and motorways lead folk from the coast and the countryside to the towns and cities. After all, for most people, as good a definition as any of a holiday is a temporary change in lifestyle. For those of us who live surrounded by fields, significantly outnumbered by sheep, this means shops, restaurants, coffee houses, theatres, museums, crowds.

It was ever thus, of course; the novels of Jane Austen are full of country folk spending the social 'season' in Bath. But that was a ritual confined to the gentry and aristocracy. Now we can all do it, for a couple of days here and there if not the season. My own Jane meets her friend Kim in Bath every December for a bit of Christmas shopping and a lot of pinot grigio, so in February 2009 when she and I went there together for a weekend, she was able to give me a guided tour, albeit a little lacking in information about Mr Darcy and Beau Brummell. It was more of a 'that's where I got your moleskin trousers' kind of tour.

An impressive knowledge of Bath's retail outlets, however, was of little use when it came to getting the cup of tea we were gasping for on the Saturday at about five p.m. The celebrated Pump Room had stopped serving at 4.30 which seemed a bit premature on a Saturday afternoon, so Jane took me into Jolly's department store, which might well have been the model for Grace Brothers in *Are You Being Served?* of blessed memory. While I visited the Jolly's gents, she went to the Jolly's caff, the promisingly named Café Zest, and asked at the counter for a pot of tea for two.

'Can you look at the sign, does it say we're closed?' said the Jolly's, but not notably jolly, employee behind the counter, gesturing to a board at the Café Zest entrance. Jane went to look, and reported that it did indeed say 'Closed'. 'Then I'm sorry, I can't serve you,' the woman replied, firmly.

I've already remarked, when describing my Blackpool B&B, on the curious capacity in this country of legions of people who earn their corn from the hospitality business to be anything but hospitable, and there is a similar failure by far too many people in the service industry to show much zest for service. As we left Jolly's I observed that there was something dispiritingly English about a woman in a café apparently quite willing to serve a thirsty customer a simple pot of tea, but instead invoking the dreaded 'Closed' sign. This reminded Jane of a line she had heard on the radio, that when the English say 'Only in England' it is with a shaking head in a spirit of exasperation, yet when the Americans say 'Only in America' it is with a smile, an exclamation of pride.

Certainly, our cousins across the Atlantic seem to have grasped the notion that guests and customers should be welcomed with a smile, except possibly in New York, where the British tradition of service with a scowl, or at any rate with a mask of indifference, seems to prevail.

But let us for now venture to old York. As well as her annual trip to Bath, Jane spends a weekend every winter, with her friends Ali and Joanna, in one of Britain's lovelier towns or cities. Ali and Joanna live in Herefordshire too, so they all need some restorative urban bustle. In 2009 they went to Cambridge and in 2008 to York, where Ali led them on an unsuccessful search for Knickety-Knackety Street, a medieval lane with a marvellously quirky name that her father had told her about when she'd told him she was planning a visit to York. They looked for it for ages, separately asking two likely-looking passers-by who naturally turned out to come, respectively, from Antwerp and Minneapolis, and were just about to give up all hope of finding it when Jane noticed a marvellously quirky name on a street sign and said to Ali, 'Are you sure it wasn't Whipmawhopmagate?' 'Oh yes, that was it,' cried Ali. 'Not Knickety-Knackety Street.'

Such are the pitfalls awaiting the rural British on holiday in urban Britain; a little knowledge but not quite enough. Still, they all had a good laugh at Ali's memory lapse, and I suppose it could have been worse. After all, in medieval London there was a quirkily named street called Gropecunt Lane, and there was one in York, too (since respectably re-named Grape Lane), not that any of us would want to seek directions to Gropecunt Lane from even the likeliest-looking passer-by.

Of all the cities in Britain, it is London that most discombobulates the visitor from up north, or out west. If you come from Shanghai or Stockholm, or for that matter Antwerp or Minneapolis, you are entitled to feel a little bit at sea in London, but as a Brit it's slightly embarrassing to feel alienated in your own capital. And if you lived there for thirteen years, as I did, it's even more embarrassing. At February half-term, 2004, having moved out of London just two years previously, we decided to take the children back to see the sights that we hadn't quite got round to seeing when we were proud metropolitans ourselves.

So we drove to London and went to Madame Tussaud's, a visit that would have been unthinkable when we actually lived in the capital. And that wasn't the only way we behaved like typical tourists; we also strayed into the congestion-charging zone and copped a £40 fine. Which, when added to the whopping Madame Tussaud's admission prices, and lunch for five at Pizza Hut, propelled the cost of the afternoon to almost £200. I kind of wished we'd stayed at home surrounded by fields congested only with sheep.

Our misadventures that day are also recorded in my book about country life, *The Pheasants' Revolt*, but deserve another airing in the context of urban holidays. It was the first time I had driven in London since the congestion charge came in. I hadn't realized that I was entering the charging zone, and even if I had I wouldn't have known what to do about it. Even now there must be thousands of British visitors to London, every year, who get caught in the same unforgiving trap.

As for the tourist trap that is Madame Tussaud's, when I lived in London I used to drive along the Marylebone Road, pitying the poor buggers standing in line on the pavement. Some wit or other once observed that the very definition of a Londoner is 'one who has never been to Madame Tussaud's', and certainly there are several sights in London that as a resident make you feel faintly superior to those merely visiting, of which the mob waiting to get into Madame Tussaud's is perhaps the most potent.

And yet there we were, part of that very mob, spending an hour on the pavement and then shuffling in to be greeted by a waxwork model of Tara Palmer-Tompkinson. Now, I don't want to get too Victor Meldrewish about this, but don't you think that the 2.7 million people a year who visit Madame Tussaud's deserve to be beckoned in by someone grander than silly Tara, a woman famous for little other than being famous? I don't suppose she's still there in the entrance hall, having faded from the limelight somewhat, but why on earth was she even there then? What would a wax-work of Tara Palmer-Tompkinson mean to all the foreigners traipsing through, unless they mistook her for Princess Anne or possibly even David Beckham, which frankly wasn't as improbable as it sounds.

Maybe it's something to do with being British that makes me so cynical about waxworks, cynicism being part of our collective psyche. Or maybe there's something particularly aggravating for a Brit to find himself being fleeced in a British tourist trap. Heaven knows I've been fleeced in plenty of tourist traps overseas (in July 2010, on our way home from a week's holiday in Turkey, I was horrified to realize that I'd just spent over £100-worth of Turkish lira on fast food for five at Dalaman Airport) but at least it's foreign money you're being parted from; at least there are some pleasantly unfamiliar smells at the snack bar. At any rate, my assessment of Madame Tussaud's was rather like Bill Bryson's assessment of Blackpool illuminations; that the waxworks would only seem seriously impressive to someone who had never seen wax before. In this age of wondrous computer wizardry, the place seemed like one gigantic anachronism.

I couldn't understand why there hadn't been some attempt to introduce some pizzazz to the experience. It was only a few months after England had won the rugby union World Cup and there was a conversion-taking contest alongside a crouching Jonny Wilkinson, plus a karaoke set-up presided over by a frowning Simon

Cowell, but in terms of anything interactive, that was about it. There was surely no need, in the twenty-first century, for waxworks to stand around quite so waxily. No need, in effect, for Madame Tussaud to sit quite so squatly on her wax laurels. And my disillusion can't just have been the product of my Britishness. Even today there must be Norwegians or Algerians or even the ever-eager Japanese going round Madame Tussaud's thinking the same.

Whatever, my grumpiness increased when I realized that to get into the adjoining Planetarium, we had to start queuing again. The admission price for the Planetarium was included in the cost of the Madame Tussaud's tickets so we felt we ought to have a look, although, as I muttered to Jane, if they'd wanted to give value for money they should have chucked in a stretch limo and dinner at the Savoy. She didn't snigger at my sarcasm because she wasn't listening. And the reason she wasn't listening was that she had spotted Jude Law, the real Jude Law, who would have been on nodding terms with many of the waxworks if only they could bloody nod. He was standing behind us in the queue, with his children, and ended up sitting in the seat next to me in the Planetarium, although he didn't stay for long because his daughter was raising hell, screaming that she was scared.

'Daddy wouldn't take you somewhere scary, poppet,' he kept saying, but she just screamed even louder until finally he barked 'right' and dragged them out even before the complicated commentary about the universe started up, which is the point at which, at a rough guess, 50 per cent of adults nod off. I don't mean to demean astronomy, which is a truly fascinating science, but when you get the chance to sit in a comfortable chair in a dark room, after traipsing round a waxwork museum with your children for two hours – in our case with a five-year-old repeatedly asking us where the woman with two swords was – you're surely entitled to a short kip.

Still, the semi-encounter with a bona-fide breathing celebrity at least gave us something to enthuse about on the way home, which compounded our status as country bumpkins visiting the city; not only had we fallen foul of the congestion charge, we had also practically hyperventilated at the sight of a celebrity.

This reminds me of my pal Ian, the guy whose brother habitually threw up all the way to the caravan-site in Borth. Ian has lived all his life in north Herefordshire, and in that time has been to London only twice. The first time was in 1989 with his first wife, when, intimidated by the crowds, the traffic, the Tube and pretty much everything else, they didn't have much fun. However, on Oxford Street Ian did literally bump into the actor Bill Nighy, whom he recognized from the telly, which pepped things up a little.

Twenty years later, with his soon-to-be second wife, Avril, Ian went to London again. And had a much nicer time, partly on account of the fact that Avril, at least, was reasonably familiar with the Tube. But here's the best bit. At Oxford Circus they emerged from the underground into the open air, where Ian straight away apologized to a man he'd semi-collided with, then looked up to see, to his uncontained astonishment, that it was the actor Bill Nighy. In 1986 something vaguely similar happened to me in America. I visited Carmel, California, and wandered around harbouring the faint hope that I might spot the town's celebrated mayor, Clint Eastwood. Sure enough, on the very next street corner, there he was, unmistakeably tall, lean and handsome, in animated conversation with an elderly woman. I responded as if someone had blown a hole in my sense of decorum with a Magnum .44, rushing up to them and asking Clint for his autograph. He turned a withering stare on me, the kind of look he gave Lee Van Cleef in *The Good, the Bad and the Ugly*, and rasped, 'I'm in a meeting.' I scuttled away.

Nevertheless, I'd been rasped at by an irritated Clint Eastwood, which seemed like a privilege of sorts. Then, the very next day, I flew to New York, and was walking along Madison Avenue inhaling, for the first time, the unique atmosphere of the Big Apple, when who should loom up walking rapidly towards me but a nervous-looking Woody Allen. This time I maintained my decorum – every syllable of his body-language shrieked 'Don't talk to me, and definitely don't ask me for my autograph' – but still, to fall foul of Clint by a palm tree in Carmel, and then scarcely twenty-four hours later to encounter Woody Allen looking neurotic in Manhattan, amounted to the kind of serendipity that you normally only find, aptly enough, in the movies. Thus it was with Ian bumping into Bill Nighy in the same crowded street twenty years apart. As a tourist it made him think, even though as an intelligent person he knew better, that the streets of London were paved with celebrities. Or one celebrity, anyway.

My parents-in-law Anne and Bob also have a lovely story about going to London as wide-eyed *ingénus* from the provinces. In fact it was their honeymoon, in March 1958. At lunch in a Herefordshire pub on their golden wedding anniversary in 2008 I asked Anne what she remembered of their wedding day, and she described running hell for leather from their reception at the Arcadian restaurant in Barnsley, hand in hand through the drizzle, to Barnsley Station. They just managed to catch the train to London, where they had three nights booked at the Kenilworth Hotel in Great Russell Street.

I asked them what they did on their honeymoon. Anne looked at me askance. 'I mean, did you see the sights, go to a show, that sort of thing,' I said, hurriedly. Yes, she said, eyes a-twinkle, they saw the sights. 'Was it your first time?' I asked. There was a fleeting but loud silence. 'In London, I mean your first time in London,' I added. 'Yes, on both counts,' Anne said, with a smile. There are times when I feel like the gaffe-prone character in *The Fast Show*, perpetually offering to get his coat. Instead, I took a glug of wine to mask my embarrassment, which is more than Anne and Bob managed to do at the Kenilworth. To Bob's horrified disbelief, it turned out to be a temperance hotel. Old Thomas Cook would have loved it, but Bob didn't. Even worse, they had mistakenly been booked into a twin-bedded room, which even the sober-minded reception staff at the Kenilworth could see was a regrettable glitch. They were moved to a double, and they still have the bill, which for three nights came to £6/18s./9d. When Anne went back to the same hotel for a conference in 1994, a standard double cost £132 per night. But at least she was able to get a gin and tonic.

Still, the moral values of the Kenilworth Hotel in 1958 clearly didn't stop them having a good time. They both recall their honeymoon with great affection, which perhaps says something, although I'm not quite sure what, about the predilection among Britain's modern honeymooners for a fortnight in Bali or Barbados, the subject of a later chapter.

Moreover, Anne and Bob went home to Barnsley with at least one honeymoon anecdote that they were able to share. At a restaurant near the Palladium one evening, they noticed their fellow diners staring at them, and couldn't understand why until a young woman came over and excitedly asked Bob, 'Are you Tommy Steele?' She went away unconvinced even when he said, in a broad South Yorkshire accent, that no he wasn't.

Back in Yorkshire, I might add, there were a few people similarly unconvinced about their reasons for getting wed. The nuptials had been organized fairly hastily, which to some scandal-mongering mischief-makers meant only one thing. But in March

2008, when Anne told a neighbour that she'd just celebrated her golden wedding anniversary, the neighbour understood. 'Yes, it's ours next Friday,' she said. 'Were you in a hurry for the tax, like us?' Apparently there were financial benefits if you got married before the end of the tax year, which isn't very romantic, but never mind. Romance-wise, running hand in hand through the drizzle to Barnsley station, as newly-weds, takes some beating.

8

Cliveden, Canadian hot tubs, and colonic irrigation

To Anne and Bob, in 1958, the Kenilworth must have seemed tremendously imposing, so heaven knows what they'd have made of the Savoy or the Connaught or the Ritz, had such places been remotely within their honeymoon budget.

Today it's not so hard to picture a young, fairly impecunious, newly married couple really pushing the boat out to stay somewhere smart, irrespective of their background. Most Englishmen sometimes like to make somebody else's home their castle, and increasingly they can. The past half-century or so has seen social barriers if not dismantled, then substantially lowered, and certainly the nation's grand hotels are no longer exclusively or even predominantly patronized by toffs. Much as I loathe the obsession with celebrity chefs, the residencies in smart hotel dining-rooms of the likes of Gordon Ramsay and, before him, Marco Pierre White, have helped the democratizing process. See them on the telly; splash out to eat their food. It's an equation as enticing in Billericay as it is in Belgravia. And helpfully, the distribution of wealth today is less uneven than it was fifty years ago. I dare say it's as common to find a plumber and his wife checking in at the Dorchester as it is a duke and duchess, and three cheers for it. I don't mind wealth determining who stays in these places, but class shouldn't be a factor, not in the twenty-first century.

Nor is it any more at Cliveden, where in the 1930s the Astors hosted the nobs who favoured appeasing Hitler – the so-called Cliveden set – yet where in June 2007 the Liverpool and England footballer Steven Gerrard married his girlfriend, former nail technician Alex Curran, in front of an altogether different and frankly less squalid Cliveden set. Jeffrey Bernard, famously dissolute and still-lamented author of the *Spectator*'s Low Life column, got it right when he said, 'I've met a better class of person in the gutter than I have in the drawing room.' A little further up the M40 that same weekend, incidentally, the Chelsea and England footballer John Terry married his girlfriend, Toni Poole, at Blenheim Palace, ancestral home of the Dukes of Marlborough. I hurrumph as much as anyone at modern footballers' preposterously large wages, but, however slackly the wretched Terry was later discovered to interpret his wedding vows, surely it counts as progress when the social event of the year at one of the nation's great estates is the wedding of a boy from one of the nation's ropier council estates.

On the other hand, too much democracy isn't always a good thing. In 1992, before we were married and more significantly before we had children, Jane and I stayed at Cliveden for a night. It was a massive treat, the more so when we found we had been upgraded to the almost risibly plush Shrewsbury Suite; so called, we decided, because it was roughly the size of Shrewsbury. But then we started leafing through the leather-bound comments book, and found that comments books in posh hotels can be liabilities just as they are in holiday cottages. The people who'd stayed in the room just prior to us had written: 'Roy and Emma had great rumpy-pumpy in the Canadian hot tub. Thanks a mil, Cliveden.' This put an abrupt end to the cheerful delusion that we were padding across our rich bedroom carpet in the elegant footsteps of the aristocracy – who might be quite prepared to have sex in public places but almost certainly wouldn't boast about it. It also kept us well away from the Canadian hot tub, not so much because we were worried about any lingering body fluids that Roy and Emma might have left; more because we didn't want to luxuriate in the same water as people who favoured the expression 'rumpy-pumpy'.

Still, in fairness to Roy and Emma, Cliveden has rather a heritage of concupiscence, and perhaps they felt that with a quick shag in the hot tub they were simply paying homage to the notorious coupling of the Secretary of State for War John Profumo and the 'showgirl' Christine Keeler, who supposedly were introduced to one another by the swimming-pool, in 1961. When we were there in 1992, the head butler, the splendidly named Michael Holiday, told us that on the day the house had opened as a hotel, six years previously, he had noticed a sullen middle-aged woman sitting with two men in the entrance hall. It turned out that the men were a reporter and photographer from a popular Sunday newspaper, and the woman, of course, was Keeler. For Profumo, by then in his seventies and wholly rehabilitated thanks to his commendable charitable works, there was never much respite from the scandal that bore his name. All the old stories were exhumed when Cliveden became a hotel, and three years later the film *Scandal* came out, so the whole thing reared up all over again.

There can't have been many extramarital affairs lasting just a few weeks which seemed so evocative of an era, and have continued to fascinate so many people for so many years.

The colourful history of Cliveden didn't just start with the Astors, however. Previous owners included the nineteenth-century MP Sir George Warrender, a famously lavish host nicknamed Sir Gorge Provender by his friends, and a century or so before him Frederick, Prince of Wales, eldest son of George II and a man with the sad distinction of being best known for his epitaph: 'Here lies poor Fred, who was alive and is dead, there is no more to be said.' And that despite the fact that poor Fred commissioned the masque which included 'Rule Britannia'; thus was the world's first performance of 'Rule Britannia' given at Cliveden on 1 August 1740.

There are stately homes and grand houses all over Britain that have been turned into hotels, and all of them positively ooze history, not always quite as oozily as Cliveden, but sometimes even more so. I love going to these places, when we can afford to, and even when we can't, and I love immersing myself not in their Canadian hot tubs but in the stories of their pasts. In February 2009 Jane and I grabbed a night at Lucknam Park near Bath, which was built, we read on the hotel website, by a wealthy Bristolian called James Wallis with the fortune he made from importing 7000lbs of tobacco from Virginia to England in 1680. I half-hoped to spot his ghost puffing away in defiance of the hotel's strict no-smoking policy.

Most of these places have strict no-smoking policies, and while that prompts no argument from me, increasingly and regrettably there is a sameness about Britain's country-house hotels, a generic dimension as if they were super-posh Best Westerns. This is a consequence of commercial pressures: financial woe betide the swish hotel that doesn't have a spa, for example. And the menus, by and large, seem interchangeable. No hotel chef worth his Maldon sea salt will countenance a menu that fails to make a song and dance about the locally sourced ingredients, which often yields some silly, utterly superfluous name-checks on the menu. At Lucknam Park, for instance, I had 'slow-cooked Burford Brown egg, truffled baby artichokes and leeks, Parmesan and Richard Vine's shoots' followed by 'sirloin of Tim Johnson beef'. I mean, all credit to Richard Vine for his truly excellent shoots, and to Tim Johnson for his most succulent beef, but is this information really conveyed to customers on a need-to-know basis, or simply because the chef thinks it makes him, or less commonly her, look good?

Strangely, the pride these places take in sourcing their ingredients from just down the road does not apply to their hiring policies. On the contrary, it is no longer unusual to spend a weekend in a country-house hotel in even the most remote part of the British Isles and encounter not a single British member of staff. I don't make this observation in a spirit of rampant nationalism, I should add. Indeed, if I owned a country-house hotel I'd probably want a dollop of French flair and an injection of Swiss efficiency around the place. But I'd also want some old-fashioned British gentility, and that's the ingredient that's becoming hard to find.

Two or three years ago, Jane and I, and the children, checked into an elegant country-house hotel in the Cotswolds for a night. I'd just had a small windfall and we'd decided to celebrate in the best way we know. But the receptionist who checked us in and then showed us to our rooms was German with, much as I hate to perpetuate stereotypes, a decidedly chilly, clinical manner. Which is not to say that it should have been a chirpy English rose from Didcot showing us to our rooms but, on the basis that first impressions endure, it was an unfortunate introduction.

On the other hand, a foreign dimension is sometimes just what these most British of institutions need. And just to prove that I'm not anti-German, our Lucknam Park breakfast was served by a perfectly delightful young woman from Bavaria, who pressed us to try a 'smurfy'. This we took to be another Wiltshire speciality, locally sourced, until she came back with a smoothie. 'Ah, a smoothie,' I said. 'Yes,' she said, 'a smurfy.' Similarly engaging was the Lucknam Park sommelier, a Frenchman whose effervescence, had it come in a bottle, would have soaked not just our table but all tables near by. 'Peach, lychees, apricot, it is, as you say in England, top banana,' he enthused about our choice of white wine. And when we asked the waitress if we could have a glass each of dessert wine he bounced over like a Gallic Tigger to explain that the wine we had so astutely chosen came from 'shrinkled grapes'.

Captivated by him, and by the palpable feeling that we were in a room in which cutlery had clattered through the centuries (the wonky old cheese trolley in particular looked as though it had seen action in the Crimea), we took so long over lunch that we left no time to digest it, or to sober up for that matter, before heading to the spa for our late-afternoon massages. I started undressing with the horrible feeling that when the masseuse started on my abdomen, she might be able to feel Richard Vine's shoots and possibly Tim Johnson's beef. Jane had a facial and a head massage, which seemed a lot more sensible, but later reported that she'd been unable to stop herself dribbling with sensory pleasure while the eager young therapist worked on her scalp.

There is, indeed, a whole new code of etiquette that the British must learn, now that every even semi-swanky hotel has a spa. Even Butlin's in Bognor Regis has a spa, with aromatherapists and everything, and a sign outside the sauna saying 'It ain't half hot, mum'. I quite like that air of informality. Too often in spas I've turned up for a relaxing massage and left feeling about as relaxed as if I've just fluffed a job interview. But that is all to do with being English. The whole world knows us for our *politesse*, in fact if you Google the word *politesse* it offers 'politesse en anglais' and 'politesse anglais', as if Englishness is that venerable French word's very definition. Yet typical English politeness and the modern spa experience are not wholly compatible. I once felt myself compelled to apologize for my hairy back to a massage therapist at a hotel in the West Country. She blushed, and generously murmured that she'd seen a lot hairier. The rest of the session passed in silence.

Both on the part of the person doing the massaging and the person being massaged, I would assert that there is something inherently un-English about the full-body massage, which involves a degree of somewhat intimate touching of, or by, a complete stranger. Not for nothing is this full-body treatment also known as a Swedish massage, the Scandinavians being far more liberal than we are in matters of complete or near nudity. And while I wouldn't want to cast all the British, or more specifically the English, as emotionally repressed, and I know that comparatively few of my compatriots were sent away to boarding-school at the age of eight, I do know quite a few who were, and you can see how profoundly strange it must be for a middle-aged chap who was scarcely ever touched by his own mother to have his bare shoulders and thighs kneaded, in a hotel spa, by 22-year-old Hayley from Harpenden, if not 23-year-old Kimberley from Kettering. Not unpleasant, let me add, just strange.

I once talked to a fellow journalist about this and he admitted to me that he had once had a massage in a five-star hotel in the Far East, during which the masseuse was impeccably polite, calling him 'sir' all the time, but that when she got down to the general area of his groin she said, matter-of-factly, 'Excuse me, sir, would little sir like a massage?' Now, I'm sure there's never any such impropriety in smart establishments in this country (although there are doubtless some of my gender who live in hope of having their little sirs attended to), but even in my experience of having had perhaps a dozen entirely respectable massages in British hotels, I always feel just a faint air of awkwardness about the situation.

Overseas, oddly enough, I feel no such self-consciousness. If I'm being given a massage by a comely young Italian or Spanish woman who speaks hardly a word of English, then I can just lie there and take pleasure in a good pummelling. Once, in a hotel in Puglia, a bare-footed Brazilian lady asked me to take all my clothes off and then, as I lay (face down), walked up and down my prostrate naked body. Happily, neither of us spoke the other's language and so could immerse ourselves in the professional relationship of client and customer. But if there's someone with her hands precariously close to my bare bottom with whom I could just as easily be having a conversation about the weather, or *Coronation Street*, it just doesn't feel quite right, somehow. And that, of course, is because I'm British.

An Italian hotelier once told me about a man who turned up to have a massage in the hotel spa and was left alone by the female massage-therapist to take his robe off and put on the standard-issue cotton thong that was just big enough to cover his private parts. When she returned to the room he was lying, face down, on the bed with his bottom exposed and the thong pulled tightly over his head; having never had a massage before, he'd convinced himself that it was some sort of face-mask. I hardly need to tell you which country he came from.

But it's not only as customers in spas that the British are awkward; our national characteristics don't always lend themselves particularly well to staffing such places, either. In 1990

Jane and I had a weekend at Ragdale Hall, the 'health hydro' in Leicestershire. I'd been sent to write about it by the local news-paper in north London that I was working for at the time, the *Hampstead & Highgate Express*, on the slightly tenuous basis that Ragdale Hall's absentee owner lived in Hampstead. So I felt obliged to experience as many treatments as possible, one of which was a session in a flotation tank, a completely dark cham-ber half-filled with saltwater. In 1990 I'd never heard of flotation tanks before, but I was intrigued by the promise that it would afford me complete relaxation and a wonderful sensation of weightlessness in an environment of total darkness and silence. And indeed it might have done so had there not been a persist-ent drip somewhere in the chamber, which far from affording me total relaxation, afforded me growing irritation. Also, the hydro-therapist on the outside of the tank, a plump young woman with purple hair, kept shouting, 'Are you alroight in there, Mr Voiner?' in a broad Leicestershire accent. I lay there naked in the saltwater feeling more and more tense, which wasn't the idea at all.

In fairness, I've heard that Ragdale Hall these days is a much slicker operation than it used to be, and if the plump young woman has stayed on to become a plump middle-aged woman, I'm sure she has made great strides in the important business of making guests feel relaxed. After all, spas in general have come on apace since the early 1990s, just as the Great British Public has become more used to being pampered and pummelled and even having its colons irrigated, whatever that means, exactly.

But as a general rule I still think that the British, whether on the receiving end or dishing it out, remain constitutionally unsuited to the spa experience. That's partly why places like Ragdale Hall have become so popular as destinations for hen weekends, or at least girls' weekends away, because in company you can have a bit of a giggle at the indubitably strange spectacle of lots of over-weight people plodding around in dressing-gowns. I know they call them robes but to the British they will always be dressing-gowns, and of course to the British the dressing-gown is really meant to be worn in the privacy of one's own home, seen by nobody except one's own family or on occasion, if you decide to throw caution to the four winds, by the postman. I'm sure my wife Jane is not untypical of her nationality when she says: 'I hate going down in a hotel lift to the spa, wearing a robe and those daft hotel slippers. When the lift stops at the next floor down and other people get in dressed in normal everyday clothes, I always feel like an escaped lunatic.' Many of us know the feeling.

9

Girls, golf and G8 summits

Jane now takes centre stage in this book, because it is only with her help that I can examine the phenomenon of the 'girls' weekend away', and compare it with the similarly interesting yet markedly different phenomenon of a group of blokes going away together. There are different kinds of girls' weekends away, of course. But what I'm picturing here is not the group of giddy twenty-somethings spending the weekends getting hammered, stuffing themselves with chocolate and trying on each other's clothes, but the middle-aged mums getting hammered, stuffing themselves with chocolate and trying on each other's clothes. Indeed, that the generic term for this sisterly getaway is a girls' weekend is practically on its own a reason for doing it; middle-aged mums like to refer to themselves and their mates as girls.

Jane goes away twice a year with a group of female friends, and once a year just with her mate Kim, on that Christmas-shopping sortie to Bath. Usually in February she goes somewhere for three nights with five or six women she befriended when we lived in Crouch End, north London, for eight years in the 1990s and early 2000s. They all had babies at around the same time and have remained close, but Jane is the only one who has moved out of the city, so their weekend destinations are always rural, alternating between East Anglia and Dorset, to provide the majority of the party with a welcome dose of country air. On her annual weekend away with her Herefordshire friends Ali and Joanna, as already chronicled, Jane heads for the city, to give them all a welcome dose of some urban frenzy.

But the destinations are irrelevant; what's more significant is how a few days away with like-minded female friends has become, for many British middle-aged women, such a greatly prized fixture in the calendar. After all, our mothers' generation never did it. I can recall my mum once going to London overnight with her friend Nina Taylor from across the road, I think to see a ballet, but that was all. By contrast, my dad, who was a horse-racing nut, went to Paris almost every autumn with at least one pal, for the Prix de l'Arc de Triomphe meeting at Longchamp. The same applied in Jane's house when she was growing up. Her dad might occasionally head off for a weekend to walk a stretch of the Pennine Way with a couple of buddies, but for her mum there was no equivalent. And that's not because my dear mother-in-law is a browbeaten domestic drudge; far from it, she's a forthright, spirited character who forged a highly successful career as an educationalist, and is a feminist in all the best senses of the word. Yet there was never any question of her taking off for a weekend with her fellow mums, to a hotel or a rented cottage, to give them some respite from childcare. Even if they could have afforded it, the girls' weekend away simply hadn't been invented.

I suppose what transformed things was the changing domestic

roles of men and women, which gathered pace in the 1980s and by the end of the twentieth century had profoundly altered the cultural landscape. In the 1970s and earlier it would have been nigh-on unthinkable for a group of married women to tootle off together for a leisurely weekend away, leaving their husbands to look after the house, the stove and the kids. But by the 1990s the roles of men and women, in the home as in the workplace, were no longer anything like as prescribed as they had been.

In 1993, when Jane was pregnant with our first child, I went with her to a series of ante-natal classes in the genteel north-west London suburb of Brondesbury Park. By then there was nothing remotely progressive about that; in fact it was more unusual for a woman to turn up to ante-natal classes on her own. I can't pretend that I actually looked forward to those classes (though I still treasure the one truly memorable fact I learnt there: that if a man's bladder were powered by a muscle as strong as the uterus, he could pee across the Thames), but it felt perfectly natural for me to attend.

However, one Wednesday evening I skipped the class on breast-feeding so that I could stay at home to watch an England football match on the telly. Jane wasn't bothered, but the teacher, and even some of our other classmates, could hardly conceal their disapproval. It showed how things had changed, all part of the continuing emancipation of women, whereby men increasingly shared – and more to the point were expected to share – the child-rearing burden.

The notion that no decent mother would leave her small children in her husband's charge for more than a few hours, let alone an entire weekend, had become as irredeemably unfashionable as the notion that it was the man's duty alone to bring home a wage packet. Moreover, where it had probably never even occurred to our mothers' generation that they were entitled to the occasional break from domestic hassle or tedium, our wives and girlfriends were, by the 1990s, cheerfully prepared – all too cheerfully, in some cases – to hand over the baby-milk formula and head for the hills. Today, if you Google 'girls' weekend away', you are presented with no fewer than 22,800,000 options to look at, and no end of hotels presenting themselves as the perfect destination. It's a growth industry in its own right.

On their February weekends, Jane and her mates always stay in a rented cottage, usually a swanky one, because splitting the cost between six or seven makes it affordable. I've never particularly wanted to know how they pass the time on those weekends, though after returning from one of them a few years ago she did reveal that while they'd been sitting around downing a few bottles of wine one evening, the conversation had revolved hilariously, and for quite some time, around the whimsical question 'If you were a fruit, what fruit would you be?' It was then that I realized the acuity of John Gray's famous line about men being from Mars and women from Venus. For two or three nights every August I go away on a golfing trip with a bunch of male friends, and I think it's fair to suggest that if there is ever a lull in the post-prandial chat, I don't ask my mates to ponder the existential question, assuming a parallel life in the fruit bowl, of what fruit they would most like to be.

I don't offer this thought in a spirit of sexist condescension, I should add. There's plenty that we do talk about on our golf trip, plenty of songs sung, plenty of gags told, plenty of meaningful in-jokes indulged, that don't hold up to even semi-intelligent scrutiny. But it shows how the lads' trip and the girls' weekend diverge. Jane and her friends – bright, well-educated, grounded women – also spent one evening competing to see how many Maltesers they could each fit in their mouth. There is something about a same-gender holiday that seems to make teenagers out of mature, responsible British adults. Hence, I suppose, 'girls' weekends away, and weekends away with the 'lads'.

To facilitate further investigation of the Mars–Venus syndrome, I invited Jane to talk me more comprehensively through her girls' weekends. They tend to start, she said, with everyone 'running around squealing' as they explore the bedrooms and decide who's sleeping where. Not something that happens on our golf trips. There then tends to be a subtle grapple for supremacy between those who like everything organized to the nth degree, with each cooking and washing-up session pre-assigned, and those who prefer to let everything just unfold. The politics and power shifts of the girls' weekend away would do justice to a G8 summit and, good friends though they all are, there is evidently always a moment when Friend A is doing the cooking and Friend B, watching, says 'Oh, do you do it like that?' Meaning, of course, 'What a stupid way of doing it.' According to Jane, this ritual exchange invariably involves scrambled eggs. It is an oddity of the British, of which more in the next chapter, that we simply cannot seem to agree on the best way to scramble eggs.

But they don't just stay indoors cooking, eating and drinking on these jaunts. There is always a hearty walk, and always at least one example of what has become known as 'a shopping moment'. This occurs on the obligatory visit to the nearest town 'when Kirsten tries a little skirt on, and we all get very excited if she buys it. Then she tries it on for us again when we get back to the cottage and we all get very excited again.' I think this was the point at which Jane realized that her evocation of the girls' weekend away did not quite match the actual occasion. 'It's a lot of nonsense, really,' she added, defensively.

I can hardly be judgemental. When I was a student at St Andrews University, my friends and I formed a football team named after the pub in which we did most of our drinking, the

Dunvegan Hotel. The Dunvegan Dribblers played together for three seasons, after which we all graduated and went our separate ways, but continued to meet up somewhere in the UK for a couple of days every August, to play golf. We now proudly, tongues only slightly in cheek, call ourselves the Old Dribblonians and in 2010, back in St Andrews, twenty of us got together for our twenty-fifth annual hooley.

Naturally, the aggregate weight has increased since 1985 in more or less inverse proportion to the amount of hair that has fallen out, but when we look at each other we pretty much see – and consequently act like – the 23-year-olds we used to be. The club song – 'Oh I do like to be a Dunvegan Dribbler' to the tune of 'Oh I do like to be beside the seaside' always gets an outing, and many of us have party pieces that are ritually trotted out at our customary black-tie dinner. Mine is an impersonation of George Formby singing 'Leaning on a Lampost'. My friend Steve 'Pussy' Baxter's is always a Shakespearean monologue – Henry V's rousing address on the eve of the Battle of Agincourt – which, depending on how drunk he is, often involves him leaping on to the table, scattering and sometimes shattering assorted pieces of crockery and glassware. Alex 'Pratty' Pratt gives us his impressive rendition of Meatloaf's 'Bat out of Hell', suitably re-named 'Pratt out of Hell'. Davey 'The Boss' Hamilton, Chris 'Baz' Barry and Dom 'Howie' Howard always, to great acclaim, do their synchronized impressions of Jimmy Savile and Bruce Forsyth. And we are all a sight closer to fifty than twenty, in fact closer to fifty than forty-five. So, as you can see, I am ill-qualified to accuse Jane and her mates of immaturity, for trying to accommodate a record number of Maltesers in their mouths.

I suppose these trips effectively represent an antidote to the responsibilities of work and parenthood, which for most people in their forties are pretty onerous. So becoming twenty-three or even thirteen again intensifies the 'escape' element of the trip, something less easily achieved if you're on holiday with your family and need to be a responsible parent. At any rate, as far as I can gather, Jane's girls' weekends and my Old Dribblonians golf trips are pretty representative of middle-aged Brits on short breaks with their friends. Swap Maltesers for Revels, or 'Bat out of Hell' for 'Bohemian Rhapsody', and it might be you.

In many other countries, there is no such practice as the weekend away with same-gender friends. I have a female Portuguese friend who assures me that over there it is unheard-of for a bunch of women to hole up together for a weekend; in fact in Portugal there's not even such a thing as the girls' night out, at least not among married women. Once you're married, you go out with your spouse or not at all. That's not so in the rest of the English-speaking world – America, Australia, Canada, New Zealand, South Africa – but do gaggles of Norwegian women get a break from their husbands and kids by digging in for weekends among the fjords eating mjaltesjers? Would twenty Frenchmen on a golf weekend end up having a sing-song, taking it in turns to deliver their well-oiled (in more ways than one) party pieces? I think it's probably fair to assume that they'd steer well clear of Henry V's speech on the eve of the Battle of Agincourt, but in any case I doubt whether such a thing would happen. Away from home we Brits seem to have a different formula for enjoying ourselves than people of other nationalities.

For men, sport or some other kind of physical activity is more often than not the excuse to go away together. It might be to play or watch golf, cricket, rugby or football, it might be to go walking, cycling, climbing or fishing, but rarely is a weekend away presented as just an opportunity to be together, even if that's effectively what it is. Also, in my experience anyway, it's far less common for two heterosexual men to go away together than two heterosexual women. When they do, it's not long before some-one makes a 'gay' jibe, which they might even pre-empt by making one themselves. I have two good male friends, neither of them even slightly gay, who occasionally take short walking holidays together, sharing rooms in pubs along the way. To not a few among their wider circle of friends, these expeditions are cheerfully known as Nick and Gary's 'Brokeback Mountain' trips. We are an unforgiving, and of course mildly homophobic, nation.

When larger groups of men go away together, nobody thinks it at all odd. Nor is it, though I'm mindful of some of the scenes late at night on our Old Dribblonians trips. It was sobering, though, and I use that word cautiously, to discover a few years ago that our traditional late-night sing-song, give or take the odd Shakespearean soliloquy, is not even remotely unique to us. We were in the Machrie Hotel overlooking the delightful Machrie golf links on the Hebridean island of Islay, lustily going through our usual repertoire, when a sweet-looking waitress came in and starting dishing out well-thumbed song-sheets. Written on them were the words to practically every song we liked to sing, the great singalong numbers by Elvis, David Bowie, Queen, Simon & Garfunkel, the Drifters, the Rolling Stones and Rolf Harris. I think they even included the lyrics to Ernie (the Fastest Milkman in the West), the party-piece of my friend, the Reverend Angus MacLeod. And while it was nice to get all the words right to all these songs after so many years of trying, it was also just a little disconcerting to know that at the Machrie Hotel, week after week, month after month, year after year, other golfing parties had been doing exactly the same thing.

What a quarter-century's worth of experience of these trips also offers is a useful insight into the recent evolution of the British golf hotel. Or maybe it's more of an insight into the evolution of my friends and me. At any rate, there was a time when all that was required of such places was a bed, plenty of hot water, and a well-stocked bar with a liberal after-hours policy. Perhaps as a consequence, that was generally all that was provided. And still is, in many cases. In fact, there are still lots of hotels throughout the British Isles, catering predominantly for parties of golfers, or fishermen, that fall short even of those requirements, the management's assumption seemingly being not that they're lucky to have our business, but that we're lucky to be under their roof. They also count on the belief that groups of blokes won't be too discerning. But groups of blokes have become more discerning, and many of these establishments have duly got better. Where there is a dispiriting lack of improvement, however, is on the catering front.

In Britain, chefs are now as famous as pop stars. The latest book by Delia Smith, Jamie Oliver or Nigella Lawson is as common in the nation's bookcases as the authorized King James version of the Bible used to be. We are supposed, as a people, to have reached a common understanding of the basic precepts of good cooking and good eating. Yet these precepts have somehow failed to reach the kitchens of the average golf hotel. Or of the average hotel, for that matter. Is there a more gloomy spectacle, for Brits holidaying in their own country, than the buffet breakfast in a mediocre hotel? I can't think of one. The gruesome vats of congealing baked beans, stewed bacon, pallid mushrooms and watery scrambled egg, being kept warm, but not alive, by cheerless heat lamps. The flimsy little stainless-steel teapots with their ill-fitting lids. Those miserable stunted pots of jam. The cold, limp slices of bread masquerading as toast. When did the fabled Full English Breakfast become so emasculated?

Sometimes, of course, you just know from every other aspect of a hotel that its Full English will be horrible, and probably best avoided. The really disappointing breakfasts are those served in hotels that have promised something better. But as a description of a Full English that lived right down to expectations, I can't improve on the following account in *The Times*, in 2010, just after the Grosvenor Hotel – in where else but dear old Blackpool? – had been voted, by contributors to the travel-review website TripAdvisor, the grottiest hotel in Britain.

The writer, the aptly named Stephen Bleach, had also been despatched to check out the previous year's winner, the Cromwell Crown Hotel in west London, which had him retching on the threshold. By contrast, he wrote,

The Grosvenor hardly smells at all. It's as if they aren't trying. To the rooms. This is more like it. Along the gloomy corridor, about half the battered doors have their numbers scribbled on in biro. Nice touch. After rejecting a minuscule single with a window that won't close, I'm 'upgraded' to room 110, a 'double'. It's tiny, and the furniture is falling apart. The light is a neon strip. The wiring looks highly dubious. The walls are cardboard-thin and the bed has a hideous flowery duvet cover and lime-green sheets. It's grim.

Nul points for interior design, then, but grim and grime are two different things. Where's the filth? The carpet's threadbare, but it's been vacuumed. The bedding's clean. The shower room's old and grotty, but there's nothing scarily organic lurking. There's one key test left. Gingerly, I strip the bed – and, finally, the Grosvenor lives up to its billing. Both mattress and duvet boast a rich, swirling cloud pattern of stains, testament to years of strenuous use. The general squalor of the place clearly hadn't put previous guests off their stroke.

Stains or not, there was no backing out now. I spread out a sleeping bag and tried to sleep. After a long and troubled dream about an invasion of alien maggots, I went down to try the 'hearty full English' promised on the website. The beans were an orange slurry; the fried bread was like a grease-soaked pan-scrubber. The rest I can describe only by sight. There's a limit, and that sausage was it. I was out of there.

Who could blame him?

10

Scrambled egg, scones and Schleswig-Holstein

There are, of course, plenty of hotels the length and breadth of Britain serving excellent breakfasts, so it is perhaps unfair to focus on those that get it disastrously wrong. But even the finest example of the Full English Breakfast as we know it today would have caused no end of mirth among the more affluent Victorians, who were responsible for the notion that the first meal of the day was also the most important. The Industrial Revolution started it, as it started so many modern customs, because it was clearly so important to commence a day at the mill or the factory on a full stomach. So even the working classes tucked into lavish platefuls of eggs, bacon and sausages, although it was the gentry and aristocracy who had the really awe-inspiring breakfasts, featuring all kinds of bizarre dishes: Miss M. L. Allen in her popular 1884 book *Breakfast Dishes for Every Morning of Three Months* positively trilled the praises of snipe on toast.

By Edwardian times, the breakfast sideboard was groaning even more and so, no doubt, were the Edwardians. To the fat fellow who gave his name to the era, the 21st-century definition of a Full English really would amount to a preposterous joke. Gabriel Tschumi, a chef at Buckingham Palace from 1899 to 1932, recorded in his memoirs that while Queen Alexandra was content with only *oeuf en cocotte* and a little cold meat in jelly for breakfast, King Edward VII liked to find room in his formidable belly for eggs, haddock, chicken, woodcock and devilled kidneys.

But even the more muted Full English, of the kind we all yearn for when holidaying in England, or for that matter the Full Scottish, Welsh or Irish, is hardly ever accomplished well these days. Even the toast is rarely right, and if they can't get the toast right, what hope the black pudding? After all, the first thing a child learns to cook is bread; in fact for the writer Philip Morton Shand, old Etonian and grandfather of Camilla Parker Bowles, the entire public-school system was 'amply vindicated in that it teaches boys to make toast'. He concluded that 'it may be an abominable action to beat a boy for a bad translation of Livy, but it is certainly laudable to beat him for clumsily burning one's toast'.

I'm not sure about that, but I do know that making toast is the simplest task in any kitchen, yet getting it warm to the breakfast table seems to be the hotelier's equivalent of splitting the atom, the difference being that someone did eventually work out how to split the atom.

Different establishments confront this fiendish challenge in different ways. Regrettably, there appears to be an increasing vogue in British hotels for those absurd Heath Robinson-esque toast-it-yourself machines, whereby you place a piece of bread on what amounts to a heated circular conveyor-belt, and loiter idiotically while it chugs around and back to you.

Maybe it's just me, but these things always have the effect of making me anxiously proprietorial about my rotating piece of bread. I stand there like a nervous parent in a park playground, waiting for his precious child to finish a turn on the roundabout, and not daring to avert his eyes for even a second, lest the kid should be abducted. Or in my case, the piece of toast, carried off to be abused with Flora margarine and honey, rather than the more wholesome butter and raspberry-jam treatment that it would have got had it stayed with me. Then there are the hotels, usually the swankier ones, where they think that the toast will stay warm if they envelop it in a heavy linen napkin, but it never does. And of course the hapless toast-rack has long been discredited as a practical way of keeping hotel toast warm.

Almost as elusive is the answer to the scrambled-egg question, which seems to tax hoteliers much as the Schleswig-Holstein question taxed nineteenth-century diplomats, but ought not to, because really, while I can see that genuine talent is required to keep toast warm, making decent scrambled eggs really shouldn't be a problem for anyone. And yet it is.

Whenever Jane and I stay in a British hotel or a pub, we apply one measure of excellence above all others: the scrambled-egg test. It is unbelievable how many places fail. We've had scrambled egg that hasn't been scrambled, and even scrambled egg that didn't appear to contain egg. The rule for scrambling eggs is not difficult, and it amounts to this: scrambled egg should never wait for you; you should always wait for scrambled egg.

The buffet scrambled egg kept warm under heat lamps breaks this rule disastrously, and I have already lambasted it, but the scrambled egg served bespoke on a plate is all too often just as dismal. We were once having breakfast at a pub in Northumberland, where the waitress's face visibly fell when I asked for my eggs scrambled. She then disappeared through the swing-doors into the kitchen, and didn't emerge for some time. It became clear that her job was to prepare our breakfast as well as serve it, and also that scrambled egg was not her forte. What we eventually got was a watery substance flecked with yellow that looked as though a small, sickly bird had vomited on to the plate. But that doesn't describe the taste. The taste wasn't as nice as that.

It is holiday experiences such as this that make people resolve, the next time, to go abroad. That, and the maddeningly unpredictable British weather, which as somebody once said only half-jokingly, has been the world's most powerful colonizing influence. Certainly, anyone who naively thought that global warming might cast a bit more sunshine over the British summer was rudely disabused of the idea by the gruesome summers of 2007, 2008 and 2009, followed by the only marginally better one of 2010, and in a way a similar phenomenon applies to food. Nobody doubts that there has been an eating-out revolution in this country over the past couple of decades, with the deep-fried brie-and-cranberry parcel now more ubiquitous in country pubs than the steak-and-kidney pie. But revolutions can sometimes effect too much change for their own good. In the frantic rush to drizzle everything with raspberry vinegar, the basics of good, honest British cooking have been eroded. It is perfectly possible to have a poor meal when holidaying in the French or Italian countryside, and even more possible in their towns and cities, but still, regrettably, a damn sight likelier in the UK.

Let me, though, now turn to a culinary staple of the British holiday, or to be more specific of the English holiday, that remains, on the whole, pure and untarnished. I refer of course to the cream tea, which is, with the possible exception of fish and chips, what foreigners vacationing in Britain, craving something utterly traditional, most like to eat.

We Brits, meanwhile, can treat ourselves to an old-fashioned cream tea as often as we like. And yet we don't. Do you know any Brits who routinely have cream teas when they're *not* on holiday? I don't. It would somehow seem extreme, even decadent.

It's not that we're a puritan lot. We like to let our hair down, and heck, sometimes even our trousers, as much as the next nation, but we do like to ration our pleasures. A good cream tea is one such, and by all accounts has been for the best part of a millennium, if not longer. According to Wikipedia, which admittedly means it just might be a fact invented by a bloke in Leighton Buzzard with nothing much to do one Saturday afternoon, there is evidence to suggest that that the tradition of eating bread with cream and jam was already well established at Tavistock Abbey in Devon in the eleventh century.

Certainly, for many hundreds of years, successive generations of British cooks have devoted themselves to perfecting the scone and its numerous cousins. I have a marvellous book called *Good Things in England*, written in 1932 by Florence White, who was effectively the country's first freelance cookery writer. Her book is a collection of recipes from medieval times on, and the baking chapter alone is like a tour through the counties and the centuries, containing recipes for, deep breath, Devonshire Chudleighs, Scarborough Muffins, Somersetshire yeast bread, Cumberland Girdle Cakes, Bran Brack, Cornish Splits, Lancashire Bun Loaf, Yorkshire Spiced Loaf, Riddle Bread, Ripon Christmas Bread, Norfolk Rusks, Lady Arundel's Manchet, Cornish Manchants, Huffkins, and, from a recipe sent in by Miss Bright of the Northern Counties School of Cookery in 1929, the splendid-sounding Singin' Hinnies.

So it is hardly surprising that there are many regional variations of the cream tea, even if it is still most associated with Devon and Cornwall. The traditional Devon method is apparently to cut the scone in two, covering each half with clotted cream, then dolloping strawberry jam on top, whereas in Cornwall the cream tea never used to feature a scone at all, but consisted of the Cornish Split, a sweet white bread roll, for which the recipe in *Good Things in England* came from a Mrs R. Bennett, may she rest in yeast.

In 1982 a reporter for the *New York Times*, Sandra Salmans, wrote an article specifically about the British tradition of the cream tea, in which she described yet another variation apparently known as 'thunder-and-lightning', 'a thick slice of bread spread liberally with clotted cream and honey'. I'm willing to take her word for it, although about fifteen years ago I did read a travel feature about London in the *New York Times*, one of the world's great newspapers, in which the writer expressed genuine surprise and disappointment that not once during his stay did he experience a proper pea-soup fog. I imagine he was also slightly miffed not to bump into Sherlock Holmes. At any rate, the point is that an intelligent paper like the *New York Times* is not beyond peddling a romanticized, Hollywood image of England, so it's entirely possible that its reporter Ms Salmans waxed a little over-lyrical about her cream teas.

On the other hand, who wouldn't get lyrical about a good cream tea? In her *New York Times* article, Sandra Salmans shared what she had learnt from her journey through south-west England, that 'the tea should be freshly brewed and the scones baked that day'. But, she added, 'it is the cream that sets Devon teas apart. This is neither the cream that one puts in coffee nor the sweetened whipped cream served on desserts. This is clotted cream, a golden, rich, heavy cream so thick that one can stand a spoon in it, so high in calories that one loses count. Yet in the mouth, clotted cream seems almost sublime.'

H. V. Morton, in his classic travel book *In Search of England*, published in 1927, had a similarly sensual experience across the border in Dorset. At a tea shop in Christchurch he enjoyed 'basins of Dorset cream, pots of jam, puffy cakes oozing sweetness, ramparts of buns and crisp rolls'. But at the end of his rhapsody came the stab of guilt that proved that here was an Englishman, not a sybaritic American or Australian or Frenchman: 'I stood up heavily and strode out up the green avenue to the ancient Priory, feeling rather ashamed of myself.' Only an Englishman could feel ashamed after a cream tea.

Morton had conceived his book while lying in what he was convinced was his death-bed, in Palestine. He reckoned that he was dying of spinal meningitis, and even though he was a Londoner, when he pictured the England he felt sure he would never see again, the images were of thatched cottages and woodsmoke, and no doubt cream teas; the England of his holidays. 'This village that symbolises England sleeps in the subconsciousness of many a townsman,' he wrote in the first chapter of *In Search of England*. 'A little London factory hand whom I met during the war confessed to me, when pressed, and after great mental difficulty, that he visualised the England he was fighting for – the England of the "England wants you" poster – as not London, not his own street, but as Epping Forest, the green place where he had spent Bank Holidays.'

In the same trying circumstances I think we'd all be the same as the 'little London factory hand' Morton recalled with such casual condescension, for the lasting impact of holidays on our imagination and memory is out of all proportion to the time they consume in our lives. When we British lie back and think of England, or Scotland, Wales and Northern Ireland, do we picture our homes, schools and offices, or the country that we know from our weeks, weekends or merely day trips away: the rolling hills, the windswept beaches, the majestic cathedrals, the idiosyncratic tea shops? Or even shoppes.

All of which brings me right back to the cream tea, and in particular to the one served at the Emporium, a tea shop in a building nearly 600 years old, in Drapers Lane, Leominster, Herefordshire. Willing to make almost any sacrifice in the course of researching this book, I decided to sample a typical cream tea in a notably idiosyncratic tea shop, for there are few finer places in which to study the British on holiday. I asked Jane to join me on this intrepid exercise. The Emporium fitted the bill perfectly.

In a way we cheated by going somewhere barely five miles from our house, but that neither of us had ever stepped into the Emporium before more or less proves my point, that most Brits indulge in a cream tea only when they're away from home. Actually, we've broken that unwritten law by going several times since, for the Emporium is gloriously quirky, while at the same time managing to be wholly typical of a certain kind of tea shop, or even shoppe.

We all know them from our trips around Britain: enough eclectic knick-knackery on the shelves and the walls to sink the *Ark Royal*, oilcloth-style tablecloths with a flowery motif, kitsch little signs such as 'If you see folk without a smile then give them one of yours', but most of all that powerfully evocative smell, a smell that could only be a traditional tea shop, just as the smell of a launderette could only be a launderette.

The other thing that so often characterizes such places is the low murmur of holidaying couples, or occasionally families, all abiding by another unwritten law, that the British on holiday keep themselves to themselves. Sometimes, indeed, couples on holiday don't even speak to each other, so there is silence, punctured only by the occasional rattle of a willow-pattern saucer, or the clink of a knife on a willow-pattern plate. Not that this is the case at the

Emporium, which is run by a hugely charismatic woman called Suzie, who could engage a Trappist monk in animated conversation. And Suzie, I should add, comes originally from Penzance, so her cream teas are very fine indeed. But in one of the rare silences that wasn't filled by Suzie's booming bonhomie, Jane turned to the pair of elderly holidaymakers at the next table – we knew they were holidaymakers because of the guidebook on the table, the cagoules carefully draped over the backs of their chairs, and the fact that they weren't saying anything to one another – and said cheerfully, 'Can you recommend the lemon meringue pie?'

It was an innocuous question, yet what the woman evidently heard was 'Can you lend us eleven magpies?' At any rate, an expression of profound bemusement crossed her face, but of course it was simply the bemusement that comes from being spoken to by a stranger in a tea shop. 'Yes, it's very good,' she muttered, when she had recovered her composure, and I was reminded of another pub Jane and I once stayed in, the Griffin at Felin Fach, on the edge of the Brecon Beacons National Park. It is a wonderful place, with comfortable rooms and fantastic food, but also the rather daring policy of putting everyone who stays overnight around the same breakfast table. Which, the morning we were there, led to three or four conversational overtures on our part, swiftly aborted when we realized, or were reminded, that on the whole the British on holiday really do like, especially over breakfast, to be left alone, thank you very much.

11

Poirot, paparazzi and prime ministers

The fundamental reserve of the British was never so clearly illus-
trated to me as on those ten holidays we spent in Cornwall,
staying in the same room in the same hotel for the same ten days
every summer. The hotel was the Treglos, a classic English seaside
hotel of the sort where you are required to dress for dinner; the
kind of place Agatha Christie might have written about, with
Hercule Poirot and Captain Hastings earnestly discussing over a
breakfast kipper the significance of the gold signet ring missing
from the hand of the old gentleman found poisoned in the bridge
room.

We weren't the only people who went to the Treglos at the same
time year after year, and so we got to know, and eventually
befriend, many of our fellow guests. But, boy, it was slow going.
A fleeting conversation about the weather one year might be
followed twelve months later by a slightly more in-depth chat

embracing not only the weather but also the travails of the England cricket team, followed the next year by a drink on the terrace and the year after that by not only a drink on the terrace but also a round of golf. You get the picture. And had it not been for all our children playing together, kids generally being immune to the social inhibitions of their parents, I doubt whether any of us would have moved beyond that fleeting exchange about the weather. Yet by the time we stopped going, we had made firm friends of two or three other families, the kind of friendships that we expect to last for ever.

Moreover, in the case of a lovely woman called Angela, it transpired that back in the 1970s my late father and her father had been business associates; indeed that on the day my dad died – of a heart attack on a train in early 1976 – he had been travelling to London to meet her dad. My father's name, Allen Viner, was as well known to Angela and her sister in their youth, as her father's name, Roy Dickens, was known to me. Yet it took seven years for Angela and me to make this extraordinary connection. That's the British for you; circumspection at all times, even on holiday.

Until we got to know our fellow guests, we relied largely on my mother-in-law's eavesdropping ability. Anne and Bob came with us to the Treglos every summer and, in the absence of Monsieur Poirot, Anne provided the powers of detection. She would sit at the dinner-table wearing an inscrutable half-smile, appearing to be listening to our conversation, when in fact she was keeping an ear on the conversation of the couple at the table behind. 'It's her second marriage, his first,' she would then report, adding, in a conspiratorial whisper, 'She has a son by the first marriage who's a convert to Buddhism.' Then there'd be a pause as she leant back, then forward again. 'And he's a second-cousin of Alan Titchmarsh's wife.' Back. Forward. 'Although he's never met her, apparently.'

Our other impeccable, although always discreet, source of information about our fellow guests was the *maître d'*, Wally Vellacott, a tall, imposing-looking fellow with a thick head of white hair. Wally was not so much a *maître d'* from the old school, as a *maître d'* who trained the people who taught *maître-d'* classes in the old school. He was the prototype, never fazed by any situation, not even the one in which he had found himself in the early 1970s when he was summoned to a guest's room and there found the guest and two nubile young women wearing only towels. Wally was invited to stay for 'a drink', but politely made his excuses and left. The guest, incidentally, was the actor Donald Pleasence; since Wally told me about his encounter I've never been able to watch *The Great Escape*, in which Pleasence played the myopic forger, Flight Lieutenant Blythe, without thinking of Wally's own great escape.

Wally had a seemingly limitless fund of stories about the Treglos, although one of my favourites was told to me by a fellow guest, Mark, one of those who, eventually, became a good mate. Mark and his family had been spending their summer holidays at the Treglos for longer than we had, and he told me about the old night porter, Henry, a fabulous character sadly now on duty behind the big front desk in the sky. One night, after a good deal of wine had been taken, Mark asked Henry if he had seen active service during the Second World War. 'Far East,' grunted Henry. 'Special Operations. Used to parachute us behind the lines and we took out the Japs one by one. Crept up behind them and slit their throats.' He demonstrated with a corkscrew.

'You'd never manage to creep up on me without me hearing you,' said Mark, winding him up.

'We'll see about that,' said Henry.

And thus it was that a couple of nights later, Mark woke up alongside his wife Sara at about four a.m. to find Henry the night porter looming over him in the gloom, slowly drawing a finger across his throat. 'Gotcha,' he muttered, then silently receded into the night.

I love that story, although it wouldn't have gone down too well with the Special Branch officers who more than once checked out the Treglos during Margaret Thatcher's long tenure as prime minister, for the very good reason that many of her entourage, including her hapless son Mark, used to lodge there while she stayed in a house down the lane owned by her friend Lord Wolfson. Thatcher was notoriously holiday-shy, apparently regarding holidays in much the same way that she regarded sleep, as a wholly unwelcome distraction from the business of prime-ministering, but for a few summers during her premiership her advisers managed to persuade her to take a few days in Cornwall. There is even a picture somewhere of her and Denis taking a stroll on the lovely Constantine Bay beach, coincidentally – or perhaps not so coincidentally – the same stretch of coast where another Tory prime minister, David Cameron, was later snapped on his summer hols with his wife Samantha, shortly before Samantha rather unexpectedly gave birth to their daughter Florence Rose Endellion.

The British have always been strangely and perhaps unhealthily fascinated with prime-ministerial holidays, our fascination usually stoked up by newspapers in need of news fodder during August's so-called silly season. In August 2010 the picture of the Camerons at Daymer Bay, a few miles north and across the Camel estuary from Constantine, was even accompanied, in a paper as eminently sensible as the *Independent*, by a column focusing on their choice of holiday wear. 'Only someone deeply institutionalised wears smart loafers on a coastal path,' mused the deputy fashion editor, Carola Long. 'That polo shirt, too, is rather dark and dour for a summer holiday; a bright Tory blue would have been a bit more jaunty. But it could have been a lot worse.'

Also fuelling this interest in the prime-ministerial hols is a widespread, unedifying but very British sense of righteous indignation concerning the destination, cost and duration, which down the years has made the prime minister's choice of holiday an absurdly sensitive topic. A week at Daymer Bay is an irreproachable choice, of course. But when Stanley Baldwin was PM, he used to forsake 10 Downing Street for the pleasures of Aix-les-Bains in the foothills of the French Alps for an entire month. Today, that would amount to political suicide.

Indeed, even if a 21st-century prime minister were to stay with his family at Butlins in Minehead, there would be those accusing him of political posturing, or of wilfully inconveniencing all the other Butlins holidaymakers with his security needs. But PMs don't do that, of course. Very often they enjoy nice freebies in a villa or château belonging to a rich friend or foreign potentate, which brings them excoriation for not doing something a little more humble. And as ex-PMs they can push their boats out – or better still, other people's boats – even further. Winston Churchill in his twilight years holidayed merrily on the yachts of friendly tycoons such as Aristotle Onassis and Lord Beaverbrook, although not without a few barbed comments from his critics back home.

In those days, though, before tabloid newspapers designated themselves our moral guardians, criticism didn't amount to much more than those few barbed comments. It is said that, following his crushing defeat in the 1945 general election, Churchill cheerfully cashed in on his international prestige by negotiating a special £4-a-day rate at the Hôtel de Paris in Monte Carlo, and it's amusing to consider what the *Sun*, the *Mirror* and the *Mail*, to say nothing of satirical TV programmes such as *Have I Got News For You?*, would have done with that kind of information these days.

However, Churchill's biographer Roy Jenkins, the son of a

miner and for a time a Labour chancellor of the exchequer, although never exactly a man of the people, saw nothing wrong in prime ministers taking plush foreign holidays, loftily remarking 'Do we really want to be governed by pygmies in boarding houses in Bognor?' It was a reasonable point, if rather insensitive towards those of perfectly average height who routinely, and cheerfully, holiday in Bognor boarding-houses. Yet it could be argued that there is more dignity in paying your way in a Bognor boarding-house than ringing round your wealthy mates in the hope that one of them might be able to free up a wing of his castle. The Blairs were particularly shameless in this regard, luxuriating in the hospitality of Cliff Richard (Barbados) and Bee Gee Robin Gibb (Miami), among many others. Cherie even admitted as much in her memoirs, describing herself and Tony as 'house-bandits'.

Characteristically, Gordon Brown was much more frugal with his holiday choices, or at least his wife Sarah was. In the summer of 2008, after it had been announced that the Browns would be vacationing in the Suffolk resort of Southwold, Gordon let it slip that he hadn't known where he was going himself until he 'read it in the papers'. It was probably a joke, but quite possibly not. Either way, he couldn't win. Some were affronted by the idea of a prime minister so remote from real life that he wasn't even consulted on the family holiday destination, while others wondered what kind of political capital he was trying to make by pretending not to have been consulted. Who knows, there were maybe even some who took it for the inoffensive quip it was meant to be, and laughed.

Whatever, at least Brown, unlike his predecessor, was supporting the British tourist industry, and as a classically genteel English seaside resort, Southwold was an irreproachable choice. That may also have been the attraction for a politician Jane and I encountered there *circa* 1994. We were spending a couple of nights at the charming Swan Hotel, which at the time represented a rare blow-out, and at dinner one evening were startled to hear a familiar stentorian voice issuing from a large man seated, with his back to us, at a nearby table. 'No broccoli for me,' boomed the Reverend Ian Paisley MP, in exactly the same uncompromising tone with which he used to tell the world that Gerry Adams supped with the devil.

Back then Paisley was a big IRA target – in fact targets didn't come much bigger – so we were a teeny bit disconcerted to find ourselves sharing a hotel dining-room with him, while at the same time being intrigued by the spectacle, right there before us if not in glorious Technicolor then certainly in surround sound, of such a high-profile politician on his holidays. Would we see him with his trousers rolled up and a knotted hankie on his head, searching for skimming-stones on Southwold's shingly beach? We tried surreptitiously following him round, until we decided that we were probably starting to arouse the suspicions of his security men. But we saw enough to treasure the incongruous sight of the Reverend Paisley and his thunderous Ulster vowels in holiday mode.

After all, as Michael White wrote in the *Guardian* in 2008: 'Politicians on holiday never quite look at ease. Relaxing is not what statesmen are supposed to do. That has been part of the sport for photographers ever since early experiments in the holiday photo-opportunity emerged at the start of the 20th century. The sight of Lloyd George digging his garden in Wales must have prompted voters to wonder if he'd ever held a spade before.'

As White also noted, ever since William Gladstone was pictured felling trees on his holidays, politicians have tried to buff their image with the electorate with a spot of carefully staged paddling, or ice-cream licking, or indeed gardening. But some prime ministers, admirably if naively, have not compromised on their choice of holiday destination. In the early 1960s, the aristocratic Harold Macmillan, and the even more aristocratic Alec Douglas-Home (a fourteenth earl, no less), were happy to be photographed on their favourite grouse moors, doubtless convinced that voters would be reassured to see the governing classes indulging in a spot of traditional recreation. The Labour Party leader Harold Wilson, who in the modern phrase was media-savvy enough to affect the use of a plebeian pipe even though he apparently preferred cigars, must have rubbed his hands with glee when he saw pictures in the newspapers of Tory grandees spending their holidays mass-murdering grouse. And it wasn't only newspapers. Macmillan and Home 'gave the game away by allowing themselves to be photographed for grainy black-and-white TV', wrote White, 'a concession to popular curiosity which would lead to paparazzi snaps within a generation'.

In 1964, after thirteen years of Conservative government and lots of dead grouse, Labour took power. For the next twelve years, 10 Downing Street oscillated between Wilson and the Tory leader Ted Heath, and with the burgeoning influence of the media, the prime-ministerial summer holiday became the subject not just of annual coverage, but also comment. Heath liked to spend his holidays at the helm of his yacht, *Morning Cloud*, and while sailing was undoubtedly a genuine enthusiasm, the photographs didn't hurt in bolstering the manly image of a confirmed bachelor commonly assumed, like all confirmed bachelors, to be cautiously and covertly gay.

Wilson, meanwhile, spent his holidays in the isles of Scilly, birdwatching in shorts and sandals, and, if you believed the impressionist Mike Yarwood, saying to Mrs Wilson 'Oh, Mary, come and listen to this' in his slightly nasal voice over and over again. He was as genuinely fond of the Scillies as Heath was of yachting – except when he thought that the passing trawlers were

Russian spy ships in disguise, sent to eavesdrop on his telephone conversations – and would in due course be buried there. Yet Wilson and his advisers, just like Heath and his team, scrupulously ensured that every holiday yielded several photo-opportunities, to make him look like a man of the people.

Across the Atlantic, incidentally, successive presidents used their holidays to cultivate the same kind of folksy image. It started more than 100 years ago when Theodore Roosevelt made sure he was photographed hiking, fishing and shooting. It may even be that his famous refusal to shoot a bear cub, which is supposedly how the teddy bear got its name, was a cynical manoeuvre to win hearts, minds and, therefore, votes. By the end of the twentieth century, movers and shakers at the White House needed no convincing of the political power of a holiday. Dick Morris, who masterminded Bill Clinton's successful re-election bid in 1996, actually warned Bill and Hillary to stay away from Martha's Vineyard, where the Kennedys had had their holiday compound, on the basis that his populist image would be tarnished by the Vineyard's perceived elitism. Clinton wasn't happy to be told where to go and what to do on holiday. Sarcastically, he asked whether a round of golf would be permissible if he wore a proletarian baseball cap, or if he could go fishing as long as he promised not to catch anything? But Morris was probably right. These things can make a difference.

12

Butlins, Bognor and Boney M

This book is about the British on holiday, not American presidents, and still less Russian intellectuals, but bear with me. My sister-in-law Vera comes from a family of famous Russian intellectuals – famous in Russia, at least, where a handsome St Petersburg street is named after her late grandfather, Dmitry Likhachev, considered to have been the world's foremost authority on Old Russian language and literature. Vera grew up in the Soviet Union of the 1960s and 1970s, when perestroika was scarcely a glint in the eye of Mikhail Gorbachev or anyone else, and tells stories of her childhood holidays that, as someone heading around the same time for places like Barnstaple and Largs, I listen to with wide-eyed incredulity.

Vera and her family were compelled to spend their holidays at a resort called Koktebel, on the Crimean peninsula in what is now Ukraine. This was a privilege accorded to very few; in the 1960s

Koktebel was intended as a resort for writers and academics only, one of several such places around the country known by the Soviets as *dom tvorchestva*, meaning 'houses of creativity'. The idea was that all these brilliant thinkers would congregate and swap ideas in an environment conducive to relaxation, ultimately for the greater glory of the USSR. There were other holiday resorts reserved for the exclusive use of artists, actors, musicians, leading members of the Communist Party and top military personnel, but in Koktebel the holidaymakers were fiercely cerebral types; there was an excellent library, and a cinema which occasionally showed films that elsewhere in the Soviet Union were banned for the dreaded, catch-all 'ideological reasons'.

These institutions, along with a large park, were impeccably, even lavishly, maintained. The accommodation, however, was not so salubrious. Vera's family had to share a house with the family of another intellectual, and even within the house there were rigid hierarchical rules. 'The most desirable place to sit was on the verandah,' Vera told me. 'But you could only sit on the verandah if you were the most famous writer present, or had the highest rank in the Academy of Sciences.'

All this sounds bizarre to British ears, the more so if you imagine the same thing happening here, and start wondering what seaside resort would be chosen as the one exclusively for intellectuals? Lyme Regis? St Ives? Probably not Southend. On the other hand, if you think about our own holiday camps, from the first Butlins, which opened in 1936 and was an instant hit with the working classes, to the modern-day Center Parcs, which resound with the cries of little Ruperts and Arabellas, it's not hard to recognize a kind of social streaming. It might not have been conceived and administered by moustachioed men sitting at big government desks with pictures of Stalin on the walls behind them, but it's there, all the same.

In the summer of 2006 Jane and I took the children for a long weekend at the Center Parcs in Wiltshire, otherwise known, if only on the Center Parcs website, as the Longleat Forest holiday village. I had resisted the idea of Center Parcs for ages – I don't really know why – but Jane and the kids were dead keen, and when our good friends the Claytons suggested that we all go together, the thing was booked and paid for before I could register any opposition, or even offer my favourite bit of trivia about Center Parcs, namely that its curious spelling is actually incorrect in every language. In Britain it should be Centre Parks, in America it would be Center Parks, and in French they would spell it Centre Parcs.

Going with another family made sense, at least. That way, if we all hated it, we could convivially hate it together, having fun being catty about the facilities and our fellow guests. Also, the Claytons enjoy cooking, and eating, as much as Jane and I do, so whatever the cooking facilities, the quality of the self-catered dinners would be guaranteed. We booked two adjacent 'comfort villas'.

Incidentally, this business of going on holiday with another family, or other families, is another relatively recent phenomenon among the British. Not so long ago, certainly within my lifetime, a family holiday was, for almost everyone, a resolutely private undertaking. When and why families began to go away together, I'm not sure. It has long been a common practice for two or more couples to holiday together, but the unwritten rule tended to be that, once children entered the equation, the family became a single holidaying unit. My wife's theory is that ours is the generation that wrought the change, being younger at heart than our parents were at the same age, or at least less accepting of the ageing process. So holidays have become less children-orientated, in the sense that the priority is no longer for the kids to have a great time; these days, the adults want to whoop it up as well. Going with other adults makes that easier, while also providing playmates for the kids so that they can be more self-contained.

At the same time, going on holiday with another family can be fraught with pitfalls. We have done it very successfully over the years, but also rather unsuccessfully. One of the more enjoyable was to a small Italian resort south of Naples, Santa Maria di Castellabate, in the mid-1990s, but I do remember Jane remarking only half-jokingly to me that in beachwear she felt self-conscious about her bottom, which I hasten to add is perfectly proportioned, because our friend Mandy's bum was so small and pert. 'When we wander down to the sea together I find myself gripped by an impulse to walk backwards,' she said. 'Do you think Mandy would find that strange?'

All sorts of problems can arise. Sometimes, the chemistry between husband A and wife A can do strange things to the chemistry between husband B and wife B. Or the two sets of parents have different ideas about keeping the children in line. Or about bedtimes, or mealtimes. At any rate, on holiday you can discover things about even your dearest friends about which you previously had no idea.

None of this applied to our weekend at Center Parcs with the Claytons, but that was partly because we were aware of our differences before we set off. We're a pretty sporty lot, they are resolutely unsporty, so while I went off playing tennis with the kids, they did other stuff. Mercifully the sun shone, fitfully. Otherwise we would have been compelled to spend even more hours than we did in the vast covered swimming area, the kind of indoor pool to which I am semi-allergic. Maybe there's a word for it; fakepalmophobia, or something. Whatever, I'm not usually a misanthrope, but the amplified cries of over-excited children playing in machine-generated waves, combined with the oppressive humidity, in general make me feel about as well disposed towards the under-tens as W. C. Fields, or King Herod.

So maybe British holiday camps are not for me. Certainly, I was left feeling slightly underwhelmed with Center Parcs, perhaps partly because I'd heard so many lavish testimonials from people who'd been, but also because I had a vague sense of being ripped off. We'd paid £545 for three nights in our comfort chalet, but it was no better than mediocre, and although we mostly cooked lavishly for ourselves, the restaurants we did try veered between average and downright nasty. I can now recall only one of them, a pancake house, but when I do I find traces of bile rising in my throat. British restaurants specializing in savoury as well as sweet pancakes, with one order emerging from the kitchen smothered in whipped cream, and another topped with ham and pineapple, should in my considered view have died with the 1980s. These days they should either be avoided, or better still, firebombed. But the children wanted pancakes, so that was that. Sometimes, there's no escaping that old British holiday dictum that as long as the kids are having a lovely time, everything else follows.

Of course, it's easy to be sniffy about holiday camps these days because there are so many alternatives. It wasn't always so. William Heygate Edmund Colborne Butlin was a South African-born entrepreneur who was smart enough in the mid-1930s both to recognize a shortage of holiday accommodation in Britain, and to cash in with a solution. The welcome new phenomenon of the paid holiday propelled such multitudes of people to the seaside that there simply weren't enough hotel and boarding-house beds to cope; in fact ministers even discussed the possibility of employers staggering holidays, to relieve the pressure on the resorts.

In 1936, the year before the Holidays With Pay Act was passed, Skegness in Lincolnshire – 'Skeggy' as it was known to folk working the coalfields of South Yorkshire and Nottinghamshire –

became the proud home of Billy Butlin's first holiday camp, on the 200-acre site of what had been turnip fields. This shiny new Butlins (the apostrophe was soon dispensed with) was promoted by a poster campaign, showing a cheerful, bewhiskered fisherman saying 'It's so bracing!' And the fisherman wasn't kidding: there were flurries of snow on the very day that the camp opened – Easter Saturday 1936. But Butlin wasn't put off by the vagaries of the British weather, and nor were his customers, not with a week's holiday costing only 30 shillings. The Skegness Butlins was followed in 1938 by a camp at Clacton-on-Sea in Essex, the nearest stretch of seaside to London's East End.

In his highly academic, yet highly readable book *The Delicious History of the Holiday*, Professor Fred Inglis draws a close parallel between the Butlins camps and the summer camps of the Third Reich, 'boisterous, happy, communal affairs given just the slightest nudge towards the Führer by cheerful, good-looking young men and women in well-dressed shirts and shorts and the swastika on their upper arms'.

At Skegness and Clacton, happily, there were no swastikas. Nor, almost better still, was there the more prosaic tyranny of the boarding-house landlady. Inglis reckons that there can be no exaggerating the influence of resorts such as Blackpool and Scarborough on both the topography and social life of the holiday camp; even the rows of small, neat chalets evoked the back-to-back terraces houses of northern towns. But there was no monstrous Blackpool landlady to shout the odds or lock out customers between ten a.m. and tea-time. It is said, in fact, that part of Billy Butlin's inspiration for his holiday camps came from a miserable childhood holiday on Barry Island in Wales, later immortalized if not exactly glamorized by the TV series *Gavin and Stacey*. The poor fellow was locked out of his B&B all day, doubtless by a landlady who looked very much like Stacey's

formidable friend Nessa. It was an inconvenience he felt holidaymakers should never have to confront. Butlins holiday camps
were open all day. And there were plenty of people willing to look
after the kids. In the 1930s, these were revolutionary holiday
concepts.

For Inglis, the early holiday camps represented the 'true gene-
sis of mass vacationing', and in 1946, an East Ender called Fred
Pontin got in on the act, turning a former US Army base at Brean
Sands in Somerset into the first Pontins. His was always a smaller
operation than Butlin's, but Fred Pontin was a pioneer too. He
introduced self-catering, an idea that his rival Billy Butlin had
always sneered at, and he even took Pontins to Spain, urging
people to 'Go Pontinental'. In 1963 the Pontins near Torquay
became home to Britain's first outdoor artificial ski slope, a might-
ily exciting concept for the early 1960s. But an artificial ski slope
didn't make the same impact on Britain in 1963 as four talented
musicians from Liverpool, and it is the ghost of Billy Butlin, not
that of Fred Pontin, who can now boast that a stay at one of his
holiday camps directly inspired the influential look adopted by the
Beatles.

'When I was a kid, I went with my parents and my brother to
Butlins Holiday Camp at Pwllheli,' Paul McCartney recalled in an
interview in 2007.

> I had a vision ... what do you call it, an epiphany? I was by
> the swimming-pool, and we were such a funny family, a little
> bit Alan Bennett. From a door in one of the buildings, I see
> four guys walk out in a line. They were all dressed the same.
> They all had grey crew-neck sweaters, tartan twat hats, as we
> used to call them, tartan shorts, and rolled white towels
> under their arms. They just walked on, and that was it for
> me, it was just, 'Yes! That is so cool!'

They were in the talent show. Then I went to see them in the talent show and they wore grey zoot suits, and they were from Gateshead, and they won. So when we came to be the Beatles, I said: 'You know what?' And I told everyone about this epiphany. And so we ended up in suits, and we all wore the same. We were part of a team that looked alike, in our uniforms. I was always keen for the Beatles to have uniforms, so we didn't just look like any four guys. It was a unit. I always liked that. It was one of my thrills with the Beatles.

Perhaps I've lived a sheltered life but I confess I'd never heard of tartan twat hats until reading this interview. McCartney was talking to an American journalist and I can only assume that he was even more bewildered by the reference, and indeed the reference to Butlins Holiday Camp at Pwllheli. Apart from anything else, not even the Welsh can spell Pwllheli, so what chance a fellow from upstate New York? But, also, Butlins is one of those proper nouns that only mean something if you've grown up in Britain, like *Blue Peter*, Jimmy Savile and Angel Delight. Britain or Ireland, anyway. In February 2010 I took an Aer Lingus flight from Malaga to London and, shortly before the plane landed at Gatwick, one of the stewardesses came on the public-address system and informed us that this was her colleague David Le Page's last flight with Aer Lingus, that he was going off to Butlins to be a redcoat, and she and the crew wanted to wish him the best of luck for the future. Very sweetly, there was a round of applause from the passengers, or at least those of us who understood. Next to me was a Spaniard who spoke fluent English, yet I could see his bemusement at the information that this young man was about to embark on a new career as a Butlins redcoat.

Some years after the entertainers at Butlins were dubbed red-coats, their Pontins counterparts were given the name bluecoats, which I think we can assume was not the result of an intensive executive brainstorming session (in the 1980s sitcom *Hi-de-Hi!*, even more derivatively, the entertainers at Maplins Holiday Camp were yellowcoats). Still, there are a lot more household names on the list of famous former redcoats, among them Jimmy Tarbuck, Michael Barrymore, Dave Allen and Des O'Connor, than there are on the list of celebrity ex-bluecoats (headed by Bobby Davro, and when Bobby Davro is at the top of a list you don't want to spend too much time scrutinizing the bottom). One summer in the late 1940s, the Skegness Butlins also employed two redcoats called Livingstone, a husband and wife, who took their young son Kenneth with them. Many years later, interviewed for the My Life In Travel slot in the *Independent*, the former mayor of London Ken Livingstone cited that summer as his earliest holiday memory. In the same slot a few months later, the broadcaster Gabby Logan traced her earliest holiday memory to a Pontinental resort in Torremolinos. She was five and was voted Princess of the Week. If it were only for giving so many people happy and enduring holiday memories, Fred Pontin and Billy Butlin deserve to be treasured by posterity. But they did much more than that.

If Butlins had the edge for entertainers, Pontins had the catchier advertising campaigns, the simplest but most effective of which was a series of TV commercials in the 1970s which ended with Fred Pontin himself saying 'Book early' and giving a thumbs-up to the camera with a slightly inane grin on his face. This lasted for ten full, rather disconcerting seconds.

I was introduced to him once, in the mid-1980s. My stepfather was a member of the Variety Club of Great Britain, and took me with him to a Variety Club lunch at the Hilton Hotel on Park Lane. Sir Fred, as he was by then, was seated at our table. 'This is Sir Fred Pontin,' someone said to my stepfather Norman and me, whereupon Sir Fred gave us an inane grin and held his thumb up for a slightly uncomfortable length of time, to my uncontained delight. It wasn't the 1970s advert I would have stepped into given the choice – I'd have preferred to share a hammock on a desert island with the sultry Martini girl, or the even sultrier Cadbury's Flake girl – but, all the same, it was great to be given a personal thumbs-up by the famous Fred Pontin.

Between them, without the slightest doubt, Pontin and Butlin redefined the British holiday. And the holiday camp they manufactured was, according to Inglis,

the source of some of tourism's richest innovations. It implied the all-inclusive holiday, that freedom brought about by handing oneself and one's family over to the organisers in order not to suffer the intolerable freedom of organising everything oneself. In Britain, snobbery being an art-form in that country, non-camping vacationers turned up their noses at the regimen and timetables of Mr Butlin, not noticing of course that the same criticisms could be made of the high-status Swan's Mediterranean Cruises, with lectures by Sir Mortimer Wheeler on the Acropolis in the morning, and a not-to-be missed performance of *The Trojan Women* in the amphitheatre at 5pm.

Inglis is right to cite the snobbery of the British. I remember being guilty of it myself in the 1970s, when a schoolfriend, Gary Rimmer, told me that he and his family were off to Butlins at Minehead for half-term. I don't think I sniggered outwardly, but inwardly I did, and I'm sure I wasn't the only one. When I went to Largs and Barnstaple, my parents and I stayed in a hotel, albeit of the austere, pebble-dashed variety. I bet Gary had more fun.

In *The Delicious History of the Holiday*, Inglis writes about the holiday camp as a thing of the past. 'Their day is now done,' he asserts, and I suppose he means that in terms of their dwindling influence. But Butlins is still very much alive, and still a target for lofty middle-class disdain. As evidence, let me offer an extract from a review in the *Sunday Times* of a 'We love the 1970s' over-eighteens adult break at Butlins in Bognor Regis.

Sipping wine poured from a tap into smeared plastic glasses, my fellow sufferer and I sat next to a bald best man with an obscenity scrawled across his forehead, and a groom-to-be wearing a shirt covered in graffiti of the 'I take it up the ***' variety. Our table was sticky with spilt drink and covered in empty shot bottles (three for £5). The carpet looked as though someone had been sick on it. I suppose we should have known what to expect on a 'We love the 1970s' break at Butlins, but the sheer scale of the raucousness – and I came with an open mind – was a complete surprise.

Of course, just as paranoia doesn't mean they're not out to get you, so lofty middle-class disdain doesn't mean it's not warranted. I'm in thrall to the memory of the 1970s as much as anyone; I've written two books on the subject. But unless the *Sunday Times* writer was exaggerating wildly, and I suspect she wasn't, that 'We love the 1970s' weekend sounds gruesome indeed. Yet it by no means tallies with everyone's experience of Butlins. We have a friend, Alan, who recently went to the Minehead resort for four nights over Christmas with his wife and two children, and came back positively enthusing about the experience (which incidentally cost a not-unreasonable £670 for all four of them, inclusive of accommodation, breakfast and dinner). Spending the festive season at Butlins might not tickle everyone's fancy, but it certainly tickles quite a few. Alan reported that more than 3500 guests were catered for on Christmas Day, plus 1200 staff.

Alan also brought back the Butlins brochure to show me, and significantly the front cover featured the kind of family of five you wouldn't be at all surprised to run into in the mezzanine restaurant at the National Theatre, or at a Boden sale. I suppose that somewhere along the line Butlins, perhaps looking enviously at the numbers flocking to the Center Parcs resorts, must have made a policy decision to target Britain's middle classes, aiming not for the pink pound or the grey pound, but the Boden pound.

Even by 1992 they knew they had to evolve to survive. A journalist friend of mine went that year, and wrote afterwards that 'time has been called on the eternal conga of glamorous grans and knobbly-kneed grandpas, banished by lean young aerobics instructors, saunas and solariums; gone are the plates piled high with bangers 'n' mash, and in with your crepes (served, hilariously, not in a creperie but in a creperia). Why, there's even Butlins' own brand of bubbly.'

Despite all that, there were still plenty of Brits who wouldn't be seen dead at Butlins in Bognor, or anywhere else. But already there was an alternative. From the start – which remarkably is as far back as 1987, in Sherwood Forest – Center Parcs had cachet with the middle-classes, not least because the concept had originated on the Continent, in the Netherlands.

It's a funny thing about the British; we sneer at the French, the Germans, the Italians, the Swedes, the Spanish, the Swiss and pretty much everyone else in Europe for all kinds of reasons, and yet the catch-all adjective 'Continental' has always been synonymous with style – obviously what Fred Pontin was hoping to cash in on with the word Pontinental. I'm old enough to remember when boring old sheets, blankets and eiderdowns began to give way to duvets, which in the early days went by the seductively glamorous name 'continental quilts'. To sleep under a continental quilt, *circa* 1972, was to be touched with enviable sophistication.

Considered scarcely less sophisticated around the same time were those heading off on a 'Continental holiday'. And as for the concept of 'motoring through the Continent', that immediately made even Mr and Mrs Pettigrew from the hardware shop on the corner look like Prince Rainier and Princess Grace, which in the case of Mrs Pettigrew, who had both a glass eye and a gammy leg, wasn't easy.

There are certain places, come to think of it, that even now demand the word 'motoring' over the word 'driving'. You really can't drive across the Continent, you can only motor, and a balmy English summer's day can surely only find you motoring through the Cotswolds, not driving. And yet you can drive through France just as you can drive through Stow-on-the-Wold. Odd, but I digress.

I'd certainly have been better off either driving or motoring down to Longleat for our Center Parcs weekend there in 2006. Our visit fell in the middle weekend of the Wimbledon tennis championships, which as usual I was covering for the *Independent*, while lodging for the fortnight with my sister-in-law Jackie, who conveniently lives a twenty-minute walk from the All England Club. So I was looking forward to seeing Jane and the children after a week apart, but wasn't able to get away from my reporting duties at the tennis until 6.25 p.m. on the Friday. The last direct train to Warminster, the nearest station to Center Parcs, left Waterloo at 7.18 p.m.

I feel that the story of my trip to Warminster that warm July evening belongs in this study of the British on holiday, simply because every holiday begins and ends with a journey, and journeys in this little island of ours are sometimes fraught with absurd difficulties, albeit, in this particular case, difficulties of my own making.

First I had to scurry back to Jackie's house to get my case. I would have taken my weekend stuff with me for the day, enabling me to go directly from the All England Club to the station, but for the fact that the Gillette Mach 3 Turbo razor nestling in my washbag would have set off a major security alert, possibly involving armoured vehicles. And the line 'What do you think I'm going to do with it, pounce on Venus Williams and shave her armpits?' – which I might very well have felt tempted to utter – would probably have landed me in jail overnight. They don't appreciate sarcasm, those security guards.

Anyway, I calculated that I had ten minutes to get from Jackie's house to Wimbledon Station, then perhaps another ten minutes waiting for the next train to Waterloo. Allowing for fifteen minutes' travelling time, that would leave three minutes to get off the Wimbledon train and on to the Warminster train. It was touch and go. It was also, let me add, a searingly hot day. By the time I got to Jackie's I was sweating buckets, and by the time I got to Wimbledon station I was sweating water butts.

At Wimbledon Station I paced up and down willing the Waterloo train to arrive, forgetting the old kettle law – that the more you will a train to arrive, just as the more you will a kettle to boil, the longer it takes. Finally it rolled in just before seven, and by the time lots of hot and sweaty passengers were disgorged on to the platform at Waterloo, there was one notably hotter and sweatier than the rest. I had the three minutes originally anticipated to catch the Warminster train, but first I bumped into every one of the millions of people swarming like flies, of whom the Kinks sang so hauntingly in 'Waterloo Sunset'.

I caught the 7.18 to Warminster with about twenty-five seconds to spare, and settled into my seat with the sweat now cascading off me. As is obligatory in all British train compartments during a heatwave, the air conditioning had either broken down or, more likely, wasn't there in the first place. So I was still sweating fifteen minutes later, as the train began to slow down to make its first stop. To my disbelief, a row of signs announced 'Wimbledon'. It simply hadn't occurred to me that I might be able to catch a direct train to Warminster from Wimbledon and save myself the stressful journey into central London. It was further confirmation, a year or two after I'd queued for ages to get into crappy old Madame Tussaud's, that I was now a fully fledged hick, properly befuddled by the capital. Still, at least I saw the funny side. Indeed, for the chap in the next seat, the misfortune of rubbing shoulders with the Incredible Sweating Man was now compounded by an outburst of slightly crazed laughter. 'Why do they always sit next to me?' I could hear him thinking.

That is just one brief chapter from the tragi-comedy that is my record of travelling round the UK. It is a tragi-comedy that will be recognized by anyone who has ever holidayed in this indubitably wonderful country of which we are all rightly proud – a story of trains that are overheated or underheated or just packed to the gunwhales, or delayed or cancelled altogether; a story of endless motorway tailbacks and major roadworks in the least convenient places at the least convenient times. But I have one sneaky trick for cheating Britain's routine travel mayhem, for which I congratulate myself every year. On bank holidays, I never venture further than ten miles from home.

13

Bank holidays, *Brief Encounter* and barking madness

The bank-holiday travel nightmare is a British institution no less than the Bank of England. And like the Bank of England it is governed by certain immutable laws, one of which decrees that, on those few days of the year when we could really do with a smoothly functioning railway system, there will be reduced services and engineering on the line, forcing the few trains that haven't been withdrawn to travel at half-speed. The effect of this is to drive even people who would rather travel by rail into their cars, and the nation's motorways and A-roads duly grind to a polluting, blaspheming halt.

Already in these pages I have chronicled the worst traffic jam in the history of Britain's roads, the 50,000-vehicle tailback that crippled a long stretch of the M6 one memorable day in 1987, earning a mention in the *Guinness Book of Records*. You won't be surprised to learn that the day in question was Good Friday, not that there was anything good about it, if you were one of the estimated 200,000 people stuck on the motorway between Charnock Richard and Carnforth. For some, of course, the name Carnforth evokes the film *Brief Encounter*, the station there having provided the principal backdrop for David Lean's classic 1945 story of repressed English sexuality and desire, scripted by Noël Coward and starring Trevor Howard as a kindly doctor and Celia Johnson as the suburban housewife, with whom, to put it in unforgivably contemporary language, he wants to get his end away. Yet for the purposes of this book Carnforth evokes another picture of England altogether: bank-holiday traffic, bumper to bumper on the M6.

There is nothing about the bank-holiday traffic jam to inspire affection, and yet as a staple of British life no less than the bongs of Big Ben, or Bird's custard powder, or *Coronation Street*, or for that matter *Brief Encounter*, its inevitability is somehow reassuring. Like Stonehenge, it is part of our very landscape. And, like Stonehenge, it rarely moves.

The bank-holiday tailback also inspired, from one of the country's cleverest writers of situation comedy, David Renwick, one of his cleverest scripts. In *The Beast in the Cage*, an episode of *One Foot in the Grave* first transmitted in February 1992, the action never strayed from the inside of Victor Meldrew's car. Anyone teaching the art of sitcom writing ought, in my humble opinion, to start with that episode of *One Foot in the Grave*. Like the episodes of *Porridge* set entirely in Fletcher's cell, it showed that the finest comedy depends above all on character, and that with great characters there is no need to have a complicated scenario involving a cat, a ladder, a kipper, a rolled-up magazine and a tin of paint. The hapless Meldrews and their friend Mrs Warboys did nothing but sit in a mostly stationary car, yielding a half-hour of wonderfully inventive comedy.

But much as we laughed at Renwick's brilliant dialogue, we also laughed at the sheer familiarity of the Meldrews' predicament. Sitting in a never-ending traffic jam on bank holiday is practically part of what it means to be British. Never mind the citizenship test that civil servants give to foreigners applying for British passports, they should just make them sit on the M6 or M25 or M3 for four hours, moving a mile and a half, on a bank holiday. Anyone who can handle that without touching the horn – because unlike almost anywhere else in the world Britain's motorway traffic jams unfold in near silence – plainly deserves a passport.

But of course the bank holiday and the traffic jam were not always synonymous; there weren't many traffic jams before 1960, yet, as already recorded in this book, the bank holiday was enshrined in law almost a century earlier, in 1871. The father of the bank holiday was Sir John Lubbock, a Liberal politician and banker who was also a cricket nut, and thought that bank employees should get more holidays to play and watch his beloved game. Before his Bank Holidays Act was introduced, banks were closed on only four days of the year: 1 May, 1 November, Good Friday and Christmas Day. Lubbock's new legislation added Easter Monday, Whit Monday, the first Monday in August, and Boxing Day, which for a few years afterwards were known, by a deeply grateful workforce, as 'St Lubbock's Days'.

Not everyone was thrilled, however. Some old fuddy-duddies cited the Romans, who by the turn of the fifth century AD were observing around 115 public holidays a year, and whose empire collapsed not long after. Apparently, the later Roman emperors, on assuming power, used to declare new public holidays as a way of keeping the populace sweet, and clearly it wouldn't have done to abolish the old holidays, so more and more were added to the calendar until there was hardly any time left to hold the empire together.

In 1871 there were some who felt that the Bank Holiday Act was a licence for idleness, and that the British Empire could end up going down the same pan as the Roman Empire had. And that was long before the introduction of a two-day weekend further indulged the idle by reducing the working week. In 1897, the year of Queen Victoria's Diamond Jubilee celebrations, the empire still extended over a fifth of the world's land surface and a quarter of its population, while not even the combined economic might of France, Germany and the United States matched that of Britain. The *New York Times* on the day of Victoria's Jubilee boasted that America was astutely clutching the right set of coat tails. 'We are a part, and a great part, of the greater Britain, which seems so plainly destined to dominate this planet,' declared an editorial. The *New York Times* has changed its editorial line somewhat since then.

Whether the decline of Britain as the world's foremost industrial power had anything to do with the proliferation of holidays, though, is debatable. Besides, it was the Americans, the new economic master race, who came up with the idea of a two-day weekend after just five days of work. By the turn of the twentieth century it was reasonably common for employers to give their workers Sundays off, not least because increasingly powerful labour unions demanded it, but in 1908 the boss of a spinning mill in New England nobly instituted the five-day week to accommodate his Jewish employees, whose sabbath fell on a Saturday rather than a Sunday. They could have taken Saturdays off and worked Sundays, but to do so would apparently have offended the Christian majority, so everyone at the mill got two days off, a revolutionary idea given significant forward thrust when it was adopted by automobile tycoon Henry Ford – a notorious anti-

Semite, ironically enough – who felt not only that increased leisure time would make his assembly-line workers more productive but, also, that two consecutive days off would encourage working people to take weekly road trips in his new, shiny, affordable Model T Fords.

I don't suppose that anyone reading this book has ever enjoyed weekends quite as much as those Ford factory workers did, on the basis that anything taken more or less for granted goes uncherished. Conversely, anything you have to fight for is treasured. In the early 1900s even the men of the Metropolitan Police had to threaten strike action before they won the right to work for six rather than seven days a week. Meanwhile, Britain's two million domestic servants – without a union or anyone at all representing their interests – went on slogging for six-and-a-half days a week if they were lucky, because it was only those with benevolent employers who got half-day holidays.

So it's no wonder that the Victorians enjoyed their bank holidays more than we do now. As Hugo Barnacle (and if that's not the greatest name ever to grace a newspaper byline, I can't think what is) wrote in a 1996 issue of the *Independent*: 'They [the Victorians] prized their scarce leisure time, and a mere bank-holiday works outing to Margate or Blackpool could be one of life's climactically happy moments. Not a few marriage proposals would result from these excursions and the mood they engendered – meaning, in turn, that not a few of us are here because of them.'

I like the idea of tens of thousands of us owing our existence to a bank-holiday romance in 1882, but for Barnacle the notion was actually part of a gloomier thesis. 'The British Sunday', he wrote, 'has improved somewhat from the state of sheer existential horror that characterised it until a few years ago, but it is still liable to be spent in a kind of slack lassitude accompanied by dark thoughts of

Monday. Something of the same gloom hangs over our bank holidays.'

It's true enough. Even within the past fifty years bank holidays have become less meaningful than they were, not that the burghers of Brighton will complain, for on England's south coast in the 1960s, practically the definition of a bank holiday was a pitched battle between mods and rockers. Over Whitsun weekend in 1964, the fighting on the Brighton seafront lasted two days. Not all former bank-holiday institutions should be mourned.

Another, the Notting Hill Carnival, survives. But it has manifestly lost its joyous, carefree air in recent years. Which is perhaps because bank holidays, more than carnivals, have lost their power to excite us. Let us not write them off altogether, though. Jane and I reached a decision some years ago to greet every bank holiday with modest plans. Instead of loading up the car and cramming as much mileage as possible into the day, we would venture nowhere very far – by which I don't mean the nearest retail park, for there is scarcely anything more dispiriting on a bank holiday than trudging round Argos – but instead seize the opportunity to visit places and see things that are usually overlooked simply by being far too close. It might be a National Trust property, a museum, or just an interesting shop you've never been in, or a hill you've always admired. Whatever, it means a lie-in, no traffic jams, but still the late-afternoon glow that comes from doing something worthwhile with your day.

On New Year's Day 2007 we decided that our modest bank-holiday outing should be a walk in the Malvern Hills. We had lived scarcely half an hour away for more than four years yet had never set foot in the Malverns, and the first day of a new year seemed like a good time to put that right. So with our friends Tom and Claire, plus our three children and two dogs, and their four children and two dogs, off we strode through hammering rain to the spectacular summit of British Camp, an Iron Age hill fort.

By the time we got there I felt no drier than I had in the shower that morning. But the discomfort was drowned by the exhilaration: the torrential rain had at last begun to ease, and the views were spellbinding. Everyone was having a good time, not least the dogs – our two, Fergus and Bonnie, and their two, Lucy and Widget. But when finally we got back to the car park, we realized that Widget, Tom and Claire's young Jack Russell, was missing. We called and called, but the light was starting to fade, so everyone except Tom and me piled into their Land Rover and headed home for some tea and crumpets. Manfully, the two of us turned back to search for Widget.

We decided to split up, but after forty-five minutes I had found no sign of the missing dog, and occasionally I had heard the hopeful cry of 'Widget!' from the other side of the hill, so I assumed that Tom hadn't managed to find her either. I trudged back towards the car park, thinking somewhat despondently that their children would always remember their New Year's Day walk with us as the occasion that they lost their beloved little dog. When I reached the car park, however, there was a beaming Tom with Widget in his arms. 'She was in the pub,' he said.

Like me he had been on the point of giving up hope, but had gone into the bar of the Malvern Hills Hotel to ask if anyone had by chance handed in a missing dog. He was promptly handed a wet but happy Widget, who had seemingly wandered into the building on her own, and had subsequently been cared for behind the bar. We had a good laugh about this, then put Widget in the car with Fergus and Bonnie. Tom kindly offered to buy me a fortifying drink before we headed back, and rarely had the thought of a large brandy seemed so appealing, so we phoned Claire to break the good news, then headed back across the road to the hotel. But just as I was removing my boots by the door, the barmaid who had handed Widget back to Tom appeared in front of us. 'I'm sorry,' she said, sounding anything but, 'but if you're wet you can't come in.' She was adamant. They'd had enough wet people in the pub that day, she said.

The Malvern Hills Hotel, I should emphasize, stands at the foot of the Malvern Hills, across the road from a car park that is used exclusively by walkers. I was literally speechless. A damp dog had been given food, drink and shelter; two damp but cheerful human beings, gagging for something to drink and with money to spend, had been turned away. From a pub. On New Year's Day. Sometimes, this is the maddest country on earth. No wonder we feel it does us good to leave it behind from time to time.

PART TWO

The British Abroad

14

Passports, pyramids and propaganda

The first thing we need when leaving the United Kingdom for a holiday, of course, is a passport. Like most Brits, I have a love-hate relationship with my passport. I love its power to whisk me past a beetle-browed man in a uniform, but hate its incorrigible tendency to go missing at the least convenient moments. Anyone who has never known that horrifying moment when you think you've lost or forgotten your passport and feel a rising tide of hysteria, or has never stopped the car on the way to the airport to verify that the passports are in the flight bag even though you checked three times before you left home just four minutes earlier, can only be a practitioner of Zen Buddhism.

The comedian Michael McIntyre has a very funny routine about the moment you can't find your passport, and it's funny because practically everyone has had that experience in or on the way to the airport or ferry terminal, checking for the passports by patting the pocket repeatedly, neurotically, until suddenly you don't feel their reassuring bulk. And then there's total panic, until you realize that you've started patting the wrong pocket.

Sometimes our passports confound this obsessive checking. I should think that most of us have either ourselves turned up to the airport without a passport, or with the wrong passport, or an expired passport, or know somebody who has. In the case of our friends Ali and David a few summers ago, it was the dreaded expiry date that clobbered them. They were due to fly with their three children from Birmingham to Bordeaux to stay with Ali's brother for a week, and made sure before leaving the house that they had all five passports. As they didn't travel abroad very often, they even checked the top passport – David's – to make sure that it was still valid. Which it was. And because they'd all been issued at the same time, that meant they all were.

Except that it didn't, and they weren't. The passports belonging to David and Ali were valid for ten years, and were within their expiry dates by three weeks less than five years, but the children's passports were valid for only five years, and were therefore three weeks out of date. The woman at the bmibaby check-in desk apparently derived rather smug satisfaction from pointing this out. But couldn't they board the flight anyway, they asked, and take their chances at French passport control, where in all likelihood their passports would get scarcely more than a cursory glance? Out of the question, said the bmibaby woman. I suppose it's something to do with the name bmibaby that you expect their employees to be if not exactly pink, gurgling and cherubic, at least vaguely cheerful examples of humanity. This woman was anything but. By the time they shuffled disconsolately away from her desk, they had the distinct sense that they'd made her day. 'You know those television programmes where people at airports will go to great lengths to help to get you somewhere,' says Ali now. 'Well, she was the opposite.'

David phoned the minibus driver who'd dropped them at the airport and asked him to come back, and while they waited they considered various solutions to the problem. Should they drive to Liverpool to get new passports issued? Heck, should they drive all the way to Bordeaux, and risk the out-of-date passports at the ferry terminal? Should David's parents look after the kids while Ali and David flew to France on their own? In the end they decided to junk the holiday, and with it the £645 they'd paid for the flights.

My friend Jonny ended up even more out of pocket following a passport-related nightmare of a different nature. Over New Year in 2008 he and his family – wife Catherine and four young sons – were due to spend a week at Marsa Alam on the shores of the Red Sea in Egypt. As always, the passports were Catherine's responsibility – a responsibility she took extremely seriously – and four days after Christmas they set off in a taxi from Southport to Manchester Airport certain that they had satisfied the requirements of the usual 'passport, tickets, money . . . passports, tickets, money' mantra.

They arrived at the check-in desk at Manchester Airport an hour and forty minutes before the flight was due to take off, and Catherine counted the passports out of her handbag: one, two, three, four, five. Jonny's was missing. She counted them again: one, two, three, four, five. Still missing. There then ensued a moment of high comedy, at least as Jonny tells the painful tale now. At the time it wasn't the slightest bit funny when Catherine started pulling out random pieces of paper from the bottom of her handbag, scrutinizing each of them – a shopping list, a Sainsbury's till receipt, a theatre leaflet – in the hope that it might have miraculously metamorphosed into a passport. It was like the scene in the 'Gourmet Night' episode of *Fawlty Towers* when Basil starts rummaging in the trifle in the hope of finding the elusive duck *à l'orange*.

What Catherine had forgotten when stashing the passports in her bag was that she and Jonny had travelled home from their last foreign holiday separately, and his passport had subsequently stayed apart from the others. Jonny generously describes the atmosphere as 'tense' while they discussed what to do, reaching the decision that Catherine and the boys would catch the flight as planned, and Jonny would call the taxi back and scream back to Southport – an hour's drive away at least – for his passport, hoping against hope that the flight to Marsa Alam might be delayed.

It wasn't. When you want them to be, they never are. There was no chance of Jonny making it back to the airport in time, so with Plan A torpedoed he stayed at home and called Gaynor, the travel agent who had booked the holiday for them, in the hope that she might work out a way to get him out there. After all, it was freezing outside. The thought of being at home for a week, over New Year, while the rest of his family gallivanted in the Egyptian sun was too much to bear.

By contrast with the unhelpful bmibaby woman, Gaynor promised to leave no stone unturned. But she called back with gloomy news: there was only one flight a week from Manchester to Marsa Alam, and, although there was another flight a couple of days later from Gatwick, it was full. The splendid Gaynor said she'd keep trying to find a solution, however, and called back again an hour later. Jonny was to fill his wallet with sterling, Egyptian pounds, US dollars and euros, just to be prepared for all eventualities, and head back to Manchester Airport, where he was to catch the nine p.m. Lufthansa flight to Frankfurt. Following a few hours' stopover in Frankfurt he would catch another Lufthansa flight to Cairo, where he would arrive at four a.m. Since

Cairo Airport was no place to be at four a.m., Gaynor had booked him into a nearby hotel, where he could spend the day, before catching an internal flight from Cairo to Marsa Alam at 5.30 p.m.

And thus the adventure began. Another whopping taxi fare back to Manchester Airport, then the Lufthansa flight. Just to amuse himself, Jonny had a frankfurter in Frankfurt, then continued on to Cairo, where I'm sure he would have had a coconut pyramid if a) they sold them there, and b) it wasn't four in the morning. After buying a visa to get through customs – a nasty trick they also spring on you in Turkey, I should add – he was asked by a smart-looking Egyptian gentleman if he wanted a car. He said he did. The man escorted him out of the terminal. The story thereafter is best taken up by Jonny himself.

Outside the terminal the smart-looking man seemed to disappear into thin air, and a threatening-looking man took his place. He led me to an unlit car park which only had one car in it, with five or six more blokes sitting on the bonnet, smoking. I did wonder at that point whether I'd ever see Catherine and the kids again, but anyway, he charged me eighty Egyptian pounds to take me to the hotel, and I tried to open my wallet without any of them seeing how much cash I had in there.

We got to the hotel about 5.30 a.m. – it clearly doubled as a brothel, by the way – and I went to bed, but I woke up about three hours later and thought that I ought to make the most of my day in Cairo. So I asked at the hotel if there was time to take a tour of the pyramids. They said there was, just, but they would need to get me a private driver. So this guy turned up and set off through the streets of Cairo at about 80mph. I still don't know how we failed to kill even a single pedestrian. Then, as we approached Giza, where the pyramids are, he said that to speed up the process of getting in to see them, I would need to hire a camel. By an amazing coincidence, he had a cousin with a camel.

So we got out of the car and ran across a four-lane freeway to where a bloke was standing with a camel and a donkey. This was the cousin, who said he'd rent out his camel for sixty euros. The driver explained the situation, that I was an Englishman who wanted to see the pyramids but didn't have much time before I needed to get back to the airport, so the cousin helped me up on to the camel and we set off semi-galloping through the back streets of Giza to the military entrance to the pyramids, where he bribed a policeman to let us through. It was at this point that Catherine texted me to say 'Where are you now?' I texted her back to say 'If I told you, you wouldn't believe me'.

Anyway, we shot round the pyramids in super-quick time, and got back to the car, but on the way to the airport we pulled up outside a building that the driver told me was a papyrus museum. In fact it was a shop, owned by another cousin. I was basically held hostage there until I bought some papyrus pictures, and then we carried on to the airport, just in time for the flight to Marsa Alam.

And to think that the whole adventure, and the hundreds and hundreds of pounds it cost, could have been avoided by Catherine checking more carefully that she had all six passports in her bag. But then there for the grace of God – or a man in a uniform who thinks he's God – go all of us.

Still, 3500 years of human experience should have taught us to approach borders with everything we need to cross them. The concept of a document entitling people to move between countries, or city states, dates back to at least 1500 BC and indeed back to Egypt; drawings found in a tomb in Thebes show a line of ancient Egyptians in what appears to be the world's first known queue at a passport office. What a shame Jonny didn't see that image on his whirlwind tour by camel; he would have appreciated the irony.

As for the actual word 'passport', it started cropping up in England around the middle of the sixteenth century, and clearly derived from the French word 'passer', although nobody seems quite sure whether the 'port' bit originally related to actual ports, or was taken from the French word *porte*, meaning gate, because the early passports were required to travel within countries as well as outside them. At night there were usually soldiers stationed at the gate in a town or city wall, demanding identification. And of course, for about as long as humans have held legitimate passports, other humans have held forged passports. The diarist John Evelyn recorded a journey to Paris in 1650 on which he used counterfeit papers.

Evelyn lived to tell the tale, but a false passport ended up being the death of William Joyce, the wartime traitor better known as Lord Haw-Haw. It's hardly a holiday yarn, but it's nevertheless a story worth relating. On 28 May 1945, two weeks after the unconditional surrender of German forces, two British army officers, Captain Alex Lickorish and Lieutenant Geoffrey Perry, were collecting firewood near their base on the German-Danish border. They were watched by a thin, unkempt man, whom they took to be a local peasant, but suddenly he called out in English, telling them where they could find more wood. It was an unwise move. Lickorish and Perry were both in the Intelligence Corps and they instantly recognized his voice as that of Joyce, whose lurid propaganda had been broadcast on the wireless regularly since 1940. 'You wouldn't happen to be William Joyce, would you?' asked Perry, with admirable politeness, whereupon Joyce reached into his pocket and Perry, less politely this time, shot him in the buttocks. For a man who had been such a pain in the arse for five years, it was poetically fitting treatment, although it turned out that he was unarmed, and actually reaching for a German passport declaring him to be one Fritz Hansen. When they searched him, however, they also found a German military passport in the name of William Joyce. The contemptible Lord Haw-Haw, whose broadcasts had never really been taken seriously but who was nevertheless considered by many British people to be a prize every bit as juicy as some senior Nazis, had been captured.

There were all kinds of complications, however, largely concerning the archaic laws of treason. Joyce seemed likely to be charged under the Treason Act of 1800, which included unrepealed sections of the 1708 Act and the 1695 Act, hardly appropriate for the mid-twentieth century and with loopholes that a clever counsel could exploit. So the Treason Act of 1945 was hastily drawn up, intended to make a treason trial procedurally similar to a murder trial. And Joyce was held in hospital in France until the act had been passed so that his trial would inaugurate it. But there was one further complication. It turned out that Joyce's British passport had been obtained fraudulently in 1933. Could he be prosecuted for treason if he wasn't a British citizen?

He had been born, in 1906, in Brooklyn, New York, to an English mother and a father, Michael, who had also been British – born in 1836 in County Mayo, Ireland – but in 1894 had renounced British nationality and become a naturalized American, making his son unequivocally American. In 1909 the family returned to Ireland, and six years later moved to England, but in 1933 when Joyce – by now a leading member of Oswald Mosley's British Union of Fascists – applied for his British passport, he lied on his application form that he had been born in Ireland and was therefore British.

Acquiring a British passport by fraud no more makes a person British than wearing a dog collar makes you a vicar. Joyce was still an American and in September 1940, moreover, having scarpered to Germany, he took German nationality. So it was a dual American-German national who was charged with three counts of high treason at the Old Bailey in 1945, presenting those intending to invoke the new Treason Act with a challenge. Joyce did not deny his broadcasts, but questioned whether they were even the business of a British court.

The prosecution rose to the challenge, arguing that treason depended not on nationality but on allegiance, and that since Joyce's fraudulent passport afforded him the protection of the British Crown, he owed it allegiance in return. This was accepted by the judge, Mr Justice Tucker, but, even so, he had to direct the jury to acquit on the first two counts of treason, which related to broadcasts Joyce had made after his UK passport had expired in September 1940. From the third count, however – that William Joyce, on 18 September 1939 and on numerous other days between 18 September 1939 and 2 July 1940 did aid and assist the enemies of the King by broadcasting to the King's subjects prop-aganda on behalf of the King's enemies – there was no escape. On 19 September 1945, Joyce was sentenced to death. He appealed on the grounds that a British court had no authority to try a foreign national for offences against British law committed on foreign soil, and one wonders whether, these days, that might have got him somewhere, maybe with Michael Mansfield QC on his case. But in 1945 there was no appetite for liberal angst. His appeal was dis-missed, as was a further one to the House of Lords, and on 3 January 1946, at Wandsworth Prison, Lord Haw-Haw was hanged. Killed, as Martin Lloyd puts it in his fascinating book *The Passport: The History of Man's Most Travelled Document*, by a passport he should never have had.

All of which brings me to my old schoolfriend Mike. I hesitate to bracket Mike with Lord Haw-Haw, but one night when we lived in London I was awoken at about two a.m. by the phone ringing. The caller was Mike, who is a musician, and was on his way to Germany for a week-long series of gigs. He and his band had set off in their van from the Manchester area and were due to board a ferry at Dover at five a.m., but somewhere towards the end of the M1 Mike realized to his horror that he'd left his passport at home. There was no time to head back for it, and for some reason it was important that they boarded an early-morning ferry. So Mike worked out that they had just enough time to make a detour to our house in Crouch End. Assuming I would lend him my passport.

It would, of course, be an irregular request at the best of times. At two in the morning when you're bleary with sleep, it was bewildering.

'So, let me get this straight,' I said, yawning, 'you want to borrow my passport for a week?'

'If that's OK, yeah,' said Mike, brightly. 'It's not as though they ever check the photo or anything. When you're in a van you just hand the bloke six passports, he has a quick look at them, then hands them back and waves you through. We reckon we can be with you in about half an hour.'

Now, Mike and I have been friends since we were thirteen. I was his best man. I love him like a brother. But we don't look like brothers. And besides, even though I took his point that the passport people on both sides of the Channel weren't likely to scrutinize likenesses, even though he promised not to drop me in it even if he was caught, even though I wasn't planning to go anywhere in the next week, I felt deeply uneasy.

There are some things about which I feel viscerally proprietorial: my wife, my children, my collection of 1960s and 1970s football annuals, and my passport. So I said no. Whereupon Mike promptly phoned another mate in London, who said 'Sure, no problem'. Whether that meant that I should be less precious about my passport, or that Mike's other mate should be more precious, I'm still not sure. Either way, from Ali and David at Birmingham Airport, to Jonny on his semi-galloping camel, to William Joyce arguing quite literally to save his neck, to Mike's little quandary on the M1, not to mention the millions of people on this planet whose lives would be immeasurably improved by crossing a frontier here, a border there, it is extraordinary how such a small, innocuous-looking booklet has the power to influence, for better or worse, a person's day, week or, indeed, his or her entire life.

15

Suitcases, security, and St Christopher

A frequently repeated statistic, especially in Britain, is that fewer than a quarter of Americans own passports. This tends to be cited as an example of their parochialism, or worse, not least in an article written in 2008 in the *Guardian*, by John Patterson, who accused stay-at-home Americans of being 'ridiculous, paranoid, pathetically insular and grotesquely self-pitying'. I don't like that kind of wishy-washy ambiguity. He really ought to have been more forthright.

Patterson was referring to those Americans who prefer not to travel overseas because of their security concerns, but in my experience – and I have lived in the United States, and visited countless times, so I like to think I know what I'm talking about – the multitude without passports just don't see the point of leaving the home of the brave and the land of the free. It's less to do with security than with expense, logistics and, to be sure, a certain insularity, but also the multifarious holiday opportunities on their own soil.

For the British, of course, things are different. In fact just about the opposite criticism applies, and I have already levelled it at those of my compatriots who sally forth for the Algarve and the Costa del Sol, for Lanzarote and Ibiza and Corfu, without ever having seen Bath, Edinburgh, the Peak District, the Gower peninsula or the Yorkshire Dales. On the other hand, it was the adventurism of the British, that very willingness to sally forth, that brought these little islands an empire and put the Great in Great Britain, as Norman Tebbit would express it. It might be a bit fanciful to see the family arriving at Luton Airport in good time for their easyJet flight to Malaga as the spiritual descendants of Sir Walter Raleigh, Captain Cook and Dr Livingstone, but when you live on a comparatively tiny land mass surrounded by water, the desire to see beyond the horizon is part of what makes us tick as a nation.

In medieval times, it was militarism, religion and trade that propelled the British overseas. But by the seventeenth century there was another objective to foreign travel: education. In 1670, a Catholic priest called Richard Lassels coined the term 'the Grand Tour', meaning the increasingly popular scholarly pilgrimage through France and Italy which was intended to broaden the minds of young British aristocrats.

Soon enough there was even a formal itinerary for the Grand Tour, taking in Paris, Venice, Rome and Naples. But many of the Grand Tourists maintained a keen British disdain for foreign customs that lives on today. Which of us can fail to find echoes of favourite family xenophobes, or of the likes of Mr Sedgwick – who lived down the road from me when I was a child, went to France once and swore he'd never go back – in the words of Tobias Smollett, a cranky Scotsman who was very possibly a forebear of

Victor Meldrew? In his catchily titled 1766 book *Travels Through France and Italy: Containing observations on character, customs, religion, government, police, commerce, arts, and antiquities,* Smollett wrote of his encounters with the French that: 'I was almost poisoned with garlic, which they mix in their ragouts, and all their sauces; nay, the smell of it perfumes the very chambers, as well as every person you approach.' Mr Sedgwick didn't put it quite like that, but he was of exactly the same opinion.

Not all the wealthy young Grand Tourists welcomed the exercise for its mind-broadening opportunities. Plenty of them actively resented the packed schedules, and Samuel Johnson wrote dismissively of the 'confused remembrance of palaces and churches' with which they arrived home. This whistlestop cultural tour of Europe is not exactly unknown today, with American and Japanese couples in matching Burberry raincoats replacing those eighteenth-century British aristos. In fact the title of a film released in 1969, about the phenomenon of the whirlwind European tour, applies as much today as it did in 1969 or indeed 1769. *If It's Tuesday, This Must Be Belgium* starred Suzanne Pleshette as an American tourist and Ian McShane as a lascivious tour guide, and it's still enjoyable, not least because it reminds me of a marvellous conversation I once overheard on the Eurostar to Paris, between a teenage American girl, travelling with her parents, and an English lad from Yorkshire.

The girl was sitting separately from her folks, and the English boy, clearly unaware of their presence, started enthusiastically chatting her up. He asked where she was going, and where she had been. 'Oh,' she said, 'we've spent three days in England and it was so cool. Yesterday we went to Westminster Abbey in the morning, and Leeds Castle in the afternoon.'

'Leeds Castle?' he said. 'I didn't know there were a castle in Leeds.'

'Oh sure,' she said. 'It's just beautiful, with, like, a moat.'

'Blimey,' he said. 'I grew up just near Leeds and I never knew that. But London in t'morning and Leeds in t'afternoon, that's a right lot of travelling. How long did it take you to get to Leeds, like?'

'Like, about an hour,' she said.

'Bloody hell,' he said.

And so it continued, with her talking about Leeds Castle in Kent, and him trying to picture a moated castle with crenellations and a portcullis somewhere near Elland Road. I didn't intervene, just sat there quietly cherishing the misunderstanding, and reflecting that even Leeds Castle in Kent was quite a follow-up to a morning tour of Westminster Abbey.

As for the heyday of the Grand Tour, the French Revolution in 1789, for fairly obvious reasons, brought it to a rather abrupt end. And by Victorian times, fifty or sixty years later, the intellectual impulse had diminished somewhat. More and more people were looking to southern Europe as a place to indulge the new-fangled concept of a holiday as an exercise in, if not necessarily hedonism, then pure, uncomplicated leisure. However, it was the poetry and the paintings inspired by the Grand Tour that had put the idea in their heads. I suppose we would have found Mediterranean beaches without Lord Byron and his friends but, as our old friend Professor Fred Inglis writes in *The Delicious History of the Holiday*: 'The Mediterranean by way of Rhine and Rhone defined the actuality of the Grand Tour and, for two centuries thereafter, filled to the brim the average vacationer's imagination. No wonder, therefore, that when mass leisure mobility burst open the doors of the air terminals, so many people were heading for the birthplace of their favourite pictures of paradise.'

No wonder indeed. And what of this mass mobility? In 1950 only one Briton in fifty had a passport, but by 1965 it was one in eleven. And what made the difference was the invention (naturally enough by a Brit, Frank Whittle) of the jet aircraft, which in turn gave rise to evocative new expressions such as 'the jet set'. The world's first commercial jet service was launched in 1952, from London to Johannesburg, by the dear old British Overseas Airways Corporation (BOAC). The plane used was the de Havilland Comet, so quintessentially and fabulously British that it took its name from Geoffrey de Havilland, the aviation pioneer who had not only helped to win the Second World War by designing the Mosquito bomber, but was also a cousin of the actress Olivia de Havilland, who before the war had famously played Maid Marian to Errol Flynn's Robin Hood. Heroines don't come more British than Maid Marian.

Still, I ought to temper this little burst of jingosim by pointing out that the de Havilland Comet, in its earliest incarnation as a commercial jet, was not exactly the safest form of transport known to man. It was a hit with passengers, but regrettably it was also, on occasion, a hit with mountains. By 1958 there had been three refinements of the original model, however, and that autumn the new Comet 4 offered, for the first time, a non-stop service across the Atlantic. The inaugural non-stop transatlantic passenger flight flew on 4 October 1958, admittedly with a refuelling stop at Gander in Newfoundland. Pan Am's rival 707 service started just three weeks later. The jet age had well and truly begun.

Going on your holidays by aeroplane in those early years was, of course, a hugely glamorous undertaking. And Britain's shiny new airports duly acquired a glamour all of their own. In 1955 the young Queen Elizabeth formally opened London Airport's first permanent terminal building, portentously declaring that 'this airport, standing on the edge of the old world and looking towards the new, is now a key port in the complex network of international air traffic'. Actually, to be more strictly accurate, she said 'stending on the edge of the old world' and 'the complex network of internetional air treffic'. I sometimes wonder what heppened to the Queen's old vowel movements. And on the subject of movements, I have heard a similar cut-glass voice announcing on a 1950s newsreel clip about London's burgeoning airport that there were now 'more than fifty movements an hour at peak periods'. The same thing once happened to me in France. But we'll come in a later chapter to the British holidaymaker's difficulties with foreign food.

For now, let's stick with airports, which throughout the 1950s and well into the 1960s were destinations in their own right, visited by people who lived in the general vicinity – and even by some who didn't – even if they had no intention ever of stepping on a plane. After all, I very much doubt whether there was anywhere else in the Staines area in 1957, for example, where you could buy a cup of coffee after eleven o'clock at night. But you could at London Airport, later to be renamed Heathrow after Heath Row, the tiny Middlesex hamlet it so terminally, in more ways than one, obliterated.

You had to work harder for your thrills back then. As a family treat Jane and her sister Jackie were, in the late 1960s and early 1970s, taken by their mum and dad to the Woodall service station near Sheffield on the M1. Had they lived near an airport, they probably would have gone there instead. Not only were the Woodall visits considered treats, by the way, but if they were on their way home from a Sunday afternoon out of doors, they were required to take a change of clothing for Woodall services. It's scarcely any wonder that our children hear stories like that and refer to the era in which we grew up as 'the olden days'.

Whether our kids have as much magic in their lives as we did at the same age is questionable, however. When Jane was a child she and her family didn't go on foreign holidays – Flamborough Head and later the Isle of Wight were as far as they got – but I did, and I can remember standing enraptured before the frantically click-ing airport departure boards, the so-called Scolari boards named after the clever Italian fellow who invented them. They have since been widely replaced by computer-operated screens, but in those days they presented an utterly thrilling whirr of exotic foreign place names: Bombay, Bangkok, Buenos Aries, Bratislava, Beirut, and that's just the Bs.

We didn't go anywhere like that, of course. The foreign trips my parents took me on were package holidays, carefully picked out of glossy brochures, sometimes to three-star or on occasion four-star hotels in Majorca and Ibiza and Portugal that were illus-trated only by 'artistic impressions' which, now that I think about it, should have warned us that we might just be going to stay on a building-site.

In the 1960s, holiday brochures were generally treated as holy writ. But that began to change, as more and more people arrived – in Spain especially – to find that the promised sea view was obstructed by a forest of cranes, and that that was the least of their problems. For comedy writers this was perfect fodder. *Carry On Abroad* (1972) was duly set in the Spanish resort of Elsbels, with Kenneth Williams as Stuart Farquhar, the oleaginous Wundatours rep, trying to console his customers – including Sid James as pub landlord Vic Flange, whose main holiday objective was getting Barbara Windsor, as sexpot Sadie Tompkins, on her back – when they arrived to find their hotel run by Pepe (Peter Butterworth) and Floella (Hattie Jacques) only half-finished. I probably don't need to add that Charles Hawtrey, in what regret-tably was his final *Carry On* role, played a mummy's boy called Eustace Tuttle, for you to get the full picture.

I can't remember being taken anywhere quite as awful as Pepe and Floella's joint in Elsbels, although, once you had to compromise your choices because of the cost, the accommodation could get decidedly iffy. We were never well-off, and whenever there was a relative abundance of what my dad called 'readies', the poker table and the 3.15 at Uttoxeter usually used to account for them. But we did go on a foreign holiday most years, and I suppose he managed to curb his gambling habit to put money aside for it. The Horizon and Thomson brochures were as familiar to me as some of my school textbooks, and scrutinized with far more enthusiasm, albeit, as I entered my teens, because they offered a rare opportunity to look at teenage girls in bikinis.

But for now let's return to airports, which became such an intrinsic part of the holiday experience, not to mention a drain on the holiday budget even before folk had left the country. Airports were turned into pleasuredromes, which excites us less these days because we're so familiar with them, but in the 1950s and 1960s, the concept of Duty Free alone seemed rather fabulous and exotic. The airport authorities quickly realized that people were so excited about going on holiday that any customary wariness about spending was put on hold. They had a captive customer base, raring to open their purses and wallets, and by the 1980s it was caculated that every minute spent in an airport lounge was worth a dollar to the airport authority. A paradox developed which continues to exist today: the airline wants to get you to your destination as quickly as possible; the airport wants to slow you down. Gradually, the airport terminal turned into an extension of the high street, and that's what it remains, only without boarded-up shops and *Big Issue* sellers.

But before all that, the growth of air travel meant that people had to learn to pack differently. Before the mid-1960s, for most people, cars, coaches, trains or less frequently boats had been the standard ways of getting to holiday destinations. Packing had not developed into an art, nor had anyone really addressed the potentially crippling weight of luggage. My parents had a set of brown leather cases when I was a kid that they must have already had for decades, that come to think of it might have been wedding presents, and they got married in 1952. So by the early 1970s the cases were probably twenty years old, scuffed and splendidly characterful. I wish I still had them, although not of course to travel with. They were so heavy that even lifting them empty was a challenge.

As more and more people took to the air, that all changed. The maufacturing conglomerate ICI got on the case – quite literally – and started tinkering with vinyl and polyester. Then, one auspicious day in 1972, perhaps on the very day that my parents and I were panting through Manchester Airport with our unwieldy leather suitcases, an American visionary named Bernard Sadow, who ran a company called US Luggage, went to see the buyer at Macy's department store in Manhattan, tugging behind him the suitcase on wheels that he had invented. The 'Eureka!' moment had come at an airport a year earlier, when he was hauling one of his own large suitcases through customs and a man glided by towing heavy machinery on a dolly. Inspired, he went home and fixed a pair of casters to the bottom of a suitcase, then tied a rope to the handle. That was the contraption he took into Macy's.

The buyer was unimpressed, suggesting that nobody in their right mind would want to tow their luggage, but Sadow was undaunted. Two weeks later he made an appointment to see a Macy's vice-president, who immediately saw the potential of cases on wheels. The hapless buyer must have felt like Dick Rowe, the man at Decca Records who turned down the Beatles reportedly with the observation that 'guitar groups are on their way out, Mr Epstein'. Whatever, when the *New York Times* interviewed Sadow, then aged seventy-five, in 2000, the royalty cheques from his 1972 patent were still cramming his mailbox.

To be sure, his prototype went through a long evolutionary process, littered with people cursing as their wheeled cases toppled over while they were running for a train or plane. And it was a pilot with Northwest Airlines, Bob Plath, who in 1989 developed the small roll-aboard suitcase for flight crews. But Sadow it was who literally set the wheels in motion, and for that I would respectfully argue that he should replace St Christopher as the patron saint of travellers: wheelie cases are a simply fantastic invention. Speaking of saints, he later invented the spray dispenser for holy water, not to mention the electric toothpick, a double-whammy which I'm sure has made life a lot easier for devout Catholics prone to getting food stuck in their teeth, but it is for giving the world luggage on wheels that Sadow deserves canonization or, at the very least, hero status in this book, alongside the likes of Thomas Cook, Sam Alper and the father of the bank holiday, Sir John Lubbock.

That said, it was at least another couple of decades after his momentous visit to Macy's before people tugging their cases became a majority in British railways stations and airports. I don't know whether we were particularly slow to catch on, or whether there wasn't quite the demand for it in a country in which internal air travel requiring carry-on luggage has never been remotely on the same scale as it is in the United States, but I do know that even by the mid-1990s wheelie cases were still considered, by large swathes of Britain's male population, to be for women and wimps. That's not so any more. If James Bond himself strode insouciantly through an airport terminal pulling his little case-on-wheels behind him, nobody would bat an eyelid.

Aptly, the evolution of luggage shows how far we have come as a nation of holidaymakers. Way back in the early years of the jet age, it was actually felt that the Great British Public needed lessons in the new-fangled business of packing for flights, and indeed in the whole unfamiliar rigmarole of passing through an airport. To this end the actor Richard Wattis was hired to feature in an instructional film, and these days it's a hoot to watch, even though it was intended seriously at the time. To be sure, the lanky, bespectacled Wattis was best known as a comic actor – usually playing fussy establishment types such as the Ministry of Education mandarin Manton Bassett in the *St Trinian's* films – but in the instructional film he is presented as a sombre, worldly fellow, well versed in the complicated challenges of international air travel. We see him solemnly presenting his passport at check-in, but best of all is the scene in which he watches his screen wife (actually Wattis was, in that time-honoured euphemism, a confirmed bachelor) packing for their forthcoming holiday.

'I'm no fashion expert, Marjorie, dear,' he says in his plummy voice as she dithers over what clothes to cram into the suitcase, 'but I bet if you chose a definite colour scheme from your wardrobe, you'd cut down a lot on weight.' Then he selects a rather racy red dress for her. 'But don't let's leave this one behind,' he adds. 'It's a honey.'

These days, the notion of a public-information film telling us how to prepare for a holiday is downright hilarious. On the other hand, it's rather dispiriting that, in fifty years, we have come from dear old Richard Wattis suggesting how we might pack our suitcases, to airline personnel at check-in desks asking if we might possibly have left our cases alone for long enough for a passing terrorist to have rammed them full of Semtex. Those gentle little interrogations always mystify me. Is that what stands between us and being blown out of the sky, people being honest about their packing procedures? I'd love to know how many times in the course of a day someone says 'No, I didn't pack it myself' or 'Yes, as it happens, my cousin Sajid did give me something to take with me to New York', putting themselves through the full gamut of the security experience. At least the sniffer dogs and even those full-body scanners that allow people to see right through your clothes (when I was a boy, there were adverts at the back of *Mad* magazine for 'X-ray spectacles', promising that very same facility) make it clear that the airport staff are very keen for you to reach your destination safely. The 'Did you pack this case yourself?' question, by contrast, seem worryingly amateurish to me.

In the meantime, for the British or any other nationality going away via an airport, the endless security checks don't exactly do much to encourage that carefree holiday spirit. This of course is the price we pay for the many benefits of living in the twenty-first century: internet shopping, internet banking, iPods, iPhones and Penelope Cruz, to name but a few. And if ultimately the hassle ensures a safe flight, then which of us wouldn't remove our shoes and our belt at the invitation, usually, of a polite man in a uniform? But as an example of how state-sponsored paranoia can intrude all too rudely on the lives of holidaymakers, I have only to relate the experience of my parents-in-law, Anne and Bob, at Miami Airport in 2002.

They had flown to Miami as part of a cruise package, and were due to join the ship after a night in a hotel. After the long transatlantic flight Anne passed through immigration control, but when it was Bob's turn to hand over his passport, he was scrutinized long and hard, and then peremptorily told to go and stand against a wall. Understandably disconcerted by this decidedly unexpected turn of events, he stood about a yard away from the wall. 'Pardon me, sir, I said, "AGAINST the wall",' the immigration officer bellowed. That particular American use of the word 'sir' never fails to tickle me. It represents the thinnest veneer of politeness and cordiality on top of utter loathing, contempt and suspicion. And in my own experience, and doubtless yours too if you've ever been to the United States, US immigration officers use it like a cosh. I am but one of many thousands of Brits whose first direct experience of the land of the brave and the home of the free was a glowering fellow in a glass booth who made me feel about as welcome, to quote Billy Connolly, as a fart in a spacesuit.

But I've never had an experience like Bob's. A man carrying a submachine gun then arrived and led him away, none too gently, followed by a distressed Anne. He was taken to an airport detention centre and told to sit in a room. At no point was he informed what was going on. When he tentatively asked, he was told to keep quiet. And when Anne asked to use the toilet, she was told to find the nearest empty cell. So her first piddle on American soil, so to speak, took place behind bars into a stainless steel pan, not a scenario they had pictured when they booked the holiday with their travel agent back in Barnsley.

Finally, after several hours, they were told they were free to go. By then, the rest of the cruise party had long since departed for the hotel. And when Anne dared to ask one of the immigration officials why they had been detained, he very crassly said, 'We just picked you out to get to know you better'. One of his colleagues was marginally more accommodating, telling them that Bob happened to share a name with a guy the airport authorities were looking for. 'It just shows we're on the ball,' he said, unapologetically. But I wonder how on the ball they were? Bob was a shortish, retired mining engineer from South Yorkshire, a white Caucasian of about seventy years old, and, although I can't be sure, it wouldn't surprise me in the slightest if the man who shared his name was a 6ft 4in black guy of about thirty-five, from South Carolina.

Nor can I be sure why they were looking for this other Bob, but the clear implication was that he was a drugs smuggler. Little did my parents-in-law realize, when they set off on their package holiday, that the word package would loom so large.

16

Horizon, hypermarkets and Hoseasons

The start of the package-holiday industry can be reliably traced to a single day: 12 October 1949, a Wednesday. That was also the day on which one of the world's most notorious terrorists was born, which is a spooky coincidence, given the way in which the fear of terrorism would later cast shadows over the start of even the most basic package holiday, with armed police patrolling airport terminals. Not, of course, that the proud parents of Ilich Ramirez Sanchez, gazing at their little bundle of joy in the Venezuelan capital of Caracas that October day, could possibly have envisaged him being nicknamed Carlos the Jackal, and becoming one of the most wanted men on earth.

Anyway, more significantly for our story, while Mrs Sanchez was pushing out the Jackal, a man called Vladimir Gavrilovich Raitz, a Soviet *émigré* living in London, was setting up Horizon Holidays. The name alone was a masterstroke, horizons suggesting travel and adventure, and with Britain about to enter the second half of the twentieth century still firmly in the grip of post-war austerity, it's not hard to see why the thought of a Horizon holiday might capture the public imagination.

Raitz was just twenty-seven years old. His well-to-do family had left the Soviet Union when he was six, and they prospered further in Britain. Raitz got a degree at the London School of Economics – later the Alma Mater, coincidentally, of another immigrant travel entrepreneur, the Greek-born founder of easyJet, Stelios Haji-Ionannou – and then joined the news agency, Reuters, as a journalist. But in 1949, during a holiday at a place called the Club Olympique in Corsica – set up, as in my view not enough clubs are, by *émigré* Russian water-polo players – it occurred to him that if he could afford to charter some aircraft, he could start a business offering all-in holidays to the Mediterranean, as a sideline to his job at Reuters. When he got home he duly established Horizon, using family money, and applied to the Ministry of Civil Aviation for the right to send charter flights to Calvi in Corsica. In March 1950, following intense objections by British European Airways, the Ministry ruled in Raitz's favour, but bizarrely stipulated that only students and teachers could take advantage of these pioneering package holidays. So off he went to buy advertising space in the *Teacher's World* magazine, and the *Nursing Mirror*.

Thus were Horizon's first paying customers eleven students and teachers. Raitz was promising them accommodation, food, drink and airfare for the all-inclusive charge per head of £32 and 10 shillings, not an insubstantial sum in 1950 yet still less than half of the return BEA airfare to Nice, the nearest BEA flights got to Calvi. No wonder the airline executives were worried. Raitz showed up their exorbitant, government-endorsed pricing strategy for the outrage that it was, and in so doing paved the way for other entrepreneurial mavericks such as Freddie Laker and Richard Branson, and indeed Stelios Haji-Ionannou. Branson recognized it too, later writing the foreword to Raitz's excellent memoir, co-written with the travel writer Roger Bray, *Flight to the Sun*. 'It is often better to follow a pioneer than be a pioneer,' Branson wrote, doubting whether he would even be in business without the efforts of Raitz and Laker before him.

Laker was another true visionary, although his innovations were kindled less by far-sightedness than by sheer anger at the degree of government protection enjoyed by British Airways. By 1970, the fledgling Laker Airways and other new carriers offering to undercut the major airlines had to abide by an absurd rule which decreed that it was illegal to sell tickets below the 'internationally-agreed fare', except to members of an 'affinity group'. To get round this, Laker and others set up highly spurious affinity groups, or clubs, enabling them to fill their charter flights. But the Board of Trade soon got wise to this scam, and sent their inspectors to Gatwick to quiz passengers.

'With which club are you travelling to New York today, madam?'

'Erm, we're the Swindon Society of Baseball Lovers.'

'I see, madam. How many people are there in a baseball team?'

'Erm, eleven? Sixteen? Seven?'

'Please step this way, madam.'

The hapless passenger would then be stopped from flying, and Laker would cop a hefty fine. In the summer of 1970, in the turbulent wake of one of these raids, Laker climbed on to a chair in the Gatwick terminal and announced his plans to start a 'no-frills' service to the United States. It took seven more years for him to get the Laker Skytrain off the ground but, when it did, he offered tickets to JFK in New York for just £59, a sum the average Brit could earn in three days.

Laker's achievement, while removing the glamour and a fair amount of the comfort from long-haul air travel, was to bring it within comfortable financial reach of Joe Public. But Skytrain lasted only four years, outmuscled by the big boys who weren't notably worried when in 1985 a former Aer Lingus employee called Tony Ryan launched his new airline, still less when Ryanair began to register big losses. In 1988 a young accountant called Michael O'Leary was hired to examine the books, and recommended immediate closure, but Ryan instead challenged O'Leary to turn the business round, which he did so successfully that in 2009, merely the year-on-year increase in Ryanair's passenger numbers exceeded the total carried by Aer Lingus. In 2010, Ryanair flew 73 million passengers, nearly three times as many as BA, self-styled but patently not the world's favourite airline. Not any more. In fact it's no longer even Britain's favourite airline, a distinction enjoyed by easyJet.

Like Branson, Stelios Haji-Ioannou cashed in on someone else's vision, but if it was Laker who pioneered no-frills flying, he refined it, realizing for instance that in-flight catering could be turned from an expense into a source of revenue, much as it still pains some of us to hand over a fistful of euros for an insipid cheese sandwich. He was also the first airline baron to recognize the power of the internet.

No less than the internet, the low-budget airlines have transformed the great British holiday. They have opened up parts of Europe in particular that previously were familiar only to the resourceful, adventurous few, and have had a similarly profound effect on holiday-home ownership. While British travel agents have every reason to curse the low-budget airline entrepreneurs, who have ruthlessly cut them out of the holiday equation, foreign estate agents should strew their path with rose petals. No sooner does Ryanair, easyJet, bmibaby or Flybe open up a new service from a provincial British airport to one in provincial France or Italy (Ryanair greeting every on-time arrival with a triumphant trumpet burst), than a whole new market for village houses in need of refurbishment, at one end of the spectrum, and small castles with vineyards at the other, is created. The kind of people who in 1970 might have had a static caravan in Scarborough are now just as likely to own a farmhouse in the Luberon, inspired by Peter Mayle, enabled by Tony Ryan.

But it was Vladimir Raitz who started the whole ball rolling. Whether aware or not of their place in history, Raitz's eleven package-holiday trendsetters set off from London's second airport, Gatwick, on 20 May 1950, flying in a DC3 Dakota at 3000ft to Lyon, where the plane refuelled. They then carried on to Calvi, to be met, in an echo of those early tours organized by Thomas Cook himself, by a municipal band. That first summer, Raitz needed 350 holidaymakers to break even, and he fell about 50 short. But Horizon Holidays was up, and despite a few stumbles it stayed running. Those students and teachers who did go, staying in old US Army tents at the splendidly named Camp Franco-Britannique de l'Horizon, enjoyed precisely the kind of carefree holiday Raitz had in mind for them. In 1952, he added Majorca to his repertoire. And in 1954, Alghero in Sardinia, followed by Tossa de Mar on Spain's Costa Brava.

A year earlier, incidentally, he had also very shrewdly followed the advice of Father McDonald, curate at the Church of the Holy Redeemer in Chelsea, who suggested that he might consider taking Catholics to Lourdes. As Father McDonald pointed out, the long, tiring journey by boat, then train or coach, was singularly inappropriate for pilgrims who, in many cases, were going because they were lame or in some way unwell. So Raitz set up

Pilgrim Tours, which was an instant success. The disapproval of some leading members of the Roman Catholic hierarchy in Britain, who believed that it was a pathetic cop-out to fly to Lourdes, that a long, uncomfortable journey by road really ought to be part of the pilgrimage experience, was dealt a comprehensive blow when no less a personage than Cardinal Griffin, the Archbishop of Westminster, boarded one of Raitz's DC3s, accompanied by his principal secretary, who later became Archbishop of Liverpool and remains my favourite-named prelate of all time, Derek Worlock.

Vladimir Raitz is yet another of this book's heroes, unless of course you think it a matter of blame rather than acclaim that he tapped the first hole in a dyke through which hundreds of thousands of tourists would eventually burst. At any rate, the sunny shores of the Mediterranean would never be the same again, and there are some remarkable statistics to show just how quickly they were transformed.

In 1957, there were fewer than 3000 people living in a sleepy village south of Valencia called ... Benidorm. Fishing, farming and weaving were the main sources of income there. Yet, just three years later, Benidorm had thirty-four hotels, thirty high-rise blocks of flats, and four cinemas. And three years after that, in 1963, *The Times* percipiently described the former fishing village as 'a home from home for the English, with all the good and bad that implies'. At the same time, the similarly sleepy village of Magaluf in Mallorca was undergoing a transformation into the haven of hedonism that would eventually give it a nickname among the British 18–30 crowd: Shagaluf.

None of this could have been achieved without the collusion of the Spanish, of course, and above all their long-time dictator Francisco Franco, who considered the metamorphosis of fishing villages such as Benidorm and Magaluf into crowded tourist playgrounds to be unequivocally a good thing for his country, buoying the economy with lots of lovely foreign currency.

As for Raitz, the very least you can say about him is that, like Thomas Cook, he was a true pioneer, and a visionary. But in 1974 he lost control of his beloved Horizon, when the company was taken over by the giant package-tour operator Clarkson's. He then watched aghast as Clarkson's imploded spectacularly, leaving 35,000 holidaymakers stranded overseas, and a further 100,000 unable to claim full refunds on their cancelled holidays. 'I might have lost the company I created and I might have lost a lot of money, but I never cheated anyone,' Raitz later recalled. It's not a claim that everyone in the holiday business can make.

In some ways, 1950 to 1970 or thereabouts represented the golden era of package holidays, when it still seemed kind of remarkable that a single payment to Horizon or Thomson, or the sadly defunct 1960s operator Gaytours, could yield flights and full-board accommodation for the whole family. Thomson, incidentally, which always seemed like a British company (but was in fact Canadian), is now owned by the German congolomerate TUI, formerly Preussag, or Preußische Bergwerks-und Hütten-Aktiengesellschaft (Prussian Mine and Foundry Company). Who in Britain *circa* 1970 would ever have thought that in paying for their package holiday, they would be lining the pockets of the former Prussian Mine and Foundry Company? Times have changed.

In those early days the operators made up the rules as they went along. Doug Ellis, who later found fame as the voluble chairman of Aston Villa FC, joined the party in 1956, specializing in package holidays from the provinces, in particular Manchester and the Midlands. He formed Midland Air Tour Operators, which enjoyed an acronym very close to that of the North Atlantic Treaty Organization, and if you've spent time with Doug Ellis, as

I have, you'll know that he probably claims as much credit for the achievements of NATO as he does for the success of MATO. Whatever made him a multi-millionaire, it wasn't humility.

It wasn't lavish generosity, either. In my guise as a sports writer, I once talked to the former Villa manager Graham Turner, who recalled the midweek scouting trips he sometimes made to Scotland when he was at Villa. Ellis often used to invite himself along on these trips, but always brought packed sandwiches prepared by his wife, on the basis that the service-station prices were prohibitive.

Funnily enough, home-made sandwiches also feature in the story of Ellis the package-holiday king. In the late 1950s MATO chartered old propeller-driven Dakotas from Derby Aviation, and operated two flights a week, one to Perpignan in the South of France, which was close enough to the 'newly discovered' Costa Brava, and the other to Palma, Mallorca. The sandwiches given to holidaymakers on these flights had been prepared the night before by Doug Ellis's mum, filled with lettuce to keep them moist, and stored in biscuit-tins. And that wasn't the only way in which costs were pared down. The Dakotas had to be carefully loaded to keep them properly balanced in flight, and so all passengers had to be weighed before boarding the plane, with the occasional unpopular – or perhaps welcome – consequence that husbands had to sit separately from their wives. But Ellis couldn't afford to pay BEA a handling fee, so when customers arrived at Elmdon Airport – now Birmingham International – they had to stand on his bathroom scales.

He could certainly never be faulted for lack of enterprise. Not only did he organize the flights to the Mediterranean, he also went and bought the hotels. By the 1960s there were 600 bedrooms in mainland Spain and Majorca filled with Ellis's holidaymakers, and he owned all of them. When he saw the potential of package holidays by coach, he added a coach company to his portfolio. And as demand for self-catering holidays grew, he built a block of 734 apartments in Fuengirola. Not bad for a working-class boy from the Wirral, the son of a mechanic who died, from a respiratory illness caused by gassing in the First World War trenches, when Ellis was only three.

But I don't suppose everyone in Fuengirola blesses Ellis and his fellow package-holiday pioneers. A couple of generations ago, like so many other resorts on the Costa del Sol, it was a characterful fishing village. Yet when I was last there, in February 2010 on my way to the airport at Malaga, it could have fairly easily been mistaken for Croydon. For one thing, it was lashing with rain. For another, the public announcements in the vast hypermarket I shopped in were all in English, not even with so much as a Spanish translation. One announcement drew shoppers' attention to a special offer on a brand of medium-dry sherry – just three euros a bottle – and in that instance I wondered whether there was no Spanish translation simply because nobody Spanish would be stupid enough to drink three-euro sherry?

All of which brings me to alcohol, an ingredient almost as essential in a book about the British on holiday as paper and ink. When I was writing this book, and told people what the subject matter was, practically all of them nodded knowingly and said 'Oh yes, Brits on 18–30 holidays, on the piss in Benidorm and Torremolinos, that sort of thing?' When I mentioned it to our friendly neighbourhood butcher, Stuart Fletcher, he asked me whether I knew the song 'An Englishman on Holiday' by the rock band Thunder? I didn't, but I do now, and sure enough the lyrics powerfully evoke scenes with which we are all regrettably familiar, even if only via grim newspaper reports, and tacky TV documentaries with titles such as *Holidays from Hell* and *Sun, Sex and Holiday Madness*.

An Englishman on Holiday

Laying down in this Spanish bar
That last slammer hit me like a car
I've got the six a.m. Balearic blues
Can't even focus on my own tattoos

I had a fight with this German guy
I saw him give my little girl the eye
While he was trying hard to be so cool
I hit him with a stool

Oh yes, all right, I'll be going all night
Gonna drink 'til they take me away
I'm an Englishman on holiday

Every year I get to do the same
I meet the boys and get on the plane
We like to sing and shout out, 'Here we go'
'Cos they're the only words that we all know

We've got the loudest shirts you've ever seen
We're gonna take the beaches like a team
We've got so much duty-free to drink
Enough to float a ship

Oh yeah all right, I'll be going all night
So light the paper, get out of the way
I'm an Englishman on holiday

We never look for trouble at the start
But it always comes our way

We've got our pride and we just can't walk away

This morning I woke up inside a cell
They dragged me screaming out of my hotel
I don't remember what it was I did
But I've got this drummer banging in my head

I've got to get out 'fore I miss the plane
And next summer I'll be back again
I'll be fighting for the Union Jack
If they let me back

Oh yes, all right, I'll be going all night
Gonna drink 'til they take me away
I'm an Englishman on holiday

This song depicts a depressing and all too vividly accurate image of the hard-drinking, pugnacious Brit abroad, and actually it's not a topic I want to explore at particular length; Thunder's lyrics pretty much say it all. However, I can tell you that in Magaluf, aka Shagaluf, in the most recent year for which figures are available, more than 3000 British tourists were admitted to the local hospitals, almost all of them for drink-related illness or injuries. It's a gruesome statistic, especially when we remind ourselves that the first properly organized package trip was Thomas Cook's irreproachably wholesome railway journey from Leicester to Loughborough in 1841, laid on for fellow supporters of the temperance movement, costing a shilling and sixpence inclusive of a 'ham tea'.

Cook would have been properly aghast to learn that one of the principal attractions for those who flocked to the Costa Brava and the Costa del Sol in the 1960s was cheap booze. But there's no point my being pious about it. One of the reasons I haven't touched Pernod or any other aniseed-flavoured alcohol since 1979 relates directly to a spectacular drinking binge, followed by an even more spectacular vomiting binge, on a campsite in the South of France, during a holiday with my schoolmates Pete, Rafe and Glenn. In fairness, I was only seventeen. I wasn't getting quite so legless by the time I was twenty-seven, still less when I was thirty-seven, which is more than can be said of some of the Brits who this summer will drink themselves practically comatose on the Costa del Sol, on Majorca, on Ibiza, on Tenerife, on Corfu.

Still, when Roger Bray, in *Flight to the Sun*, makes the astute point that there was 'a cocktail' of reasons why Britain's package-holiday boom happened when it did, he doesn't mean the cocktail of sangria and Guinness pumped from the stomachs of three young Geordie women in Magaluf hospital. He also rejects his friend Vladimir Raitz's theory that it was mainly a reaction to post-war austerity, and another war-related theory, that Brits who had travelled overseas to fight were now anxious to see foreign lands in peacetime. There is some truth in both suppositions, Bray asserts, but there were many more factors, among them the Education Act of 1944, which raised the school-leaving age to fifteen, leading to the creation of more grammar schools and greater aspirations in sectors of society that had previously had limited – yes – horizons.

At the same time, the post-war demand for labour gave the working classes increased bargaining power, which in turn led to sharp wage increases. Between 1955 and 1960, average weekly earnings rose by 34 per cent, more than twice as much as the average rise in retail prices during the same period. Suddenly there was a great deal more disposable income, and what finer way of disposing of it than a fortnight abroad, an undertaking further promoted by an invention that entered the lives of ordinary British people about the same time as the package holiday itself: television.

17

Marketing, millionaires and murder

By a happy coincidence, the early growth of Horizon Holidays and the other package-tour operators occurred in exactly the same years as the explosion in television ownership. For that the catalyst was the coronation, on 2 June 1953, of Queen Elizabeth II. Millions of Elizabeth's loyal subjects wanted to watch her being crowned, although until I wrote this book I wasn't aware that the prime minister, Sir Winston Churchill, and his cabinet, had decided long before Coronation day, indeed the previous summer, that there shouldn't be television cameras inside Westminster Abbey. They thought that live television coverage, with all the lights and general kerfuffle it required, would exact too much strain on the young Queen. Which I suppose was an admirable concern, although, less admirably, several of them also apparently felt that television coverage would diminish the privileged exclusivity of the occasion for all the nobs inside the abbey. Doubtless leaving out this second consideration, Churchill conveyed to the Queen his cabinet's advice that the television cameras be excluded, to which the Queen responded with whatever might be the polite royal version of 'Bollocks!' She pointed out that she was the one getting crowned, not the members of the cabinet, and she wanted the cameras present, so there.

As a consequence of this admirable royal show of resolve, sales of television sets – mostly with fourteen-inch screens, tiny little things by today's standards – rocketed. Twenty million people watched the coronation on TV, the first time that viewing figures had been greater than listening figures, with only 12 million following the excitement on the radio. All of which might seem more than a little tangential to the story of the British on holiday, but it is directly relevant in two ways. Firstly, one of the Queen's pageboys that day was a young fellow called Jeremy Clyde, the twelve-year-old son of socialite Lady Elizabeth Wellesley (and, to see how he slots into the story, read on a few paragraphs). And secondly, the sudden proliferation of televisions was great news for those selling holidays, or at least it became great news on 22 September 1955, when commercial television began.

In truth, it took a while longer for the travel companies to recognize the value of advertising on television, but that wasn't the only benefit of the medium. By the time colour TV came in, in the late 1960s, lots of advertisers were peddling their wares against a backdrop of blue seas, waving palm trees and white sand, and the nation didn't simply respond by buying Cadbury's Flakes, Bounty bars, Martini and Campari, it also fancied a piece of the beach action. In a famous Campari advert in 1977, actor Jeremy Clyde – the very same fellow who'd been a pageboy at the Coronation – played nicely to type as a white-suited toff who, standing on the terrace of a grand plantation home somewhere in the tropics, asked model Lorraine Chase whether she had truly been wafted there from paradise? 'Nah, Luton Airport,' she guile-lessly replied in a broad south London accent, and though no one predicted it, the advert did far more good for Luton Airport than it did for Campari. More than twenty years later, the managing director of Campari International, one Enzo Visone, admitted that 'the Lorraine Chase ad was a terrible mistake', because it had completely undermined the image of Campari as an élite brand. Yet it put Luton Airport squarely on the map.

As for actual holiday advertising, intended to sell holidays, it is hard to think of many iconic examples. Already in this book I've paid tribute to Fred Pontin with his thumb held up for a bit too long, telling us to book early, but the only actual jingle I can remember from my childhood – which in my totally unbiased view coincided exactly with TV advertising's golden age – is the one for Hoseasons boating holidays.

Now is the time, to send us a line,
for your Hoseasons boating brochure

We've got all kinds of craft that'll suit you just fine,
for messing about on the water

Sailboats, canalboats and cruisers too
All Britain's waterways waiting for you ...

Annoying jingle that it was, I can almost guarantee that, if you're my age or older and remember it as vividly as I do, it will now continue reverberating in your head for the rest of the day, if not the rest of the week. As for Hoseasons, I can tell you two things about them. One, the company owes its rather curious name to the man who founded it in the 1940s, one Wally Hoseason, who was the harbourmaster at Oulton Broad near

Lowestoft in Suffolk. And, two, in February 2010 Hoseasons was sold for £51 million to Wyndham Worldwide, the American conglomerate that also owns the Ramada, Days Inn and Howard Johnson motel chains. Who'd have thought there'd be so much money in sailboats, canalboats and cruisers too?

Money, of course, is the determining factor in the British holiday experience. According to the latest research, the average cost of the main annual holiday for a family of four in this country is just over £3000, a figure that might well cause some of you to recoil in horror on account of it seeming such a lot, and others to gasp because it seems so little. Needless to add, holiday expenditure relates closely to household income, but perhaps even more closely to a state of mind. I have two professional friends who do the same job and must earn roughly the same salary, yet one of them scrimps on family holidays while the other splashes out.

The amount Jane and I spend on holidays is atypical, because as an occasional travel writer I sometimes get discounted hotel rates, and therefore we get to stay in places we could never otherwise afford. This makes me a contributor to the phenomenon known by some as travel porn. I dislike the phrase, but you know where it springs from: the idea that you can look at what you can't have, and indeed people do pore almost lasciviously over all those newspaper supplements and glossy magazines, the latter headed by the shamelessly aspirational Condé Nast Traveller, with their beautiful pictures of five-star hotels and perfect coral beaches. Sometimes they succeed in luring us away from what we can afford to what is likely to break the bank, and television has been complicit, too, down the years. Alan Whicker started it all, offering us a glimpse of lifestyles many of us could only dream about, and later Judith Chalmers took over the baton, although in fairness the holiday programmes and travel supplements have usually been careful to offer more affordable options alongside the out-of-reach, counterpointing the new resort in the Maldives with the farm holiday in the Yorkshire Dales.

At the smart resorts we sometimes go to, though, I marvel at how many ordinary-seeming people have the funds in place to pay upwards of £8000 for a week's holiday. The answer, I suppose, is that some of them haven't. At any rate indeed it is apt that the great British holiday shares the same abbreviation as grievous bodily harm, given the serious and lasting damage it does to some wallets.

For us, these holidays are not quite the outrageous freebies they are depicted as by some of our more forthright friends, bless their hearts, yet there's no doubt that the so-called 'media rate' is one of the great journalistic perks, if admittedly somewhat shrouded by an ethical grey area. I quite understand the reasoning that a writer being offered generous terms by a hotel, or airline, or tour opera-tor, might hold back on the acerbic criticism even where it is due, or conversely crank up the rhapsodic praise where it is not due, thereby compromising the interests of the only people he ought to care about, namely the readers. It's a valid point of view, and without the slightest doubt there are times when newspaper read-ers are ill-served by this Faustian pact between travel writer and host. That's why my estimable colleague at the *Independent*, the travel-industry expert Simon Calder, started to bill himself as 'The Man Who Pays His Way'. Quite rightly, he felt that readers ought to know that here was a writer giving them information without fear or favour.

On the other hand, a degree of practicality has to prevail. The travel pages of newspapers and magazines would be significantly less interesting, and less varied, if journalists only wrote about holidays they could afford to take. And even as the beneficiaries of discounts there are some – I hope I can include myself – who offer criticism where it is deserved, irrespective of the largesse on offer.

Anyway, I write all this as a prelude to recalling a feature I contributed to the *Independent* back in 1999. A five-star hotel called the Anassa had just opened in Cyprus, and the PR company promoting it in the UK kindly offered me a substantial discount on a family holiday if I would write about it. Parts of the Anassa were still under construction, but it was being marketed as such a luxurious destination that it attracted a super-rich clientele, propelling Jane, the children and me into the company of multi-millionaires. It was, to say the least, an eye-opener: women with the finest breasts share dividends could buy and their husbands, playing FTSE with each other under the marble tables. Most of them had arrived by private jet.

The Anassa was just a few months old and already by far the swishest hotel in Cyprus, perhaps in the entire eastern Mediterranean. Leonardo DiCaprio had been there shortly before us – 'small and pudgy', we were reliably informed – as had Simon and Yasmin Le Bon and family. Our fellow guests, however, were business tycoons rather than film and pop stars; indeed, the hotel register could easily have been mistaken for the *Sunday Times* Rich List. For a week I watched them behind their Gucci sunglasses from behind my F. W. Woolworth sunglasses. They were, are, an amazing breed, and not remotely impressed with their very grand surroundings. Beside the huge urns standing proudly at the top of every staircase, the huge earners were not happy. In fact, they were extremely cross. The Anassa, they thought, was not all it had been cracked up to be. Several of them had come only because the Sandy Lane Hotel in Barbados was closed for refurbishment, and they were missing the Sandy Lane badly.

At the pool, Jane and I watched in appalled fascination as two or three of the most disgruntled multi-millionaires led a kind of insurrection. Historically, the proletariat has risen against the monied classes. At the Anassa it was the other way round, as first the staff and finally the manager were confronted by growing deputations of Armani-trunked tycoons. They complained that their travel agents had told them that the indoor health spa was 'a lick of paint away' from completion. Not so, they said. They also lambasted the food, which we thought was terrific, if not very obviously Cypriot. My lobster and salt-cod ravioli in burnt sage butter and yoghurt was exquisite. But by day four we were suffering from taramasalata-withdrawal symptoms, and our six-year-old, a huge fan of the Sainsbury's delicatessen counter back home in north London, memorably asked, 'Mummy, do they have hummus in Cyprus?'

That six-year-old, I should now add, was the same child who on a more recent holiday in the Languedoc, as a sixteen-year-old, memorably asked 'What's the French word for quiche?' But that's another story. This story is about the mega-wealthy, and I can report now – although I thought better of it at the time – that the most disgruntled of the tycoons actually arranged for himself and his family to be airlifted out of the Anassa and taken to a fabulous hotel he knew in nearby Syria. Yet by any rational standards there was scarcely anything wrong with the Anassa; indeed, in the three most vital respects – bedrooms, food, service – it seemed to us as luxurious as it could possibly be.

Still, this – the tycoon and his family – represented the British on holiday no less than the tattooed thugs of whom Thunder sang, and this book must encompass both ends of the spectrum. Besides, this vast and colourful spectrum is covered by a single objective: we all go on holiday in pursuit of a good time, even if one person's idea of a truly fabulous time is another person's utter nightmare. And that doesn't simply mean that the people who go on £40,000 holidays would be miserable on £400 holidays; it can work the other way round as well. Certainly, mixed in with a fair dollop of contempt, I felt sympathy for the multi-millionaire desperate to leave the Anassa. How awful to be surrounded by such splendour and to be so utterly underwhelmed. I suppose it is, to an extent, the perennial curse of the rich.

I'd love to have introduced him to Jane's Auntie Janet and Uncle Mike. As I write, in mid-March, they have just come back from Blackpool, where they stayed at the Viking Hotel for the over-55s. They paid £260 for a week's full board, which also included free drinks and a 'wonderful' nightly cabaret. And their enthusiasm is endorsed by the vast majority of 291 internet reviews of the Viking and its two sister hotels, the Cliffs and the Claremont. The spelling of some of the reviewers leaves something to be desired, but the collective thumbs-up is unequivocal. 'Had a marvolouse time ... compere Ryan first class ... food second to none,' reckoned Cully47 from Liverpool. 'The food was plentyfull ... can't wait for our next visit,' trumpeted Driver187 from the West Midlands. 'What more could you wont?' asked Harry from Birmingham.

It is finding budget holidays in the sun, though, at which Janet and Mike excel. A few years ago they went with Saga Holidays to the two-star Hotel Vista Ora in Benidorm, paying £1800 for return flights and four weeks' full board. More recently they paid £1500 for three weeks at the four-star Hotel Turquesa in Puerto de la Cruz, Tenerife, also with flights and full board. It was January, but apart from 'a couple of storms', the weather was good. And drinks there were free every day between eleven a.m. and midnight. Much as my multi-millionaire wouldn't be seen dead at the Vista Ora or the Turquesa, still less in a pair of Primark swimming-trunks, I suppose he would applaud the value for money. That, bizarre though it seemed to us, is what he felt he was missing in Cyprus.

The hotels we stayed in on the package holidays of my

childhood were a little closer to the Vista Ora than the Anassa but, as I've already written, a foreign holiday once a year was more than most of my friends managed. I can remember holidays in Majorca, Ibiza, the Algarve, and Lido di Jesolo near Venice, the last of which was at the end of August 1971. I know this because I remember befriending a boy called Jeremy who was nine years old, like I was, and must have been blessed with a similarly vivid imagination. Back in Britain there was a massive manhunt for a 39-year-old armed robber called Frederick Joseph Sewell, who a week or so earlier had murdered a police superintendent while fleeing the botched hold-up of a jeweller's shop in Blackpool. For days the search for Sewell had dominated the news in the UK, and even pricked some interest across the Atlantic. The dead superintendent, Gerry Richardson, was 'the highest-ranking police officer yet gunned down in the line of duty in a country where policeman seldom carry guns', reported the *Sarasota Journal* in Florida, gravely. And the story was clearly still on my mind when we got to Italy because, while playing on the beach with Jeremy one morning, I became convinced that a man on a nearby sunbed, seemingly on his own, was none other than the elusive Sewell.

I passed my suspicions on to Jeremy, who agreed that, from the photographs he'd seen, this fellow was almost definitely, probably certainly, Sewell. Between us we must have read far too many *Famous Five* and *Secret Seven* books, because we decided to spy on him, and spent the rest of that day tracking his every movement. We even followed him back to his beachfront hotel, only slightly deflated by the revelation that in fact he wasn't alone, but had a wife and baby with him. After all, what could be better cover for a criminal than a wife and baby, on a beach in Italy? We kept an eye on him for another day, and then after much debate we shared the findings of our sleuthing with my parents, who privately must have roared with laughter, but indulged us by treating our detective work seriously. My dad nobly said he'd look into the matter, and somehow or other – I was too scared to watch – contrived a brief conversation with our suspect. But he had to rely on his reasonably passable German, because the bloke turned out to come from Munich. Even then Jeremy and I weren't convinced.

Anyway, had any of this happened in Southport – which frankly was a rather more likely place than Lido di Jesolo to spot a bloke fleeing an armed robbery in Blackpool – I would probably have forgotten about it years ago. But it happened on holiday, which is what has kept it, through all the intervening decades, in my head. The real Frederick Joseph Sewell, let me add, was caught in a flat in south London after forty-five days on the run which, it transpired, had taken him nowhere near the Venetian Riviera.

During the course of our detective work, Jeremy and I even managed to take a surreptitious photograph of our suspect, using my parents' camera. This was of little immediate use, since in those days you had to send off your photographs to be developed, which could take anything up to a fortnight after the holiday had ended, and that's assuming you sent them as soon as you got home. Nevertheless, I wish I still had that snatched photo of 'Frederick Joseph Sewell' on the beach in Italy. If it is holidays that provide the most vivid of childhood memories, it is photographs that jog those memories, or holiday snaps as they are still called (if only by me) even in this relentlessly digital age.

I love holiday snaps. Not other people's, of course, and like most modern families we have enough of our own to fill about three pantechnicons, but there's nothing as wholesome and heart-warming as sitting down on a wintry Sunday afternoon and leafing through the holiday albums. One of my biggest treats as a child (I must have been easily entertained) was sitting in my grandma's lounge in Southgate, turning the heavy pages of her ancient photograph albums, which were crammed with black-and-white and even a few sepia pictures of my mother and her siblings on holiday in places like Margate and Clacton, in the 1930s. For some reason, enormous stuffed animals were a big attraction for children in those days (they must have been easily entertained, too). My grandma died in 1990 and I don't know what happened to her albums (as the youngest grandchild I wish I'd been given them, instead of her Wedgwood biscuit barrel), but I clearly remember the pictures of my mum, my Auntie Dorothy and my Uncle Max, as children, perched on big stuffed tigers and rhinos.

A couple of old black-and-white holiday photos I do have date from a couple of decades later, in the mid-1950s, shortly after my mother married my father, and some years before I slithered on to the planet. They were taken in Majorca and are fantastically stylish, almost like pictures from the golden age of Hollywood. In one of them, my parents sit at a restaurant table with a couple of friends. In one hand my father seems to be holding a maraca, in the other a cigarette. Next to him my mother is wearing a comedy sombrero. It sounds borderline naff, and yet it could not look more glamorous if it featured David Niven (whom my dad rather resembled) and Rita Hayworth. In the other picture, evidently taken by my father, my mother is glugging from what looks suspiciously like a dispenser for salad-dressing, although I expect it contained wine. Again, it sounds like a typically embarrassing holiday snap, yet it oozes style and sophistication. They went on that holiday with their Liverpudlian friends Diane and Ben, who are also in the photograph, and Ben is wearing a dinner jacket. Who, these days, would take a dinner jacket to Majorca? Maybe that's why modern holiday snaps are so unstylish; we get the packing wrong. We need Richard Wattis on hand to suggest the sleek red dress. If you remember, 'it's a honey'.

While I was writing this book, incidentally, I showed my 85-year-old mother those two photographs, to see what memories they would unlock. She dated them as 1954, and recalled that the two couples stayed in one of the few hotels in Magaluf, and that one day the friendly proprietor took my dad and Ben down to a nearby beach, and said that he had been offered an opportunity to buy it, but couldn't afford to do so on his own. If they would each invest £1000, he said, the three of them would be partners. As my mum recalls it, my dad made a show of considering the offer, so as not to let on that he didn't have £1000, or even £100, to spare. If he had managed to scrape together the cash, heaven only knows what a private beach in one of the Mediterranean's most popular holiday resorts would have been worth by the 1970s, let alone today. I could have been heir to a Majorcan property fortune. Hell, that could have been me at the Anassa, plotting my escape because the flagstone path to the spa wasn't quite finished.

The point, I suppose, is that even after five or six decades holiday snaps are amazing, Proustian repositories of memories and anecdotes. Jane and I have a picture of our son Joe on holiday that prompts a more prosaic memory than my mother's recollection of the day my dad was offered half a mile of Magaluf waterfront, but is nevertheless a family favourite. It features Joe, aged five, holding up Jane's bikini bottoms, and was taken a few minutes after he had asked for his swimming trunks, so that he could go and play in the hotel pool. Jane told him that they had not yet been unpacked, and directed him to a suitcase in the bathroom. He went off to find them, then stomped back a few moments later, holding Jane's bikini bottoms. He had a pronounced lisp at the time. 'My trunkth aren't there,' he said, crossly. 'All I can find are theeth GIGANTIC panth.'

Maybe you have to be a member of our family to find it funny. But most families have their equivalent; the holiday snap or holiday slogan or holiday story that gets everyone laughing and reminds us – and frankly, with teenagers in the house, reminders are sometimes needed – why we all love each other.

18

Misfortune, madness and the Med

Not all holiday snaps ignite positive memories. We have a series of photographs of a restaurant high up overlooking a beach on the Costa de la Luz, taken as a reminder of the moment when our son Jacob, then aged two, fell headfirst out of an open window 40ft up.

It is an image that will stay with me until my last breath. A flash of blue sandals and yellow socks, me shouting 'NO!' and making a desperate lunge, and Jane screaming 'Oh my God!' as Jacob disappeared from view. By some miracle he survived relatively unscathed. Young children and drunks do survive these things, I was told later, because they don't stiffen up in anticipation. But it happened in 2001 and Jane and I still carry the emotional scars.

It was a Sunday lunchtime, and up to that point it had been a successful holiday. The weather was glorious, the Med almost warm. And yet it was doubtless because we were on holiday that we relaxed our usual vigilance. Dangerous heights had always been one of my parental neuroses; indeed, I had scrupulously moved a chair well away from the balustrade on our hotel balcony. But in the El Pirate restaurant overlooking Cape Trafalgar, the open window did not ring any alarm bells. Jacob insisted on sitting at the end of the table nearest the window, and we let him. To refuse would only have caused a scene and, besides, hadn't we just that morning seen a toddler standing proudly on the front of a motor-scooter driven by his father, neither of them wearing a helmet? The Spanish treat their children as mini-adults and it is easy to get sucked into a similar mentality. It's motor-scooters and tapas until midnight for Spanish kids. Not for them a plate of dinosaur-shaped chicken nuggets and early to bed.

But we blamed ourselves, not Spanish culture, for Jacob's dramatic plunge. In fact, our opinion of Spain, already high, shot up a hundredfold when, little more than five minutes after the accident, an ambulance arrived with a paediatrician on board. In Cadiz, forty-odd miles away, such a response would still have been impressive. But in this little scrap of a village it was nigh on remarkable. When the paediatrician's remarks – 'I can hardly believe I'm saying this, but he seems to be OK' – had been translated for us, and the shock had started to subside, we asked ourselves what might have happened in a British seaside resort? Even if the emergency services had arrived that quickly, highly unlikely on a remote stretch of coast like Cape Trafalgar, a health service starved of cash and manpower could never have got its act together sufficiently to send along a paediatrician.

Moreover, when later that day I asked the hotel receptionist to direct me to the nearest pharmacy, she did not have to scour the local newspaper for details of Sunday opening times. The pharmacy, a gleaming establishment with English-speaking staff and a rather beautiful tiled counter, was a five-minute walk away. Of course it was open. And, yes, they had infant paracetamol. Yes, they had it in suppository form in case he spat out the medicine. I was lost in admiration. I still am.

Jacob's injuries soon healed. He sustained a slight cut behind his right ear and badly grazed his right side, which caused him discomfort; yet by the Tuesday he was back in the hotel pool, his usual cheerful if alarmingly fearless self. We never knew exactly what happened at El Pirate. He must have moved his chair back, stood up and peered out, overbalancing before I could reach him. Jane and I berated ourselves for careless parenting, and were still in shock when we got home a week later, but our friends were wonderfully supportive, describing all sorts of incidents involving their own kids, in which tragedies were narrowly averted by luck rather than design. Even my mother recalled an incident she had long suppressed, in which I, as a toddler, crawled out of a window on to a parapet over the Kardomah cafe on Kensington High Street. Evidently Jacob was lucky to be alive in more ways than one.

But such are the tortures of parenthood. The accident didn't change my opinion that giving children too little independence is just as irresponsible as giving them too much. Nevertheless, the stark fact remained that we had let our youngest child fall out of a high window, and that he could easily have been killed.

On the way down he must have glanced off the side of the building, which changed his headfirst trajectory. At the bottom, he bounced off a rocky ledge on to the beach, but aghast, we did not stop to look out. We hurtled down a flight of stone steps to the beach – the longest twenty seconds I have ever endured – with terrible thoughts flashing through our minds. That we would find him dead. But this was adorable, funny, characterful Jakey, so how could he be? There was already a crowd around him when we got to the bottom of the steps, and – blessed relief – he was crying.

We were twice asked whether we wished to make a formal complaint against the restaurant, and I expect that in a more litigious society, especially America, we could have made millions. But how can you sue when something is your fault? Or is that being naive?

Whatever, in the ensuing tearful bout of self-recrimination we realized one dreadful thing. That if the worst had happened, the presence of our two other children would have provided little or no consolation. That the only one we wanted would have been the one not there. A friend of ours whose only brother died young confirmed that this tallied exactly with her mother's response, not just in the immediate aftermath of her brother's death, but miserably ever after, exerting a dreadful strain on the mother–daughter relationship.

Anyway, I include the details of Jacob's accident in this book not so much because it happened on holiday, but because it wouldn't have happened if we hadn't been on holiday. The average British person spends between 5 and 10 per cent of his or her adult life on holiday, so inevitably some holidays will be ruined by accidents and deaths. And statistically they are more likely to happen on holiday than at home, partly because we tend to undertake higher-risk pursuits on holiday and partly because we tend to be more relaxed and therefore less mindful of risk. I have a doctor friend who broke his neck on holiday in Africa once, when he was in a jeep that rolled over. He wasn't wearing a seatbelt, which would have been unthinkable in the UK, but – hey – he was on holiday. Mercifully, he made a full recovery.

Also, the foreign environment itself can make accidents more likely. In our case, the window almost certainly wouldn't have been open in an English restaurant, but also, as I have said, on holidays we all take our eye off the ball. Or the child. Or the camera. Or the handbag. That's why tourists make such juicy targets for pickpockets and hustlers all over the world. A friend of ours tells a gruesome story of wandering through Barcelona, and being approached by a gypsy woman who gave him a toothless smile, then tucked a white carnation into his buttonhole.

'How charming,' he somewhat naively thought, then reached into his inside pocket for his wallet, which was still there, with his credit cards tucked into their little slats inside it, yet all the banknotes had disappeared. A few yards further down the road was a small hotel, so he went in and asked the advice of the English-speaking receptionist, who told him that as soon as she'd seen the white carnation, she'd realized precisely what the problem was. A man sitting in the reception overheard all this, and advised my friend to go straight to the police station. Shaking his head mournfully he came over and showed exactly how the pickpocket had carried out the dastardly deed, then he stepped outside with my friend and gave him directions to the police station. You have probably guessed the denouement. When my friend got to the police station, his credit cars had gone too, pinched by the helpful bloke at the hotel. You almost have to applaud the effrontery of it.

Coincidentally, or maybe not so coincidentally, Barcelona was also where I was pickpocketed for the first – and so far, touch wood, only – time on holiday. Jane and I went for a rare weekend away without the children in the early spring of 2010, and I was mindful of my friend's story, particularly when we walked down the famous Ramblas. It is said to be one of the most pickpocket-rife streets in Europe, and I duly kept my money in the breast pocket of my shirt, underneath a jumper, patting it every five minutes in the neurotic way of the tourist who thinks he is being targeted by every thief in the neighbourhood. Happily we got back to our hotel with the money undisturbed, but I joked to Jane that I half-expected to take my trousers off and find that my boxer shorts had gone, such is the devilish reputation of those light-fingered Catalans.

The following day, we wanted to see the Parc Guell, the quirky, Gaudi-designed park overlooking the city. The hotel concierge recommended getting there either by taxi or the number 24 bus, so we chose the latter option, and when it arrived within seconds of us reaching the bus stop, and the fare was only 1.40 euros each, I congratulated myself on an economically astute bit of touristing. Moreover, travelling by bus puts you in touch with the vibe of a city in a way that sitting in the back of a cab simply doesn't. Unfortunately, travelling on this bus also put a pickpocket in touch with the 150 euros that I was very stupidly carrying in my back pocket. After surviving the dangerous Ramblas unmolested, I had foolishly lowered my guard.

As the bus filled up, becoming positively packed, I felt a fleeting contact but scarcely gave it a thought until, at the Parc Guell, I reached for the notes in my back pocket to pay for a couple of coffees. Being robbed was hugely tiresome for all kinds of reasons. In a way, worse than losing the money – which was a sufficiently large sum to be a blow but not enough to warrant the hassle of pursuing an insurance claim – was being exposed as such a mug. I'd always prided myself on being a fairly savvy tourist, yet had just presented a thief with the easiest pickings of his day, if not his week. The bus journey, which had seemed like such a knowing thing to do, had cost us 152.80 euros. By painful contrast, the taxi journey back to the hotel cost 8.50 euros.

Still, of all the things that can go wrong for the British or anyone else on holiday, petty theft is really nowhere near the top of the list. Nor, even, is falling out of windows, as long as the person taking the plunge survives without lasting damage. The worst thing that can happen is death, not just for the deceased, nor only for the stricken friends or relatives, but for everyone concerned, including the tour operator.

All of which brings me to my friend Frank, who runs a

company called World Odyssey, specializing in upmarket, long-haul trips. Frank understandably boasts of not having 'lost' anyone in the ten years World Odyssey has been in business, but before that he worked for the swanky travel agency Abercrombie & Kent, and recalls an unfortunate business in Tanzania, where an elderly Englishman suffered a heart attack while on safari. In East Africa there is a splendid organization called the Flying Doctors, whose planes will land on any makeshift airstrip to whisk an unwell person off to hospital. But the Flying Doctors have a cardinal rule: they don't carry corpses.

In this instance, tragically, the elderly Englishman died before help could arrive. But the staff at the safari lodge, sympathetic as they were, were well aware of the bureaucratic nightmare that would ensue once they had reported a guest's death. And so, according to Frank, a scene unfolded faintly reminiscent of the 'Kipper and the Corpse' episode of *Fawlty Towers*, with two strapping staff members propping the dead man upright, and helping him to the plane with encouraging remarks, for the benefit of the pilot and the on-board medic, about how well he was doing. The plane was airborne by the time the Flying Doctors medic established that he was already, in fact, a goner, and by then he was no longer the responsibility of the people at the safari lodge. Heartless, but, Frank assures me, completely true.

It is a much better idea, if you do have to pop your clogs on holiday, to do so in Europe. Another good friend, Stephen, has been running a company specializing in cycling holidays since 1985. Bents Bicycle and Walking Holidays started out and still take place mainly in what is best defined as *mittel* Europe, focusing on Germany, which has a certain logic since Stephen is not only a former British Olympic cyclist, but also half-German. He runs a terrific business and is rightly proud of having suffered only one death among his customers since 1985, but naturally wishes it was one fewer. It occurred on a beautiful summer's day, when an English couple in their sixties were cycling through northern Bavaria, scarcely a week after the husband had retired from full-time employment. This fellow's wife was ahead, and had been chatting away cheerfully for some time when she realized that he hadn't responded for a while. She stopped and turned round, and he wasn't there. Puzzled, she cycled back, to find to her incalculable distress that he'd suffered a massive heart attack, and was already dead.

Since this was Germany rather than Tanzania, there were hardly any bureaucratic hurdles. The British consulate in Frankfurt were, in Stephen's estimation, 'fantastic'. The man's body was repatriated without any hassle, and a few weeks later Stephen received a long letter from the widow, apologizing profusely for any inconvenience her husband's death might have caused the company. It is hard to imagine such a letter from anyone but a Brit: I'm so dreadfully, dreadfully sorry for the problems my husband's unexpected death might have caused you.

While writing this book I spent an engrossing couple of hours in a pub, talking to Stephen about the idiosyncrasies of the British on holiday. In fairness, I should add that it's not only the Brits abroad who have idiosyncrasies, nor is it only the tourists with whose characteristics we are perhaps most familiar in this country, principally the Americans and the Japanese. In March 2010, for example, Air New Zealand was forced to apologize for a training manual in which cabin staff were advised to keep a close eye on Tongan passengers in case 'they drink the bar dry'. They were also told that travelling Koreans demand good manners and Thais expect flight souvenirs, but it was the characterizing of the Tongans as 'uncontrollable alcoholics' that caused the biggest furore and I can quite see why they took exception.

I imagine, though, that it was rooted in a certain amount of truth. In the same way, it would be unfair to write off all British holidaymakers as cheapskates, but by all accounts we are cheaper than most. I had some experience of this in 1981 when I spent the best part of a year working as a porter in an old-fashioned three-star hotel in the centre of Paris. The Americans were by a distance the most generous tippers, and the Brits were by a similar distance the least. I don't suppose that has changed.

Getting back to my evening in the pub with Stephen, he told me some holiday tales encapsulating the best of Britishness, and others encapsulating the worst. Starting with the former, in the summer of 2005 parts of his Alpine cycling routes were washed away by a series of freak floods, and the small town of Kochel am See in Bavaria was particularly badly affected. By unhappy chance, there was a Bents party of cycling tourists, comprising several British families and one American family, staying there at the height of the emergency. While Stephen arranged to have his customers bussed to a less stricken part of the Alps, the Brits without exception mucked in with the locals, sandbagging buildings for all they were worth. The Americans, by stark contrast, abandoned their holiday, complaining bitterly.

One should always be wary of generalizations, needless to add. But this story fits with something Frank told me about World Odyssey. When Americans book with him, they almost always start by asking for the most expensive option, because they equate expense with quality. Most British customers start by doing exactly the opposite, asking what's cheapest. Naturally, the pricier the holiday, the more money Frank makes, but that doesn't mean to say that he would prefer to sell his packages in Massachusetts rather than Middlessex, because, once the Americans have paid top dollar, they expect top everything. And can rage like the fires of hell if they feel they're not getting it. This is not a criticism, by the way. On the contrary, I admire it. Brits, as already recorded in these pages, are, on the whole, the most lacklustre complainers in the world.

However, there are some holiday disasters that are almost beyond complaint. My favourite story of Stephen's is also the most toe-curling, and in some ways the saddest, concerning a young Scottish rep he employed in the summer of 2009. Stephen relies heavily on reps, whose job it is to transport baggage from one hotel to the next, while the customers enjoy a leisurely walk or bike ride. These aren't the only demands on the rep, of course, but for anyone reasonably resourceful, bright and sociable it is not the most stressful job in the world.

That wasn't how the young Scotsman saw things, however. One afternoon in the beautiful Tuscan hilltop town of San Gimignano, after just ten days of repping, something nudged the fellow over the edge of sanity. He wandered into the middle of a piazza, took off all his clothes, and set fire to them. He was duly arrested, and it turned out that he'd had psychiatric problems before, which he had omitted to disclose on his c.v. In the meantime, due to being carted off naked by the *carabinieri*, he was unable to discharge his repping duties. The first indication that Stephen received to suggest that all was not well, was when two customers phoned him in his office – which, less than conveniently in terms of crises in Tuscany, is near Ludlow in Shropshire – to say that their bags hadn't arrived. This was at 7.30 p.m. Shortly afterwards, the police arrived at the hotel and over the next couple of hours the details of the rep's unfortunate breakdown unfolded. Just after six the next morning Stephen was on a flight from Stansted to Pisa to pick up the pieces, which he estimates cost him more than £6000.

He spent two days in Tuscany sorting things out, hastily reassigning reps and making arrangements for his troubled Scottish employee to be flown home. But he still needed to rely on the goodwill of his customers, not least that of a couple from

Hampshire who were due to fly out to Pisa a few days later. By this time Stephen was back in Shropshire, and it had emerged that the Scotsman, in another act of irrational behaviour, had posted the keys for seven bike locks into the slot on the car CD player, from which they couldn't be retrieved. There was a biggish group arriving the following day, and they would need fully functioning bike locks. Luckily, Stephen had a packet of spare keys in his office, but rather than post them to Italy, he phoned the couple from Hampshire, asking if they would mind taking them out with them? They agreed readily enough, and by way of thanks he said he'd make sure that the new rep – his own son James, very speedily despatched to Italy – would stand them a drink or two. He explained that he would send an envelope containing the seven small keys by overnight delivery to arrive before nine a.m., well before they were due to set off for the airport. This he did, and the couple passed on the keys to James.

But here's the sting in the tail: this couple still had £260 outstanding on their holiday, which they refused to pay, claiming that they thought their favour to Stephen wiped out the debt. From time to time even now, Stephen cussedly sends them a letter reminding them that they owe him money, and they just as cussedly reply insisting that they owe him nothing. A vulnerable Scotsman strips naked and sets fire to his clothes in an Italian piazza, causing a former Olympic cyclist to put some bike-lock keys in the post to some people in Hampshire, causing a £260 debt to go unsettled, causing a disagreement which continues for years afterwards. It's enough to help a man understand the theory that a butterfly flapping its wings on one side of the world can provoke a tornado on the other, which until now, frankly, has always been beyond me.

19

Frogs, four Yorkshiremen, and finding ourselves

The strip in the San Gimignano piazza also serves to direct my attention towards Tuscany, for many years one of the classic holiday destinations for the British middle classes. Indeed, I remember a cartoon in a summertime edition of *Private Eye* years ago, which featured some smart Georgian houses in the background, and in front of them a sign saying 'Hampstead', over which someone had written 'Closed – Gone to Tuscany'. The notion that the whole of liberal intellectual Hampstead might decamp to Tuscany in the summer was of course preposterous, yet like all the best cartoons it carried a grain of truth. There are certain Italian and for that matter French towns where every summer you can be more or less as certain of rubbing shoulders with barristers from Lincoln's Inn Fields, and with Harley Street consultants, as you would be in, well, Lincoln's Inn Fields and Harley Street.

When I generalize about the British on holiday, I suppose I am overlooking class distinctions. The very word 'class' makes some people wince on the basis that we are meant to be less and less delineated by background and education, and hurrah for it, yet there is no doubt that holidaying Brits can be divided, very broadly speaking, into those who shop at Waitrose and those who shop at Aldi. I don't particularly want to let snobbery into these pages, but there's clearly a distinction. And the former group also includes the privileged sub-species who give their children names such as Allegra and Ivo, and whose children – let's call them Allegra and Ivo – know what a *gîte* is, for example, practically before they can walk.

I'm not entirely sure when the French word *gîte* – which originally meant simply 'shelter' – became a fixture in the middle-class Brit's vocabulary; sometime in the mid-1980s, I think, when *gîte* holidays were all the rage, and if Hampstead was 'Closed – Gone to Tuscany' during what my mother still calls the long vac, Wimbledon was 'Closed – Gone to the Dordogne'. The *gîte* holiday is no longer the exclusive preserve of the affluent middle classes, any more than Tuscany and the Dordogne are, and yet in large swathes of rural France and Italy it is still Allegra and Ivo you are more likely to hear being summoned for their tea on an August afternoon than, let's say, Kyleigh and Darren. In France, one of these swathes includes the Pont du Gard, the remarkable Roman aqueduct not far from Nîmes, in the shadow of which, in the summer of 2009, I enjoyed the amusing spectacle of Allegra and Ivo and their parents, William and Cressida (or a family very much like them) sharing a small shingle beach with several rough, hard-drinking, hard-smoking and hard-swearing French families.

Cressida and William stood it for about half an hour, during which time there was a terrible commotion when a beefy young Frenchman tattooed up to *les yeux* found a frog and cruelly popped it into his skinny sister's bikini bottoms. My family and I were stationed on a kind of rocky plateau well above this hoo-hah and, for us, half the fun lay in the behaviour of the French family, among whom the recriminations were loud and eventful, with an older family member actually punching the frog-wielding miscreant in the back of the head while the sister stood nearby screaming blue murder, and the other half of the fun provided by William, Cressida, Ivo and Allegra, manifestly fascinated and appalled in equal measure, neither wanting to stare in case it seemed impolite, nor wanting to leave in case that seemed impolite. Eventually, after what they evidently deemed a respectable interval, they packed up their wholesome-looking picnic, making sure not to leave any litter, and trooped off, doubtless never to return to the Pont du Gard.

On the very same holiday, I should add, I saw a similar culture clash in reverse, a rather chic, streamlined French family lying on sunbeds at a little seaside resort in the Languedoc while not five yards from them a loud, large and pasty family from Yorkshire unpacked their beach stuff and a row unfolded between the husband and an elderly woman with a light-purple rinse whom I took to be his mother. 'What yer looking for?' she said, as he rooted through a bag. 'Ah'm not looking for 'owt.' 'Are yer looking for water?' The word water was pronounced watter, to rhyme with platter. 'No, I'm not looking for water.' 'Water's 'ere.' 'I'M NOT LOOKING FOR BLOODY WATER!' The French family looked on down their aquiline noses. It was marvellous.

Returning to William, Cressida, Allegra and Ivo: until I grew up I never knew anyone remotely like them, nor did I know anyone who spent their holidays in rented houses – or still more

217

exotic, villas – in France or Italy. I didn't know anyone who went skiing, either. The families I knew who had money, stayed in foreign hotels. Those who didn't have money, holidayed in the UK.

In adulthood, however, I have become friends with people whose holidays as children were dramatically different from mine. Among them is my good friend James, born just five months earlier than me in 1961, and raised in one of the plusher suburbs of Birmingham, where his father was a dentist. In 1968, James and his younger brother Ben were taken by their parents from Birmingham to Yugoslavia, in an Austin 1100. Nobody I knew in Southport did anything remotely as adventurous as that.

As James recalls it now, a sort of makeshift wooden platform was rigged up on the back seat, so that he and Ben could play cards. There was no question of anyone in the car wearing a seatbelt, in the back (for the watertight reason that there weren't any) or even in the front. After all, the 'Clunk-Click Every Trip' campaign spearheaded by Jimmy Savile was still some years off, and the conventions of travelling long-distance by car were wholly unlike they are now, especially for the junior family members. In the twenty-first century children sit in the back with their iPods and iPhones, developing, in some cases, iPersonalities. For a while in the back of our own family car, until our children acquired their own entertainment devices, we had a DVD player rigged up, just to remove the faintest chance that they might at any stage of the journey, get bored. Yet my friend Becky remembers sitting for hours in the back of her dad's turquoise Morris Marina, the air thick with the mingled scents of her mother's forty cigarettes a day and Rive Gauche perfume, and if the children wound down a window by so much as an eighth of an inch there was hell to pay. Kids these days phone ChildLine for less.

For James and his family, the 1968 trip from Birmingham to

Yugoslavia and home again took a fortnight, which amounted to not very much more than driving all the way there and all the way back. But that's not to say it was an uneventful holiday. On a Yugoslav motorway the Austin 1100 suffered a blow-out, and James still remembers the sensation of the car veering from side to side before it hit the central reservation and span round to face the opposite direction. If ever there was a moment to be wearing a seatbelt, that was it, and yet miraculously no injuries were sustained, except to the vehicle, and even that remained perfectly roadworthy for the epic return journey. Indeed, James's dad drove the last 800 miles to the ferry in one go. But by the time they got back to Birmingham the car seemed to be struggling, and the man at P. J. Evans garage in Bourneville pronounced it, with just 17,000 miles on the clock, terminally worn out.

That holiday might have left a healthy family car fit only for the knacker's yard, it might have featured a crash that could easily have killed them all, but it was undertaken for the best of motives: to broaden the minds of two impressionable little boys. In that sense, it was a holiday that could trace its lineage all the way back to the Grand Tour of the eighteenth century, only with an Austin 1100 instead of a coach and four. And the following summer, with a Vauxhall Victor Estate, the car bought to replace the clapped-out Austin. That year, James's dad drove them all down to the south of Italy and back, a trip which included visits to Pompeii, Monte Cassino and, almost the main reason for the entire holiday, the grave of the legendary tenor Enrico Caruso in the Del Pianto Cemetery in Naples. Why the parents of two boys aged nine and seven might have thought that the prospect of seeing Caruso's grave would keep them happy on the back seat of a Vauxhall Victor Estate for four days, or however long it took to get from Birmingham to Naples, I really don't know. But I love the fact that they did.

The idea that holidays should educate is an enduring middle-class impulse, even if it doesn't necessarily go down well with middle-class kids. Yet by the time those kids hit their late teens, lots of them show they have absorbed the message by signing up for what is now known as a gap year, deferring their university entrance by twelve months to take off with a huge backpack for South America or Australasia.

In 1980, long before I'd heard of the term 'gap year', I did something similar myself, though I didn't get as far as Australasia; only Paris. But in those days hardly anyone from my school took a year out, as it was more prosaically known, so by the time I pitched up at the University of St Andrews in the autumn of 1981, I thought I was the bee's knees, or even *les genoux d'abeille*, for having lived and worked in Paris, finding myself a job as a hotel concierge and renting, for fifteen francs a week, a tiny, slummy bedsit on the Rue de Courcelles. I was in for a rude awakening, however, for scarcely had I shaken hands with the two guys who were my neighbours in my hall of residence, than they were telling me what they had done on their years out: I suppose the passing of time might have played tricks with my memory but, as I recall it, one had crossed the Kalahari on a giant tortoise, while the other had set up a chain of soup kitchens in Calcutta, before undertaking a sponsored journey along the Great Wall of China, on a pogo-stick. It might have been a spacehopper. At any rate, their adventures made mine look like rather tame fare.

These days even more than in those days, gap years, and the whole phenomenon of young British people travelling rough in their teens or early twenties, are prey to tremendous one-upmanship, a kind of inverted holiday snobbery whereby the further you have ventured off the beaten track, the more kudos you can claim when you get home.

The more privileged the child, the hairier the gap-year experience is a very general rule of thumb, so general that there are thousands of exceptions every year, of public-school boys and girls looking no further than daddy's firm or farm, his hedge fund or his hedgerows, for their first sustained experience of the wider world, and comprehensive-school kids heading off for Papua New Guinea or Bogotá. But the children from more affluent backgrounds tend to have wider horizons, and there are all kinds of reasons why: family encouragement; family money; a wider network of contacts in far-flung parts of the world; the familiarity of leaving home for a year when you've been used to being waved off to boarding-school from the age of eight; or, again, simply the same impulse as all those eighteenth-century aristocrats, some of whom might well have been ancestors. Whatever, it is no coincidence that many of the writers of the generally excellent *Rough Guide* books – started in the 1980s by another visionary, Mark Ellingham, who saw a gap in the market for meeting the information needs of backpackers on low budgets – are decidedly posh.

Since 1982, when Ellingham wrote his inaugural *Rough Guide to Greece*, the world has opened up dramatically to backpackers. That was also the year when my mate Mark Sutcliffe and I went InterRailing, considering ourselves downright intrepid for crossing eight European borders in a month, and for busking on foreign streets to supplement our beer fund. But we stayed firmly in western Europe. Now, the former Eastern Bloc countries are on the backpacker's radar, not to mention huge swathes of South America and the Far East. And on the radar not just of the backpacker, of course, but of the more moneyed traveller too. The world has become smaller and safer, with only Africa presenting as many no-go areas for the British tourist as it did thirty years ago.

For previous generations, it was military service that turned boys into men, girls into women. For many now it is adventures on the Inca Trail or the Burma Railway, which has to be considered a sign of progress. Who knows, their A–Z of safe, viable destinations might one day extend from Afghanistan to Zimbabwe, taking in North Korea and the Democratic Republic of the Congo.

For parents – and I write as the father of a girl who is soon to finish school, and is determined to travel either before or after university – all this is a source of some angst-fuelled ambivalence: we encourage our kids to see the world, and we're proud of them when they do, yet we worry like hell about them getting back in one piece, or joining a cult in Mexico, or a hippie commune in Kathmandu. My friend Alison has a friend called Helen, whose grandmother always used to warn her against travelling abroad, her bizarre but completely heartfelt concern being that 'you might get stolen and end up as a sex slave in Asia Minor'. And this when Helen was only going camping in Brittany. Meanwhile, where some people see concerns, others see business opportunities. Trading on the parental angst are an increasing number of companies specializing in gap-year trips, and offering a degree of organization and security for your child as he or she takes off for page 93 or 117 of an atlas in which Europe is covered by pages 1 to 30.

That said, the worried parent's ultimate repository of faith and trust is the child, who is also the source of all the anxiety. All you can hope is that your child behaves sensibly, even in a risky situation, and especially with the growing participation in extreme sports as part of a gap-year or foreign holiday. Even as I was writing this book, a female British student died in the Alps, crashing into a rock face on a zip-wire, having declined to wear all the routine safety equipment. And scarcely a year passes without a British person, usually aged between eighteen and thirty, meeting with a tragic accident while white-water rafting or bungee-jumping in some distant land. On which subject, my daughter Eleanor tells me that when her friend's older brother went bungee-jumping in Australia, the instructor who shackled him to the elastic cord waited until he had stepped off the parapet, and then yelled 'Wait a minute, mate, I haven't checked your . . .' All in the name of good Aussie humour.

It is a happy irony, though, that as horizons have broadened, as extreme sports have proliferated, so communications have improved. For Mark and me, our only contact with home was the odd postcard from Innsbruck or Rome, if that. Even if we'd managed to figure out how to operate a public payphone in Austria or Italy, we would have baulked at the number of coins required. Now, there are internet cafés everywhere. Thanks to Skype, we don't even have to wait for the photographs. We can actually see our loved ones, and marvel at their Australasian or South American tan.

Jane and I have some dear friends, Kim and Will, whose daughter Grace (state school-educated, and without wealthy parents, I should add) took off to South America with a mate, prior to starting at Leeds University. Grace didn't sign up with a gap-year company, preferring to plot her own bus route, which included Bolivia's El Camino de la Muerte, the charmingly named road of death, so narrow and precipitous in parts that an average of one vehicle every fortnight is said to leave it, almost always fatally for the occupants. But it was only when she had safely completed El Camino de la Muerte that Grace Skyped home.

If Grace were the sort of young woman to wear her gap-year experiences as a kind of badge of pride, she certainly could, but one-upmanship was never her motivation. In Rio she and her friend witnessed a shooting; in Salvador they were robbed. That alone would equip her for a gap-year version of Monty Python's famous 'Four Yorkshiremen' sketch, in which four prosperous businessmen try to outdo each other by boasting about the deprivation of their childhoods. 'Robbed in Salvador, that's nowt? I were robbed and held hostage for a year!' 'Robbed and held hostage for a year, call that an experience?' 'I were robbed, held hostage for a year, then murdered.'

Whatever, Grace's experience owes everything to her own curiosity and resourcefulness, and to the fact that she has been raised by supportive, level-headed parents. That might not be everyone's opinion of parents who let their daughter put herself in a situation where she can be robbed in Salvador, but it is unequivocally mine – at least until Eleanor tells me that she fancies motorcycling through Equatorial Guinea. Notwithstanding Grace's adventurous streak and their steadfast support, though, her departure was traumatic for all three of them. Typically, she asked not to be taken to the airport, preferring to set off from Finsbury Park tube station in north London, but as her mother Kim describes it, she felt as if her heart was being tugged into the tunnel with the departing train. As for the huggy homecoming many months later, that did happen at the airport, but Kim and Will took Grace's friend Nikita with them, and the drive home from Heathrow to Crouch End was filled not with Grace telling stories of the madcap Rio Carnival, or about her rickety bus journey through Colombia, but with Nikita telling Grace all about splitting up with her boyfriend. Extended foreign holidays might still be the best way for us to find ourselves, as the self-help manuals would have it, but at the end of it all, we still find ourselves at home.

20

Parents, pals and postcards

For most of us, I suppose our parents are the biggest single influence on our holidaying preferences, whether because of the places they took us to, or the places they didn't take us to. Some of us become just like our parents in our attitude to holidays, some of us become the diametric opposites. I don't know which path my own kids will follow. We have taken them on long-haul flights a few times, to North America and the Caribbean, and I hope this will encourage them to look beyond Europe when they come to take their own holidays. On the other hand, I hope that they won't be sniffy about Europe, which surely offers more diversity, when you think about language, food and customs as well as topography, architecture and history, than any other continent.

I never went on a long-haul flight as a child, but then in those days the trans-oceanic expedition was a much bigger deal, not least in terms of comparative expense, than it is now. Taking your children on long-haul flights also means exposing them to the realities of the wealth gap, and I'm not talking about taking them to see India, or those other places in the world where Western tourists encounter truly heartbreaking poverty; I'm just talking about getting on the plane, and watching other people head for the first-class and business sections while we are herded into economy.

The cheap-seat British have a characteristically resentful attitude towards their counterparts at the front end of the plane, which usually simmers just below the surface but sometimes boils over into open, rumbling discontent. In May 2010 Jane and I took the kids to Antigua for a week, flying economy with Virgin, and on the way home the steward announced that the pilot was expecting turbulence so could we all fasten our seatbelts and refrain from using the toilets, and could the Upper Class passengers please get out of the jacuzzi. It was a joke – comfortable as Virgin Upper Class is, there aren't yet any jacuzzis – and rather a good one, playing directly to classic British inverted snobbery, whereby we prefer to look down our noses at those with more money than ourselves than to salute them for their material success in life. Anyway, the joke was swallowed whole, with an audible exclamation of indignation that the Upper Class passengers were able to spend the nine-hour journey luxuriating in hot, bubbling water, while there we were having to cope with all the travails of economy flying, such as the guy in front abruptly jerking his seat into recline mode just as you've got out the Travel Scrabble.

Even once I'd assured them that the steward was having us all on about the jacuzzi, my children begged me to pay for them to travel Upper Class sometime; I told them that their writer parents would need to produce at least one bestseller each even to consider it. Actually, it's not a bad thing for chiildren to know that you need to work hard, and perhaps enjoy an element of luck as well, to be able to afford nice holidays. When I was a kid I was made very aware of the correlation; in years when my dad had flogged enough bras and camisoles, we had a foreign holiday. And sometimes, when he sold more than usual, he and my mum used to take me abroad in the winter as well as the summer.

These tended to be educational trips. One year we went to Rome, another year to Athens. It's not their fault that all these decades later, what I remember most vividly from the Athens trip is not the Acropolis, but the gyrations of a belly dancer at a 'nitespot' that must have been deemed suitable for the under-twelves. Nor is it the Colosseum or even the Trevi Fountain that rear up in my mind's eye when I remember our few days in Rome when I was eight years old, but my father's suggestion that he might take me to watch a Serie A football match. I had never been to a proper football match before, and greeted with thrilled disbelief the idea that I might make my debut at Roma or Lazio. The disbelief was well founded, as it turned out. When my dad saw the price of the tickets he changed his mind, non-negotiably. I was heartbroken.

These are not the life-long memories they were hoping would fill my head as we traipsed the streets of the two greatest cities of the ancient world, but God bless them for trying. And actually, I wasn't entirely impervious to culture even as a very small child. When I was no more than five or six my mother and grandma took me to Amsterdam for a weekend, and to the Rijksmuseum, where we duly arrived in the room in which Rembrandt's famous painting *The Night Watch* was exhibited. I recognized it instantly, because my dad had a print on the wall of his office, above a branch of the Midland Bank in Leece Street, Liverpool. 'Look Mummy, there's Daddy's painting,' I shrieked excitedly and, as my mother still tells the story today, the English-speaking people in the room looked at us with respectful interest, guilelessly assuming that this little boy had a very rich father from whom this great work of art was on loan.

For the most part, though, my childhood memories of foreign holidays are of Spanish, Portuguese and Italian beaches, and of waiters being sent away from our table in hangar-like hotel dining-rooms because the soup wasn't hot enough. My late father had a thing about tepid soup, which sometimes he would send back three or more times if it didn't satisfy his temperature requirements, and if I'd known the Spanish for 'Right, give the fucker this, I've heated it up so it will scald the fucking paint from the walls' I'm sure I would have heard it repeatedly in the kitchens of the hotels we stayed in.

But tepid soup or not, he and my mum liked to be in one place. The motoring holiday through Europe, as experienced by my friend James, wasn't for us, perhaps partly because I was an only child and my parents didn't think it would be fair for me to sit alone on the back seat for hours on end. The kind of package holidays we took at least threw up a fair chance of my making a friend or two, which in turn stopped me nagging my dad to play table-tennis or crazy golf, giving him more time to read his latest James A. Michener novel.

I did make some firm friends on those childhood holidays, although in an era without Facebook, text-messaging and the rest, I don't recall any of those friendships enduring much, if at all, beyond the plane journey home. In adulthood I've had a few more successful stabs at keeping holiday friendships going, and in my twenties there were even some semi-lasting romances kindled under a foreign sun, but it is children who make friends most easily on holiday, their lack of inhibition an admirable thing.

I remember my own kids, on the Costa de la Luz in Spain on the holiday that Jacob fell out of the window, becoming firm friends with two little German sisters whose English was only marginally better than their German – by which I mean it extended to three or four words rather than none. Yet the British adult, as we have established, is in general not good at making social overtures to other people on holiday.

When we do, and hit it off, lasting friendships are often cemented. Maybe this is all connected with our so-called natural reserve. There's an old cliché about the difference between the Americans and the British, that Americans have a veneer of friendliness, but it's not easy to find the genuine warmth under-neath, whereas you'll struggle to get off first base with a Brit but, once you have, you'll find a real friend. I can think of people I've met over the years who have utterly contradicted both sides of this equation, but like most old clichés, as with most of the best car-toons, there's also plenty of truth in it.

Often, a holiday friendship gets no further than an annual Christmas card. In 1987 I went skiing in the Bulgarian resort of Borovets with my then girlfriend, and we met a young married couple from Devon called Sharon and Kevin. My girlfriend had skiied a fair amount before, but it was my first time, and so while she swanned off with the intermediates, I was confined to the beginners' class with, among others, Sharon and Kevin. We got on famously, as you almost have to do when you're hopelessly snow-ploughing into each other all day, and the following Christmas we exchanged cards, including cheerful updates on our skiing plans for the following year.

I never set eyes on them again, yet their cards kept coming for at least the next fifteen years, arriving one Christmas with the name of a child added, a few Christmases later with the name of another child added, and always with some scribbled information about their last, or their next, skiing holiday. We routinely sent each other change-of-address cards too, and by the year 2000, although I'd long since forgotten what Kevin and Sharon looked like, I knew that they'd been to Val d'Isère that February, that the conditions had been excellent, that they were now handling even black runs and mogul fields with ease, and that they were hoping to go to Tignes in 2001. I, meanwhile, having stopped the skiing holidays while my children were small, had nothing to offer, piste-wise, in return. I felt as though I was letting them down, indeed that might be why eventually their Christmas cards stopped coming. Either that or they ended up buried in an avalanche. Whatever the reason, I was hugely disappointed. It seemed daft but wonderful to me that a few classes together all those years earlier had prompted this annual skiing bulletin. Who knows, maybe they'll read this book and make contact again. I hope so. I want to know where they're going skiing next year.

At the other end of the spectrum from my Kevin-and-Sharon experience is the holiday friendship that blooms so dramatically that it leads to future holidays together, or even the decision of one couple, or family, to move to be closer to the other. The very best friends of our mates Ali and David, the people whose bmibaby flight to France was scuppered because the children's passports had expired, are folk they met on holiday years ago. And Jane's Auntie Jose, a marvellous character without whom no book of mine will ever be complete, at least until I write a new biography of Tamburlaine the Great or a novel set among the Norwegian fjords in the 1760s, and perhaps not even then, always comes back from holiday talking so enthusiastically about the new friends she has made that we soon feel, without ever meeting them, as if they're our friends too. There's not much we don't know about Baz and Gwen, except of course what they look like.

While we're on the subject of Auntie Jose, let me turn to the holiday postcard. The saucy English seaside postcards drawn by Donald McGill I have already dealt with, but the postcard from overseas is a different matter altogether, and Auntie Jose's, at least in our family, are collector's items. By and large, the British are good at sending postcards but not at writing them. Go into one of those antique shops that have loads of old postcards for sale at 20p each and you'll see what I mean: 'Weather fine, Mavis much better, see you on Friday' or 'Rain most days, hotel adequate, wish you were here'.

Actually, I find those large cardboard boxes of old postcards almost unbearably poignant. I can't help reflecting that those little messages home, however brief, were invariably written by people when they were at their most alive, on their holidays, and now they are dead. There is one such box permanently on the counter in an antique shop in Leominster, close to where I live, and from time to time I riffle through it, thinking of all the human emotions that those cards represent: the excitement, anxiety, joy, contentment, disappointment (with the weather, usually). While I was writing this book I bought a few at random, just to share with you. One, sent to 43 Pleasant View Street in Aberdare, mid-Glamorgan, says 'Dear Lottie and Drew, Having a nice time, weather and digs OK, All the best, Stan'. Another, coincidentally sent to the same home, but addressed only to Lottie (what happened to Drew?), says 'Dear Lottie, Having a great time. Weather – Food – Hotel – are all Fantastic. Been to Florence, Pisa and lots of other places. Beryl, Len and Hayley.'

I'm not suggesting that such postcards should be filled with Wildean epigrams – although Stan might have managed a bit more information for Lottie and Drew – but rare indeed is the UK-bound postcard bearing any evidence of wit, which is surprising, because we are a witty lot, on the whole. And if wit is rare, rarer still is the postcard that omits any mention of the weather. If a psychological profiler were to piece together an assessment of our national psyche based purely on the postcards we send one another, he would conclude that we are a nation of weather-obsessed dullards. Perhaps we are.

Children are one happy exception to this rule. Children write fantastic postcards, full of non-sequiturs and little squiggly drawings, and so packed with information in tiny writing that there's scarcely any room for the address, and the stamp has to be fixed splat over the account of dad running over a wild pig in the hire car. Another exception to the rule is Auntie Jose. Her postcards aren't long, and they usually contain a heartfelt complaint about either the hotel or some of her fellow guests, but invariably, either the complaint or some other observation is expressed with effortless and matchless skill. If you have read about Jose's postcard-writing talents in my book *Tales of the Country*, then again I apologize for repeating myself here, but I particularly cherished her description a few years ago of a hotel swimming pool that she considered too small, surrounded by white walls she reckoned too high. 'It's like a postage stamp in the middle of a squash court,' she informed us in her card, and we rejoiced in the certain knowledge that she would not have been especially pleased with herself for plucking that image from her mind; it was simply the best way of describing the silly hotel pool. If William Shakespeare himself had known what postage stamps were, and squash courts, and for that matter swimming pools, he could have found no better line of imagery.

21

Barbecues, Bergasol and bikini lines

William Shakespeare, a different William Shakespeare, was coincidentally a client of my friend Stephen's, the cycling-tour magnate, for several successive summers. This particular William Shakespeare had been a lecturer at Luton Polytechnic, and was in his late seventies by the time he started taking Stephen's cycling holidays about twenty years ago, a man of the utmost rectitude and gentility who insisted on wearing a three-piece suit at all times, even while pedalling through the Bavarian countryside on a sweltering summer's day. Stephen told me about him when I asked him if he'd had any guests he could call properly eccentric, and Mr Shakespeare fits the bill perfectly. Once, Stephen found himself on the same flight home as Mr Shakespeare, sitting just across the aisle from him, and watched in amusement and amazement as the old boy, following the announcement that seat belts were to be fastened and tray tables restored to an upright position in preparation for landing, carefully and solemnly pulled his protective cycle helmet from his bag and fixed it squarely on his head.

The true British eccentric is always a marvellous and reassuring sight a long way from home. You can imagine older Bavarians watching Mr Shakespeare bicycling serenely by in his three-piece suit, and not so much wondering how they lost the war, as realizing why they did. But there is a difference between a British eccentric and the eccentricity of the British, and it was the latter I saw in action one Sunday morning in the summer of 2005, when we were staying near Guilvinec in Brittany at a campsite for tents but also mobile homes, called the Camping Village de la Plage. Our accommodation was a mobile home – not just any mobile home, I might add, but a top-of-the-range Monaco Deluxe – and that morning the Englishman in the mobile home opposite spent four hours polishing his electric-blue Nissan Sunny. I promise you that's no exaggeration. I was setting out on my bike for our breakfast croissants at eight a.m., just as he was flexing his chamois, and he was hard at it until noon. As we left for a picnic lunch on the beach at 11.55 a.m., he was putting the finishing touches to his hubcaps. He obviously saw no reason why being on a campsite in France should interfere in any way with his cherished Sunday morning routine, and I sort of salute him for it, although it didn't stop us all sniggering from across the way.

France, being the foreign country closest to us, is where the eccentricity of the British abroad has always been most in evidence. Brittany was also where my friend Alison spent many of her childhood holidays, and she describes a sacrosanct family routine that took place at four o'clock every afternoon, when her granddad would come down to the beach carrying a tea urn. And if the tea urn weren't evidence enough of almost cartoon Englishness, he always had a knotted hankie on his head. The disappearance of the knotted hankie as a viable choice of holiday headwear seems to me a tremendous shame. But why did it disappear, and why was it only favoured by the British? That's a university dissertation just begging to be written.

Getting back to the campsite, or at least our bit, with mobile homes cheek by jowl and largely occupied by our fellow Brits, it reminded Jane of the Hoyland Common housing estate on which she'd grown up; indeed, it also evoked a housing estate in the way it fostered petty snobberies, not least ours towards the chap on the Nissan Sunny side of the street, but also towards us from all those 'proper' campers sleeping under canvas. Still, we were very happy with our Monaco Deluxe. On booking it we'd been concerned that we might feel as though we'd landed in a trailer park, but in fact the Monaco Deluxe (to which, over the course of our week there, we variously referred as a cabin, chalet, caravan, hut, house and indeed trailer, without ever feeling that we had found quite the right word) was rather stylish. It had three bedrooms, a shower room, lavatory, dining area, little kitchen with faux-marble worktops, and outside, on our little patch of parched grass, a barbecue.

There is nothing quite like the barbecue to incite one-upmanship between Brits on holiday. When we got back from our picnic that Sunday, the fellow opposite had redirected his attention from the Nissan Sunny to the barbie. And he went about it in the same thorough if somewhat anal manner, loading the charcoal practically piece by piece, and not allowing a single other member of the family anywhere near. He was clearly an expert, though. When finally he started cooking he seemed to have tongs for hands, like a Nissan-driving Edward Scissorhands. And from time to time over the next few days I caught him looking over at our less forensic, more collective approach to barbecuing, wearing a superior half-smile. He was watching when Jane poked my coals one evening, and I'm sure I saw him retch.

The Camping Village de la Plage was as good a place as any to undertake our first foreign camping holiday *en famille*, with a classy shop and a big pool with water slides. Of course, Continental campsites have always been streets ahead of their British counterparts, at least until the last few years when sites such as the one at Pencelli Castle in the Brecon Beacons, where we could have eaten off the floor of the toilet block if we'd really wanted to, have become much cleaner and more sophisticated. In the 1960s, when I was a child, only Continental campsites offered a decent chance of a successful holiday, partly of course because the sun was much likelier to shine, but also – little though my parents' generation cared to admit it – because they were better equipped and administered.

Not that it would ever have occurred to my mum and dad to take me camping; they would rather have taken me shoplifting or bear-baiting. But for plenty of British families in the 1960s and 1970s, the Continental holiday by definition involved a tent. Those interminable journeys that my friend Becky endured, the Morris Marina filled with a potent mixture of her mum's cigarette smoke and Rive Gauche perfume, were very often from her home village of Dilwyn in Herefordshire to a campsite on the Atlantic coast of France, and of course back again. This practically made Becky and her family celebrities in Dilwyn, where Tenby in South Wales counted as a daring holiday destination, and yet her most abiding memory of one particular fortnight with Canvas Holidays, in St Jean de Luz near Biarritz, is of unrelenting rain. It was also Becky, you'll recall, whose father pointed the car back towards Dilwyn after appalling weather blighted the family holiday in Ottery St Mary. It's funny how some people remember their childhood holidays being blessed with eternal sunshine; and others, with remorseless rain.

Still, one family's disastrous, argument-inducing washout is another family's fortnight-long fiesta of Snap, Ludo, Chinese Chequers and Monopoly, and Becky remembers even the rain-sodden St Jean de Luz trip with affection. But the signature experience of every one of her family's holidays in France was of traipsing unsuccessfully from one restaurant to another, looking for something that her vegetarian mother could eat that wasn't omelette and chips. In the end, though, it always was omelette and chips. 'They must have thought', says Becky now of all those mystified French restaurateurs, 'that we were bananas.' It is a singularly apt choice of word. Certainly, her mum must have been an unusually exotic creature for Dilwyn in those days: I guess there were plenty of women who smoked forty a day and dabbed themselves with Rive Gauche, but no others who eschewed meat.

Strangely, meat was very much a factor in my own first camping experience abroad. That was in 1979, the summer before I took my A-levels, and with my schoolfriends Pete, Rafe and Glenn I caught a coach to the South of France, where our plan was to find a suitable campsite, pitch a couple of two-man tents for a fortnight, and drink beer, meet girls, practise our French and laze in the sun, or, more realistically, drink beer and laze in the sun.

The coach went, via a Channel crossing, from Wigan bus station to the middle of Nice, which might not compare with the Spice Route across Asia, Route 66 or even the Pennine Way as one of the world's great journeys, although it amounted by a distance to the longest I'd ever taken, lasting twenty-two hours and yielding my first thrilling experience of a French motorway café. The service stations in Britain in 1979, and I include Woodall services on the M1 to which Jane and Jackie were taken as a family outing in its own right, were uniformly dismal places, serving food that tasting of nothing if you were lucky, and like the bottom of a cat's litter tray if you weren't. But somewhere on the Autoroute du

Soleil I had a lunch of chicken and chips, or more evocatively *poulet frites*, that for deliciousness far exceeded anything I'd ever eaten in a restaurant in my homeland. It was practically a rite of passage, and if some magazine or radio programme ever asks me to list the ten most memorable restaurant meals I have ever eaten, that simple plate of *poulet* and *pommes frites* will loom large. Come to think of it, it's highly unlikely that any magazine or radio programme ever will ask me to name my ten favourite meals so I'll have to do it without being asked (see chapter 26).

No other meal from that camping holiday sticks in my mind; clearly, no other meal had such a seismic effect on me that it remains vividly in the memory after more than three decades. But other aspects of that holiday I remember well. We ended up pitching our tents at the gigantic Camping Caravaning de la Baume site near Fréjus, which I know is still thriving, because many summers later my sister-in-law Jackie and her family based themselves there, and Jane, the children and I, coincidentally staying just along the coast, visited for an afternoon. Happy as I was to discharge my fatherly duties by the pool that day, I couldn't help looking wistfully at the carefree British teenagers having the holiday I'd had long before they were born. Holidays can do that sort of thing to you.

Other than the chicken and chips on the journey down, it's the music I remember best from that summer of '79 in the South of France. After a day or two on the campsite we befriended three nineteen-year-olds from Rotterdam whose names I can still remember – Leo, George and Bart – and even though they were a couple of years older, the seven of us became inseparable. They liked good raucous fun, were football nuts like us, and best of all they had a car, Leo's gigantic old Citroën, so we had a lift to and from the beach every day. Blaring constantly from Leo's car was a cassette on to which he'd recorded a couple of tracks from

Supertramp's recently released album *Breakfast in America*, and so it was that 'The Logical Song', played at almost deafening volume doubtless to the intense irritation of everyone else in the traffic jams through St Raphaël and Ste Maxime, became the soundtrack to the holiday. Little did I realize how apt the lyrics were for three seventeen-year-olds on the cusp of early manhood.

When I was young, it seemed that life was so wonderful,
a miracle, oh it was beautiful, magical.
And all the birds in the trees, well they'd be singing so happily,
joyfully, playfully watching me.
But then they send me away to teach me how to be sensible,
logical, responsible, practical.
And they showed me a world where I could be so dependable,
clinical, intellectual, cynical . . .

That pretty much sums it up, not that there was anything wonderful, beautiful or magical about the 22-hour coach journey home, two weeks of beer, sun and fine but unfamiliar food having exerted a terrible toll on my insides. I will spare you too much by way of detail, but suffice to say it was a gruesome experience, and of course that is another dimension to the British holiday: our vulnerability to diarrhoea, sun stroke, food poisoning, mosquito bites and every other discomfort sent to plague us in foreign lands.

I have an excellent if alarming little book unambiguously called *Bugs, Bites and Bowels* which addresses just this issue. It is written by an East Anglia-based GP called Jane Wilson-Howarth, and anyone of an anxious nature could be forgiven for leafing through it and deciding never to venture east of East Anglia, or indeed very far west of East Anglia. Take Chagas disease, which killed Charles Darwin. It is spread by the bites of little varmints called assassin bugs which, according to Dr Wilson-Howarth, 'defecate as they take their blood meal, and the parasite migrates from the bug's faeces into the victim's broken skin. If the parasite manages to get in, an inflamed swelling often appears at the site of entry . . . but the first stage of the disease is mild and sometimes goes unnoticed. Symptoms generally begin after several years, by which time treatment is difficult.'

The chances of contracting Chagas disease, you'll be relieved to hear, are very slight. One way of minimizing those chances, says Jane Wilson-Howarth, is by not sleeping on the floor of a wattle-and-daub house in Central America, which happily is a precaution that comes naturally to most of us. But she also cites some side-effects of rather more common practices that I must say I didn't know about until, while appropriately seated on the lavatory, I read her book. Apparently, hair-loss can be a consequence of long-haul flights, although we don't start moulting until three months or so later. And 'fungal infections around the genitals are common in the tropics, even in nuns'.

Paradoxically, the discomfort by which we Brits are most plagued on overseas holidays is the one most easily avoided: sunburn. There was a time when we didn't have the slightest awareness that sunburn was the slightest bit bad for us, let alone sometimes terminally bad for us. In her teens, my own Jane had friends who on a hot summer's day in the Barnsley area – and there were some – would lie spreadeagled on their patios with sheets of tin foil spread underneath them, in the hope that it would intensify the rays of the sun and turn them brown more quickly.

The other common method in those days was to rub yourself with cooking oil, so that you might fry like an egg even in your own back garden. And not very much healthier than cooking oil was the sun lotion Bergasol, which might more aptly have been spelled Burgersol, given the enthusiasm with which people slapped it on themselves in the hope of browning like a piece of meat on a barbecue. Eventually it was banned by the European Commission's Scientific Committee on Consumer Products on account of it containing far too much of the tanning accelerator psoralen, a cancer-causing substance, but that was in 2008. Thirty years earlier, for thousands of Brits heading for the sun, Bergasol was the first thing in the suitcase. Yet Alison, the friend whose granddad used to arrive at the beach in Brittany at four p.m. every day with a knotted hankie on his head and carrying a tea urn, says 'Suncream didn't exist when I was a girl. Or if it did, we hadn't heard of it in Sheffield.'

Certainly, when I was a child, hardly anybody's sunny holiday was complete without a dose of sunburn, and in April 2010 it emerged that people in their sixties and seventies were five times more likely to be diagnosed with deadly skin cancer than their parents had been at the same age, all because of the sunburn they suffered on foreign holidays in the 1960s and 1970s, before we understood the dangers.

Luckily, I wasn't often stricken myself, because I used to suffer from a condition my mother called prickly heat. I was a perfectly robust child but my physical weaknesses were a susceptibility to prickly heat and dreadful hay fever, which could make the summer months a bit of a trial. The hay fever we tackled with Piriton tablets, which are still around but have evolved somewhat since the 1970s, when the warning that they could make you drowsy was something of an understatement; one of them could knock out a horse. Still, at least they relieved the symptoms of my hay fever, if only by rendering me unconscious for twenty-four hours. The prickly heat could only be tackled by staying out of the sun, and whenever it struck I was strongly advised by my parents to sit in 'a cool bath' for an hour. A voracious reader as a kid, I went through most of the works of Anthony Buckeridge, author of the Jennings books, while lying in cold water in Spanish hotel bathrooms.

However, as I grew older and the prickly heat vanished, I formed a new holiday relationship with the sun, formed not least by the revelation that it was good for a teenage complexion under assault from acne. Adolescent vanity is a powerful impulse, and I see it now with my own teenage children, the irresistible force that is my near paranoia about the dangers of too much sun meeting the immovable object that is their desire to look good when they get home to their friends. And of course that vanity never wholly leaves you. I can't be the only person who, having spent a fortnight only slowly downgrading from factor-50 suncream to factor-30 to factor-15, then sees the steps to the easyJet flight home as one final opportunity to give my face a full unprotected blast of hot foreign sun.

It is ironic that the suntan is now generally considered a nice, enviable thing to have, indicative to a certain extent of disposable income, because for centuries in Britain, tanned skin was regarded as the preserve of the peasantry, a consequence of labouring outside while more privileged folk stayed indoors. To achieve the sought-after pale look there were even whiteners for the skin: Elizabeth I used arsenic.

But in the twentieth century that all began to change. Just as the seventeenth-century Sussex doctor Richard Russell advocated the use of seawater to cure many ills, so, in 1903, was the Danish scientist Niels Finsen awarded a Nobel prize for his research proving the beneficial effects of sunlight on a host of infectious diseases. Soon, the tan became a symbol of both health and wealth, and it is said that when the fashion designer Coco Chanel was photographed in 1923, stepping with brown limbs off a yacht on the Côte d'Azur, the sun-kissed look acquired a spiritual home.

In Britain, naturally, there remained a degree of suspicion about the sun. Until well into the 1930s, the word 'sunbather' was pretty much a euphemism for nudist, and in June 1930 about 250 sunbathers at the Welsh Harp reservoir on the north London outskirts, many of them starkers, were attacked by a disapproving crowd – an event splendidly known as the Sun-Bathing Riots.

By the 1980s, however, nudity outdoors in pursuit of an all-over tan, and even indoors, with the help of fluorescent lamps emitting ultraviolet radiation, was commonplace in Britain. These days, there have been so many alarming stories about the dangers of sunbeds that it is a wonder anyone still does it, although there's nothing new about the curiously dysfunctional relationship between the British and that fiery orange mass of hydrogen and helium that increasingly we are not sure whether to seek or avoid; in fact it was best summed up by the late Noël Coward in his most famous song, written in 1931.

Mad dogs and Englishmen go out in the midday sun.
The Japanese don't care to, the Chinese wouldn't dare to,
Hindus and Argentines sleep firmly from twelve to one,
But Englishmen detest a siesta,
In the Philippines there are lovely screens,
to protect you from the glare,
In the Malay states there are hats like plates,
which the Britishers won't wear,
At twelve noon the natives swoon, and
no further work is done –
But Mad Dogs and Englishmen go out in the midday sun.

We're a bit more circumspect now about the foreign sun at midday or any other time than we were in 1931, yet still far more complacent than most other nationalities. Go to any beach on the

Algarve or the Costa del Sol and I can practically guarantee that the worst case of sunburn, the woman with the red raw skin that suddenly turns milky white where it hits her bikini line, or the man whose bald head looks like the surface of Mars, will come not from Rennes or Rouen, Antwerp or Aachen, but from Rotherhithe or Rotherham, Aberdeen or Aberdare.

The most wince-inducing sight, though, is of a child reddened and blistered by the sun. Among my own most uncomfortable holiday memories is feeling the winces of others while we were staying at the swanky Hotel Anassa in Cyprus with all the disgruntled tycoons. Eleanor was six years old, and spent much of one morning early in the holiday bobbing about in the children's pool. She had a hat on and we kept reapplying a high-factor suncream, but the rays still got through, and she spent the next couple of days conspicuously sunburnt. It didn't seem to hurt her and she didn't mind unduly, but I minded terribly. I felt, perhaps a little melodramatically, and perversely even more than I did when a year or so later Jacob went nose-first out of a Spanish window, as though I had failed as a father.

22

Naturism, nipples and nookie

Curiously, and I write not from experience but from what I've been told, the foreign stretches of beach on which cases of sunburn are rarest are those reserved for naturists. I suppose it makes sense; sunburnt shoulders are painful enough, but nobody wants sunburnt nipples or testicles. As I say, though, my information is second-hand. I've never been to a naturist beach and as a fairly typical Englishman, buttoned-up in more ways than one, have no overwhelming desire to do so, even by way of research. Like many Englishmen of my generation, my knowledge of naturism was gleaned entirely from the copies of *Health & Efficiency* magazine I studied as a boy, and they were scrutinized rather less because I was interested in the best places to take all my clothes off on holiday, and rather more because they offered a fleeting acquaintance with the naked female form, albeit with the pubic hair airbrushed out. I went to a single-sex school, where well-thumbed copies of

H&E were a form of currency, equivalent in value to fifty Bazooka Joes, two cans of strawberry Cresta, an unopened pack of football stickers, or a used set of poker dice.

I have only one friend who is happy to let it all dangle in public, or rather two friends, a husband and wife, Fizz and Dan. They used to spend their holidays on the Greek island of Skiathos, home of one of the Aegean's best-known attractions for naturists, Banana Beach, so named, Fizz assured me, because it – the beach – is shaped like a banana. Actually, a little more research reveals that Banana Beach is divided into three. The old naturist bit, now largely clothed, is called Big Banana, then there is a smaller more naturism-friendly area rather oddly called Nameless Banana, and finally the out-and-out nude bit. With what can only be deliberate ambiguity, this one is called Little Banana, although strangely it also goes by the name of Spartacus Beach, and I like to think it might be difficult to locate for a couple raring to strip off. 'This is Spartacus ... no, this is Spartacus ... no, this is Spartacus!'

Enough with the old movie gags. While I was writing this book, and having not seen Fizz for probably five years, I phoned her out of the blue to talk to her about her propensity for taking her kit off. Once we had dispensed with the formalities of how her children were, and how mine were, it wasn't the most obvious subject matter for a phone call between two people who hadn't seen each other for ages, but she gamely embraced the topic and recalled some happy holidays on Banana Beach, which I had assumed had been populated mainly by Germans and Scandinavians, who tend for some strange reason to be the Europeans most willing to expose themselves. Just to return for a second to my cycling friend Stephen, he tells me that on a decent spring or summer's day you can hardly see the banks of the Rivar Isar near Munich for bare breasts and buttocks, although not of the notably young and firm variety. On the beaches of southern Europe, I have noticed over the years, there is an almost inviolable law which decrees that the woman who flops down topless on the sunbed next to you, will not be 23-year-old Astrid from Heidelberg, but 71-year-old Brunhilde from Wiesbaden.

To my surprise, however, Fizz assured me that it is predominantly Brits who occupy the nudist portion of Banana Beach, although those Brits are mainly elderly couples. I must say that, of the elderly British couples I know, I can't visualize any of them starkers on a beach in Skiathos, but maybe that's a consequence of my inhibition rather than theirs. There was one year, Fizz told me, when she and the family went to Skiathos earlier than usual, and found a different crowd on Banana Beach with, as she put it, 'a lot of piercings, everywhere'. They too were British, women as well as men, but there was a different, less wholesome vibe about them.

Normally, she added, the scene there is irreproachably wholesome. 'There's nothing dodgy or embarrassing about it,' she said, firmly, and I felt a little ashamed for having approached the subject as a bit of a giggle. 'For me, it's basically all about the joy of not wearing a wet swimming costume,' she explained. 'And of course it's jolly nice to have an all-over tan.'

She and Dan stopped going to Banana Beach when their eldest child was ten, reckoning that it would soon become an embarrassment to him and his siblings to see their parents naked in public, but she felt sure that they'd go back as soon as the children were all old enough to take their own holidays. Indeed, she felt confident that she and Dan would end up as one of those elderly couples, wrinkled and brown, shuffling down to the water's edge. Fizz talked with such enthusiasm about the naturist experience that after I put the phone down I went to check out the Banana Beach website. Unfortunately, it had been shut down; all that remained was a message from someone aptly called Sunny.

Hi everyone

Sadly, the time has come to bring the Banana Beach Website to an end. The constant battle with internet hackers and pornography merchants have made it impossible to continue.

Those of you who have been fans from the beginning will know the problems we have faced. We created the website many years ago when the internet was in its infancy and Banana Beach was a secret, known to only a few brave travellers. Over the years the website has received 6.7 million visitors and the beach has become world famous.

Thank you to everyone who has contributed over the years and I hope you enjoy Banana Beach Holidays for many years to come.

Kind regards,

Sunny

I was rather sad about that, especially the bit about the porn merchants. I confess to having been guilty myself of sexualizing nudity, if only by cracking lame jokes about bananas, but it's regrettable that adults in particular do so. And when the nudity they sexualize is that of young children, it becomes not so much regrettable as warped.

And so to the United States, where Jane and I spent a terrific holiday when Eleanor and Joseph were four and two, and before Jacob was even a glint in my eye (indeed, hats off to anyone who can muster a glint with a four-year-old and a two-year-old trucking about the place).

We went for the wedding in Boston of my good friend Beth, and decided to wrap our summer holiday round her happy day, which took us to a characterful little town on the coast of Maine called Ogunquit. The beach there was fantastic, and on the first day we walked from our little rented cottage with its cute white picket fence to the shore, where the children romped naked in and out of shallow pools, at least until we realized they were drawing a crowd. 'Wow, that's primitive' was one of the kinder comments to reach our ears. 'They must be European' was another. We had never thought twice about letting our children go naked on a beach, so it was a shock to realize that we were challenging some kind of unwritten protocol, and more shocking still to think that people were sexualizing our kids, which unquestionably they were. We were a few hundred miles and a few hundred years from where the Pilgrim Fathers had landed, yet their puritanical codes of behaviour seemed firmly entrenched. What, though, was weirder? Small children innocently playing naked on a beach, or folk being seriously affronted by the sight of small children innocently playing naked on a beach?

Still, there comes a point at which words such as naked and nudity do lead inexorably to sex, and besides, how can the story of the British on holiday avoid it? I've already written about sex in Blackpool, but it applies no less to foreign holidays, a three-letter s-word almost as relevant to the way we spend those holidays as 'sea', not that I'm planning to investigate the seedy sex-holiday industry, which so besmirches one of the finest words in the English language (an evolved form of the Old English word *halig-daeg*, by the way, meaning a holy day).

One doesn't need to follow any of those revolting Gary Glitter-types to Bangkok and Vietnam, though, to realize that sex and holidays are inextricably connected, from the most romantic honeymoon to the most loveless one-night stand on an 18–30s shagfest in Ibiza. Yet what might constitute romance for one person, might be considered loveless by another. 'Don't you understand, I don't just want a roll in the hay, I need something that's going to last,' said Sadie Tompkins (Barbara Windsor) to

Bert Conway (Jimmy Logan) in *Carry On Abroad*. 'Who says it's not going to last,' he replied. 'We don't go home until tomorrow afternoon.'

There are countless variations of the holiday fling, from that one-night stand in Ibiza to stolen embraces under a foreign moon that end in long, happy marriages, from those disturbing tales that pop up in the news every couple of years of the seventeen-year-old girl from County Durham (why it's always County Durham I really don't know) who goes to Sharm el Sheikh for a week with her parents, then runs away from home so she can go back and marry Omar, the 34-year-old barman from the Oasis Palace Hotel . . . to the Shirley Valentine tale of the middle-aged woman who finds romance, but more importantly herself, on a sun-kissed Greek island.

My ever-reliable source Stephen has one of the best holiday-fling stories, concerning a happily married Englishman and a happily married Scottish woman who both went on one of his cycling holidays through the Bavarian Alps without their respective spouses, and ended up in bed together after a few too many schnapps one night. And the next night, and the next. At the end of the week they went their separate ways, and as far as he knows didn't see each other back in the UK, but the following year they both booked again, effectively spending the week as a couple and making Stephen complicit in the deception by giving them separate invoices. It's a story of adultery and betrayal of which I suppose we should disapprove, and yet there is a pleasing redolence of *Brief Encounter* about it.

A foreign holiday, of course, can do wonders for the libido. Moreover, a bit of a tan and a dimly hit hotel bar can make the most slack-jawed sales rep from Kidderminster look attractive, if only to a pointy-nosed secretary from Kettering. And, on a holiday, the usual rules of engagement go out the window, almost literally so in my own case in the summer of 1982, when I was coming to the end of my InterRailing holiday round Europe with my old schoolfriend Mark Sutcliffe. At the railway station in Nice, Mark and I, inveterate exhibitionists that we were at the time, made a deliberately ridiculous song-and-dance of saying goodbye to four English girls we'd met on the beach earlier that day. For their entertainment and ours, we wailed, we pledged eternal devotion, we blew flamboyant kisses, and when the train finally started moving, we waved an ostentatious adieu (ignoring the warning not to lean out of the window that in the course of a month chugging along the Continent's railways we had committed to heart in several languages, our favourite being the Italian, 'è pericolosa spongere'). What can I say? We were twenty years old, having the holiday of our young lives.

Anyway, a minute or two after we had sunk back into our seats, heartily amused by the fuss we had caused, the door of the compartment slid open and an attractive American girl entered. Her name was Robyn, she was twenty-two and came from California, and she told us how much she had enjoyed watching our antics back at the station. As she was travelling alone, she added, could she possibly join us? This she did, and there must have been something about being on holiday that, once Mark had fallen asleep, made me behave in a way I wouldn't normally have behaved on a train even in 1982. Suffice to say that by the time the train pulled into the Gare de Lyon in Paris, Robyn and I were an item, and while it would be indecorous of me to comment on the twenty-something sexual proclivities of a woman now in her fifties, let me just say that her attitude towards the human body was far removed from that of the censorious Americans I encountered on the beach at Ogunquit many years later. At any rate, Mark was left to continue the journey back to England on his own, while Robyn and I found a cheap Parisian hotel, and a few days later, after jacking in her plans to meet up with a girlfriend in Amsterdam, she came back to England with me for the last week of her European vacation.

By this time, a postcard had arrived for me at my mother's flat in London. It was from Ana, a girl I'd met on the Spanish leg of the InterRailing trip, and it was written in very rudimentary English, concluding with the declaration that she loved me. Ana and I had spent two evenings energetically snogging and not much more, so this came as a surprise, not least to my mum, who I presume had read it and was now also confronted with Robyn, the pretty Californian two years my senior. All of which makes my twenty-year-old self sound like something of a stud, and I really wasn't, but I offer these stories as evidence that nothing ignites a romance, or even serial romances, like a holiday. In Venice and Rome, indeed, I'd had a fling with another American girl backpacking round Europe, Andrea. And Mark hadn't had a monastic four weeks either, scoring three times, rather like the footballer Michael Owen years later, in southern Germany.

That summer, looking back, I was probably at the peak of whatever physical appeal I have ever possessed in the eyes of the opposite sex. I'd shed all the excess weight I'd carried as a decidedly lardy teenager, I was tanned, my hair had been bleached by the sun. Looking at the old photographs now, I even had a fetching growth of what would later be called designer stubble. At Gatwick Airport, Robyn and I had the kind of melodramatic farewell for real that Mark and I had staged for fun in Nice, and we stayed in touch, writing to each other every week or two, swearing undying love. A year later, in July 1983 – part of the same epic American adventure on which I would be bollocked by Clint Eastwood in Carmel, and bump into Woody Allen in Manhattan – I flew to Los Angeles, fully expecting to rekindle the affair. But there was no tan, and I dare say that a year of drinking beer at university had added a few pounds, and probably a few spots. Nor, on her own turf, did she seem anything like the fun-loving creature I'd met on the train in France. Whatever, within twenty minutes of Robyn meeting me at LA International Airport we both realized that ours had been a meeting of fit, bronzed backpackers the summer before, not a meeting of minds. Our holiday fling had been well and truly flung.

23

Honeymoons, hen parties and Harp lager

Let us turn now, though, to the most romantic of all holidays: the honeymoon. First of all, where does the word come from and what did it originally mean? According to my *Shorter Oxford English Dictionary*, it was a word knocking about in the sixteenth century, referring to the first month of married life, and may have been a variation on 'honey-month', meaning the same thing. Interestingly enough, or perhaps not interestingly at all, the Polish, Russian and Welsh words for honeymoon all still mean honey-month.

Our good if unreliable friend Wikipedia, meanwhile, predictably throws up a few other suggestions, informing us that the word derives from the ancient practice in parts of Europe of giving a newly married couple enough mead (made out of honey, you see) to last a month, hence honeymoon, although I tend to think that this is one of the facts invented by that chap in Leighton Buzzard on a drizzly afternoon. Slightly more plausibly,

Wikipedia also cites the first known literary reference to honey-moon, apparently in something called the *Abecedarium Anglico Latinum*, written in 1552 by one Richard Huloet.

'Hony mone, a term proverbially applied to such as be newly married, which will not fall out at the first, but th'one loveth the other at the beginning exceedingly, the likelihood of their exceadinge love appearing to aswage, ye which time the vulgar people call the hony mone,' wrote Huloet, the old spoilsport, appearing to define the word as the period early in a marriage when that initial powerful love between two people begins to wane. Mind you, he might have had a point in the case of a woman my friend Rosie knows, who pulled off the rather impressive trick of meeting her (second) husband on her (first) honeymoon.

Nor would Frank, who runs the travel company World Odyssey, disagree with Huloet. Frank once organized a safari holiday in Botswana combined with a beach holiday in Mozambique for a honeymooning couple, and was aghast to learn when they got home that they had complained vehemently about both lots of accommodation, even though he knew the two hotels to be first-class. It transpired that there had been 'major domestic issues' between the newly-weds, and they had taken out their irritation with each other, and doubtless their disappointment that the honeymoon had soured so quickly, on the hotel staff.

According to Frank, of the few complaints he gets from British clients about his holidays, 90 per cent stem from either marital or family disagreements, or the weather, not exactly factors within his control.

As for honeymooners in particular, he gets some bizarre requests, including one from a wealthy City of London broker who gave him ten days to organize a trip to Namibia that also had to include the actual wedding. In fact, this chap and his bride-to-be wanted, for some reason best known to themselves, to get married in a hot-air balloon. However, Frank found that there is a law in Namibia which decrees that all weddings must take place under a roof, so he arranged a church wedding in Windhoek, the capital, followed by a blessing in the hot-air balloon, conducted by a doubtless faintly bewildered priest somewhere high over the Namib Desert.

'That one was fun to sort out,' he told me. Fun? I can think of plenty of people who would have gone grey and developed a twitch in response to being given a task like that. But I suppose it helped that money was no object. Frank had another rich customer who gave his honeymoon specifications and then said 'We're going to blow the barn doors off this one', meaning there were to be no budgetary constraints. In the end it cost more than £200,000. I can see why that might be enjoyable to organize, however vulgar one might consider such whopping expenditure. For Frank, the flip side of the coin is when people call him with an utterly unrealistic financial ceiling, such as the couple who wanted a three-week South American honeymoon for £4000, including flights. 'If they'd been willing to go as backpackers I could just about have done it for them,' Frank told me. 'But even that would have been tight.'

That said, £4000 is a good deal more than Britain's average honeymoon expenditure. The latest research, conducted by *Brides* magazine, suggested that £2900 is the average sum spent on honeymoons, although among *Brides* readers, clearly a well-heeled lot, that rises to £3894. Especially interesting are the statistics on honeymoon destinations, with the Indian Ocean now by far the most popular, well ahead of Europe, and the UK (the destination for a mere 3 per cent of honeymooners) now comprehensively outstripped by Mauritius (5 per cent). How and when did we become so affluent in this country that we stopped going to Blackpool and Brighton for our honeymoons, and started going to Bali and Bhutan?

I suppose sex has a lot to do with it. Not so very long ago, the wedding night and ensuing honeymoon afforded most couples their first opportunity for full sexual congress (I have to be honest here; I debated whether to write 'a proper shag', but felt it might undermine my thesis). So in a way it didn't really matter where they went, one bed being pretty much as good as the next. But times have changed. Of all the Brits who get married this year, some 91 per cent will already have cohabited. Sex is no longer the principal purpose of a honeymoon, so instead it becomes an excuse for a fantastic holiday, perhaps even the elusive 'holiday of a lifetime' of which Tim Vine joked 'never again'. Which is not to say that sex has been wholly sidestepped as a honeymoon activity; when I phoned Deborah Joseph, the estimable editor of *Brides*, to talk about all this, she assured me that there are still plenty of honeymoon babies.

On the other hand, my assertion earlier in this book that going on holiday can be inordinately stressful because of the breadth of expectations involved, applies doubly, trebly, maybe even tenfold, to honeymoons. For our parents or grandparents' generation the stress might have been to do with sex – Could he get it up? Did he know where to put it? Would she enjoy it? – and nowadays it might be more to do with the holiday itself – Will the British Airways cabin staff go on strike? Will the hotel in the Seychelles be as romantic as it looks on the internet? Will a volcanic ash cloud ruin the whole bloody thing? Will it all be worth the colossal expense? – but, either way, the word honeymoon, with all its doubtful etymology, has come, all too often, to mean one thing: anxiety.

This might be why I don't, in truth, know many people whose honeymoon lived up to their extravagant expectations. My mother, back in the early 1950s, spent her honeymoon throwing up on a cargo ship carrying tomatoes, because one of my dad's poker buddies had told him it was a cheap way of travelling over-seas. And my wife, back in the early 1990s, spent her honeymoon throwing up because she was three months pregnant, although I'll only accept 50 per cent of the blame for that.

When my mother got married again, in 1981, the honeymoon ticked all the boxes that had gone unchecked first time around, largely because my stepfather was affluent enough to indulge them both. Come to think of it, the best honeymoons are often those on which the bride or groom, or both, has just got married for the second time, with groom, or bride, or both, more relaxed or wealthier or worldlier than they were first time round. Indeed, long-married couples sometimes have a 'second honeymoon' for the same reasons, because they didn't have enough confidence, or money, or perhaps didn't know each other well enough, when they had their first shot at it.

A few years ago I was best man for one of my oldest friends, Mike, who was getting hitched for the second time. It was my job to organize the stag party, which took place at a pub near Lancaster one Friday night. Obviously I had failed dismally in my duties as a modern best man, because according to all the conventions of the 21st-century stag party, we should have taken off to Prague for a long and riotous weekend. Almost three-quarters of British grooms-to-be nowadays enjoy stag celebrations lasting longer than twenty-four hours, and a third of them go abroad to get pissed. Not only has the Indian Ocean eclipsed the English seaside as a honeymoon destination, so have lively foreign cities as destinations for British stag jaunts. In 2010, four of the ten most popular stag destinations, indeed three of the top five, were on the Continent: Prague, Amsterdam and Barcelona ranked second, third and fifth, with London still at the top of the list and Brighton fourth. Tallinn in Estonia was eighth.

Moreover, the average spend on these foreign stag trips is currently just under £200 a head, and was rising even at the height of the so-called credit crunch in 2009, whereas brides-to-be had reined themselves in, very responsibly reorganizing their priorities to suit economically stricken times. By the end of 2009, two-thirds of hen parties lasted less than a day, and were costing an average of just over £100 per head. And of the ten most popular hen-party destinations only one of them – Barcelona – was overseas. Indeed a third of them were taking place in the bride's home town. All of which proves the injustice, first pointed out to me by my dear wife, of groups of men being called stags – intelligent, noble, photogenic creatures – and groups of women having to answer to the collective name of hens – silly, squawky, flappy things. It really should be the other way round.

Mind you, it has to be said that there wasn't much nobility about the hen party that boarded the same easyJet flight to Barcelona as Jane and me at Liverpool's John Lennon Airport in March 2010. They were all wearing small plastic tiaras except for the bride, who was wearing the full bridal headdress. And they were, it also has to be said, being just a little bit silly, squawky and flappy. On the other hand, they weren't notably drunk, unlike two stag groups on the same flight, whom we had noticed back in the terminal getting seriously stuck into the Harp lager. It was, I should add, a 7.10 a.m. flight.

I'm all for people enjoying themselves, and heaven forbid that I should sound too much like the proverbial retired colonel in Tunbridge Wells, but I do slightly wince at the idea that in Prague, Amsterdam and Tallinn, this is the most visible representation of Brits abroad. I don't care so much about Barcelona, after my pickpocket experience, but the people of Barcelona care deeply. A few months after our visit a mysterious graffiti artist began to roam the streets of Barcelona, painting lines on the streets dividing them into lanes for tourists, and lanes for native citizens. The message was plain enough: we don't want to rub shoulders with you lot, hogging our lovely streets. To which I suppose a tourist's response might be: 'Fine, then we won't get fleeced by your horrible pickpockets.'

That said, on our second night in Barcelona we spotted some of the stags from the plane, staggering, aptly enough, along the Ramblas. It was clearly these kind of people that the mystery protester had in mind. They were all wearing matching T-shirts on which were printed the words 'Spanish Triathlon', along with three pictures of stick men and three descriptions of what they were doing: Eating, Drinking, Fucking. I tried to picture a similar group of pissed-up Spaniards, wearing similar T-shirts perhaps depicting three stick men eating, drinking and fucking their way through an English Triathlon, lurching down Oxford Street or through Covent Garden. And of course I couldn't. Apart from anything else, how many Spaniards come to England for the eating?

As for the third part of this notional Spanish triathlon, let me just relate a honeymoon story told by some Herefordshire friends of ours, Belinde and her husband John. Belinde is Danish and booked their honeymoon fifteen years or so ago in her maiden name, which was Fode. It's a common surname in Denmark, apparently, but in Portugal the word 'fode' happens to be a profanity meaning 'fuck' or 'fucking'. Understandably ignorant of this, John and Belinde unfortunately chose the Algarve as their honeymoon destination, and all kinds of misunderstandings ensued, not least on arrival at the hotel, where the receptionist was too polite, or perhaps too embarrassed, to point out to them that they had written down the purpose of their stay in the box marked 'name'.

To return, though, to those stags staggering down the Ramblas in Barcelona, I really must stress that the British on holiday have historically had a much more positive impact than negative. Especially on Europe. I suppose all those other nationalities might eventually have worked out for themselves the charms of the Mediterranean as a holiday destination, but we got there first, just as we arrived first in a part of Europe as yet unexplored in these pages: the Alps.

24

Claudia Schiffer, Christianity and the Cresta Run

It's true; if any one nation can be said to have turned the Alps into a holiday destination, it was the British. Or to be even more precise, the English, at least according to *How the English Made the Alps*, a book published in 2000, and written by a fellow called Jim Ring, which makes him sound a bit like a fitness accessory, but actually he's a very good travel writer and specializes in accounts of how the British popularized parts of Europe. He wrote another book called *Riviera*, which superbly evokes the period between the wars, when the absurd Edward and Mrs Simpson led high society to the Côte d'Azur, and lesser society followed, although arguably it was the Americans (which Wallis Simpson was, of course) who did more to promote the Côte d'Azur as a holiday destination, from those arch-hedonists Scott and Zelda Fitzgerald to the multi-

millionaire Frank Jay Gould, who was awarded the Légion d'hon-
neur by the French government for effectively creating the beach
resort of Juan-les-Pins in the early 1920s, although having paid
twenty euros for the privilege of sitting on the beach at Juan-les-
Pins in August, I'm with Ring, who reckoned that a more fitting
tribute might have been the guillotine.

More so even than the Côte d'Azur, with its three corniches
weaving in and out of mountain tunnels, it was engineering skills
that made the Alps accessible. And that was where the British
came in, cleverly threading railways through the mountains and
introducing to remote villages what an early twentieth-century
diarist called 'those cardinal British institutions – tea, sanitary
appliances, lawn tennis and churches'.

Before all that, the Alps had been 'discovered' by the English
Romantics, notably Byron, Shelley and especially Wordsworth.
Come to think of it, Wordsworth was one of the greatest travel
PRs of his or any age, waxing as effusive about Switzerland as he
ever did about the Lake District. He was like a one-man *Wish You
Were Here . . .?*, on which subject my mate Stephen's cycling holidays through Alpine Germany were featured on *Wish You Were
Here . . .?* back in 1997, which cost him £4000 but was worth
every penny (naively, I'd assumed that those programmes were
made at ITV's expense, but in fact, in return for the publicity,
Stephen was expected to cover the crew's flights, car hire, hotel
expenses, drinks tabs, the lot). He received 600 phone calls in the
twenty-four hours following transmission, an incredibly potent
shot in the arm for a small company. And a Wordsworth poem in
the late eighteenth century had a similar effect.

In the 1830s and 1840s, hard on the heels of the Romantics,
came a second, more energetic wave of Brits, intent not on painting the mountains and writing poetry about them, but climbing
the damn things to the top. This had never really occurred to

native Alpine dwellers, except with a view to opening up trading routes between one valley and the next. Almost inevitably it took the British to come up with the outlandish idea of climbing mountains for fun, and among the pioneers was James David Forbes, son of the seventh baronet of Pitsligo, no less, who in 1841 successfully tackled the 13,642ft Jungfrau, despite some hairy moments 'on a slope of unbroken slippery ice, steep as a cathedral roof, with precipices at the bottom of an unknown and dizzy depth'. It had been, he concluded, almost certainly while stroking his stiff upper lip, 'rather frightful'.

In 1865, by which time the term 'alpinist' had been coined as a valid description of what some British chaps did, the intrepid and rather ill-named Edward Whymper led the first successful ascent of the Matterhorn, but lost four of his party on the way down when a rope snapped. Whymper lived another forty-six years, but the disaster never stopped haunting him. 'Every night, do you understand, I see my comrades of the Matterhorn slipping on their backs, their arms outstretched, one after the other, in perfect order at equal distances – Croz the guide, first, then Hadow, then Hudson, and lastly Douglas. Yes, I shall always see them . . .'

His fellow Victorians were not deterred by the accident, though, and when you think about modern-day climbing equipment, it's remarkable what they managed to achieve in hobnailed boots and hacking jackets. By the century's end, they even had audiences. Well-heeled Brits flocked to the Alps, if not to scale the mountains, then to stand on the lower slopes and watch as others did so. They went with Thomas Cook's tours, and those set up by another God-fearing entrepreneur, the devout Methodist Henry Lunn, a firm believer in muscular Christianity.

In the 1880s, Lunn took up the increasingly popular sport of alpine skiing, which had been revolutionized by the recent invention of the boot binding, enabling skiers to change direction (and let's not credit the Brits with everything; the binding was the brainchild of a Norwegian, Sondre Norheim). Lunn felt that a combination of clean mountain air and wholesome exercise could only be good for the soul, and who can argue with that? In 1905 he set up the Public Schools Alpine Sports Club, and three years later the Alpine Ski Club, in due course passing the baton, or perhaps the ski pole, to his son Arnold, who invented slalom racing in 1922, and in the 1930s was largely responsible for turning downhill and slalom skiing into recognized Olympic sports. In 1913 Arnold Lunn married Mabel Northcote, the granddaughter of Sir Stafford Northcote, who'd been both chancellor of the Exchequer and foreign secretary, and their marriage went swiftly downhill in the very best possible way: Mabel became the first woman to pass the challenging British First Class skiing test. She died in 1959, but Arnold (by then Sir Arnold, knighted for services to winter sports and Anglo-Swiss relations) lived on until 1974, long enough to see the company founded by his father merge with the Polytechnic Touring Association to become Lunn Poly, and long enough to see his beloved Alpine skiing embraced by every nation in the Western world.

Not everyone had welcomed the transformation of the Alps into, initially, a rich man's playground. Around the turn of the twentieth century, Henry James, esteemed novelist and professional spoilsport, positively fulminated about the damage that tobogganing and skiing were doing to the mountains. But the momentum was as unstoppable as an avalanche, and driving it were the British.

The British influence can still be seen in older ski resorts right across the Alps – Meribel in France is like Fulham with altitude – but nowhere is this more so than St Moritz in Switzerland, home of the Cresta Run. In 2001 we spent a week in St Moritz not because we wanted to take the children skiing for the first time in their lives, but because we wanted to give them their first experience of snow. Eleanor was seven and had never seen so much as a snowflake, yet when Jane and I were seven, on opposite sides of the Pennines, it snowed every winter. Southport was unhelpfully flat, but my friends in Lynton Road and I had a ritual annual trudge with our sledges to a small mound near Royal Birkdale Golf Club that we grandly called the Round Hill. My friends Jez and Chris Sykes always had a proper wooden toboggan with metal runners whereas I only had a tin tray, but it was just as effective. I didn't even mind too much that it had pictures of flowers on it, hard as it was to be macho when your makeshift sledge was covered in burgundy roses.

Snow brought out everyone's macho tendencies in those days. The annual snowball fight in Lynton Road was like the Battle of the Little Big Horn, with me trying not to end up as General Custer as snowballs came at me like small guided missiles, launched by one of the Carroll brothers. Playing cricket for the Lord's Taverners many years later I faced the bowling of Colin Croft, once one of the most fearsome of the terrifying West Indian pace attack, but not even a cricket ball delivered by Colin Croft sped past me with the velocity of a snowball propelled by Nick Carroll. Happy days. And yet by 2001 I had three children of my own, aged seven, five, and two, all untutored in the art of packing a snowball, building a snowman, steering a sledge or even a tin tray. And having seen *Bambi* a thousand times, they knew all too painfully what they were missing. Eleanor had already written to Father Christmas asking for an Amazing Ally doll and loads of snow. I thought about sending her to a self-help group: 'My name's Eleanor and I've never seen snow.'

So St Moritz it was, our week in one of the most eye-poppingly expensive resorts in the Alps, if not the world, made possible by a writing assignment and the blessed 'media rate'. And shortly after dawn one morning I took Joseph to the Cresta Run to see what real sledging was all about. The spectacle that greeted us was as eye-popping as the prices at the nearby Badrutt's Palace Hotel, where we were staying, and where we were charged the equivalent in Swiss francs of £10 to fill Jacob's bottle with milk.

It was seven a.m., and a gaggle of frightfully pukka Englishmen stood around, all wearing tweed trousers and holding shabby toboggans. I only had to read the record of the fastest times from the day before to realize the social élitism that prevailed on the Cresta; it was headed by Lord Dalmeny and just below him came Prince C. zu Fürstenberg. But most memorable of all on that cold Swiss morning was the resounding voice of the redoubtable, 66-year-old Lieutenant-Colonel Digby Willoughby MC MBE, who continued overseeing the Cresta until his death in 2007.

If anything confirmed the Cresta as a snowy corner of a foreign field that was forever England, it was, no less than the Union Jack hanging limply from the junction box, the plummy voice of Colonel Willoughby cutting through the icy morning air from a loudspeaker, sternly instructing participants to take their marks. 'Hastings to the box,' thundered Willougby, and I watched Hastings quail. This was his first time, not that Colonel Willoughby was making allowances. 'Hastings, 125.42 (seconds),' he bellowed a few minutes later. 'That's no good. You're wasting our time, not listening to instructions.' Hastings blanched. Anne Robinson on *The Weakest Link* was never as disdainfully condescending as Colonel Willoughby in full cry. It was marvellous, a little remnant of empire.

We were there in the second week of January, and had travelled up to St Moritz by train from Zurich. The squeals of amazement had started almost immediately on departure from Zurich Airport. 'Wow!' 'I've never seen anything like it!' 'This is fantastic!' 'I can't believe it!' These squeals had nothing to do with snow,

I might add; Zurich didn't have any. Nor did they come from the children. It was Jane and me, rejoicing in the beauty of a fully functioning rail system. We had to change trains twice to get to St Moritz, and had anticipated this being no easy matter with three young kids, even though our three heavy cases were travelling separately, thanks to Switzerland's blessed Fly Luggage System (but then, what was our load compared with that of the Maharajah of Hyderabad, who once arrived in St Moritz with 500 trunks, 300 pieces of hand luggage, forty tuxedos and a suitcase full of ties?).

In fact, the clerk at the airport railway station made it a painless business, carefully explaining what time each train would arrive, how long we would have to effect the transfer, and from which platform the next one would leave. Jane and I could all too easily imagine an Edinburgh-bound Swiss tourist requesting similar help at Heathrow on a cold January day. 'Which platform at King's Cross, mate? You're having a laugh. And anyway, the east-coast line is in chaos. Wrong sort of snow.' Yet in Switzerland the trains followed the timetable to the second, and while I know that Swiss precision shouldn't ever come as a shock to an Englishman reared on a more haphazard approach to time-keeping, we were lost in admiration. We pulled into St Moritz station bang on schedule, four hours, ten minutes and forty-seven seconds later.

It was snowing heavily when we got there, and darkness had fallen. We were greeted on the platform by a chauffeur in a heavy woollen cape, who, to our delight, escorted us to a one-horse open sleigh. There had been no violence on board – except when two-year-old Jacob belted five-year-old Joseph with his toy kangaroo – but in many other respects I felt as if I'd stepped into the pages of *Murder on the Orient Express*. The scene as we clip-clopped through the streets was almost laughably evocative of pre-war glamour, and our arrival at Badrutt's Palace did nothing to diminish it. Almost as soon as we arrived I bumped into a monocle-wearing Englishman who in the heyday of Fleet Street had been a distinguished foreign correspondent, and whom I knew slightly. He remembered arriving at the Palace thirty-five years earlier, just behind Noël 'Mad Dogs and Englishmen' Coward, who was with his constant companion, Graham Payn, and startled the stiff Swiss receptionist by checking in as 'Mr and Mrs Noël Coward'.

We just missed out on a similar brush with fame; Claudia Schiffer had left the day before. But as at the Anassa in Cyprus, there was money to ogle, if not celebrity. In the vast lounge of the Palace I hardly saw a woman without a full-length mink coat, a facelift or a lapdog, and more often than not, all three. The men wielded caber-sized cigars. 'A lot of them are Russian mafia,' grumbled my foreign-correspondent friend. 'The clientele rather depends on who's got money this year.'

While doubtless true, it was an ineffably snobbish remark, rather implying that only Brits with old money deserved to stay at the Palace. It has to be said that the ritzier resorts in the Alps, not unlike Benidorm and Magaluf if with a different customer profile, do not necessarily showcase the best of the British on holiday. And by that I don't just mean braying sloanes patronizing the locals, or pissed-up, off-duty squaddies picking fights; sometimes you see more subtle but scarcely more attractive British traits.

In 2008 we had our first holiday in Switzerland since the trip to St Moritz, in a pretty ski resort called Arosa in which Germans were far more abundant than the British. It had not always been so. As far as we could tell we were the only Brits staying in a nice but not especially swanky hotel called the Valsana, but in the lobby there was a framed page from the *Arosa Winter Guide 1926–27*, written in English, in which the Valsana advertised itself as 'a leading English sport hotel (all south rooms with private loggia balconies facing the ice-rink)'.

All that week in Arosa we encountered only one other British family, at the foot of the Tschuggen Express, a leather-upholstered private monorail run by the Tschuggen Grand Hotel, the Valsana's much posher sister. There was nobody there except us and them waiting to board the monorail car, and they had three children who were roughly the same ages as ours. So naturally we made tentative conversational overtures, which were firmly, unequivocally rebuffed. Instead of risking a friendly chat with us, the parents kept looking pointedly at their kids and talked only to them. 'Are you OK, Jess?' 'Yes, why?' 'Because you look a bit cold.' If Jess had been as buttoned-up physically as her parents were socially, she would have been as warm as toast. It wasn't as though we craved their friendship or anything, but honestly, why are some middle-class Brits on holiday so damned uptight? All the other nationalities we met on the slopes positively radiated good cheer.

That said, in straining not to make this book overly critical of foreigners, I mustn't tilt too far in the opposite direction, by subjecting my own countryfolk to a collective character assassination. Unarguably, some things work better in the hands of the British than they do in the hands of anyone else, which obviously doesn't include trains, but I do think, just to pluck a random example, that we could have made a better job than the French of the European outpost of the Disney theme-park empire.

It's true that I might be a little jaundiced because my family's one and only visit to Euro Disney, or Disneyland Paris or however they currently style themselves, was a more or less unmitigated disaster, sullied by relentless rain and the shock of losing Joseph, then aged four, for ten minutes – a trauma compounded by the small but nightmarish detail that like 500 other kids under the age of ten he was wearing a plastic yellow poncho with a picture of Mickey Mouse on the back. Yet even had the trip been a success

I would have been deeply suspicious of every inanely grinning Goofy and Pluto and Minnie Mouse, knowing practically for sure that there was a surly Frenchman, or woman, beneath the mask. The reason Disney theme parks work best in the United States is because you just know that behind every inanely grinning Goofy and Pluto and Minnie is an inanely grinning Brad or Chuck or Mary-Sue. Yet here in the UK I do think we could have given it a really decent shot.

25

Phrasebooks, foreigners and Fucking Hell

One department in which we are unutterably and irredeemably bad, however, far worse than any other nationality, is language. I know one shouldn't generalize but here I think I can. The Brits make no concessions, no compromises. I have a friend who once sat at a table next to a female English tourist sipping coffee in a Madrid café, and overheard the woman saying to the waitress, with no evidence that she spoke anything other than Spanish, 'Can you just pop a bit of milk in here, love?'

It's not just people in the service industry who are expected to understand English, either, it's Italian peasants selling terracotta flowerpots by the roadside in Puglia, and Greek fishermen flogging their catch on the beach in Piraeus. Yet oddly, this arrogance has served us well. To return to the Alps, the writer Jerome K. Jerome once very percipiently pointed out that it was not the poet or painter or philosopher or even the mountaineer who carried

Anglo-Saxon cultural influences to practically every Alpine valley, but the English traveller, who, unable or unwilling to learn a single word of any language but his own, sallies confidently forth, purse in hand, through every mountain pass to every village. 'One may be shocked at his ignorance, annoyed at his stupidity, angry at his presumption,' wrote Jerome. 'But it is he that is Anglicising Europe.'

The British attitude to foreign lands, in Europe in particular, is nicely summed up by a story told by Jeremy Paxman in his absorbing book *The English: A Portrait of a People*. In 1836, Mrs Frances Trollope arrived in Calais and overheard a conversation between a young man making his first visit to France, and an experienced traveller. 'What a dreadful smell!' exclaimed the young man, burying his nose in his pocket handkerchief. 'It is the smell of the continent, sir,' replied his more worldly companion.

Paxman weaves this tale into his persuasive thesis that the geography of the world has been responsible not just for the histories of different peoples, but for their psychologies. 'Could Switzerland have maintained its amoral prosperity had it not been a land of mountains?' he asks, adding that 'the very absence of a geography for the Jews is what created Zionism, one of the most powerful ideologies of the 20th century'. And he concludes that the 'first profound influence upon the English is the fact that they live on an island'.

There can be no arguing with that; as an example of our island mentality Paxman also cites a famous headline from a 1957 edition of *The Times* – 'Heavy Fog in Channel: Continent Cut Off'. And of course the number of derogatory uses of the word French speaks volumes. Syphilis alone, down the centuries, has been euphemistically referred to as 'the French disease', 'French pox', 'French gout', 'French marbles' 'French aches', and 'receiving a

French compliment'. One way to avoid a French compliment was to wear a condom or 'French letter' (which in French, neatly enough, is 'une capote anglaise', just as their version of taking French leave, meaning to bunk off work without permission, is 'filer à l'anglaise'). The disdain travels in both directions across the Channel, except of course when the Continent is cut off by fog.

Clearly, it is our distinct geography that has helped to form our view of the French, what with them being so near, yet so foreign. But it is also that geography that has made inveterate travellers of us, indeed that has made us rather schizophrenic: no other nationality has turned the casual abuse of the French practically into a cornerstone of its language, yet no other nationality has travelled so enthusiastically and in such numbers to France, garnering so much enjoyment from French food and French wine.

Such is the paradox of the British on holiday, and not only in France. Moreover, Jerome K. Jerome was dead right about our incompetence or sheer laziness with languages. For every Brit who has made practical use of a phrasebook while on holiday, there must be ten more who, preferring to bluff things out in English, have mocked the whole concept of phrasebooks. There was once some sustained correspondence in the *Daily Telegraph* on this subject, readers writing in with their favourite examples of just how preposterous foreign languages are.

One woman recalled as a child having an Austrian governess (it takes a *Telegraph* reader to boast an education at the hands of an Austrian governess), who brought with her a phrasebook covering everything that a discombobulated traveller might need in several languages. This woman claimed to have tried to memorize, aged seven, the Hungarian for 'after my wife had fallen into the ravine, I stood looking down after her for a long time'. Another correspondent invoked the website 'Living in Indonesia', where there apparently appears the useful phrase 'Kuku-kuku kaki kakak kakek-ku kaku-kaku', meaning 'my grandfather's older brother's toenails are stiff'. Can this be true? I haven't checked. But, true or not, it eloquently expresses the British conviction that all other languages are inferior to our own, even those, like Italian, that are undeniably more pleasing on the ear.

Incidentally, if you want written confirmation that Italian is a more lyrical language than English, look no further than the description of a dish I once ordered in Sardinia. It was 'Crema tiepida di piselli con molluschi profumati alla menta', a series of words you can almost imagine whispering into the ear of a lover. Its English translation, by contrast, was 'Lukewarm green peas cream with molluscs flavoured with mint', not something you'd want to whisper into anyone's ear, least of all that of a lover.

And yet the conviction that English is the best of languages is one we all take on holiday, giggling uncontrollably when those well-meaning but hapless foreigners fluff their efforts at translating their own languages into English, and I can't honestly exclude myself. I was delighted, in a restaurant in La Clusaz in the French Alps a few years ago, to order 'The Piece of Beef With Big Salt and His Marrow Bone'. Poorly expressed in print, it was, of course, inexpressably delicious on the plate.

A friend of mine, Sally, recently sent me a whole load of examples of these clumsy or over-literal translations spotted down the years by British travellers abroad:

In a Bucharest hotel lobby: 'The lift is being fixed for the next day. During that time we regret that you will be unbearable'

In a Paris hotel lift: 'Please leave your values at the front desk'

In a Japanese hotel: 'You are invited to take advantage of the chambermaid'

In a hotel in an Austrian ski resort, a request 'Not to perambulate the corridors in the hours of repose in the boots of ascension'

On the menu of a Polish hotel: 'Salad a firm's own make; limpid red beet soup with cheesy dumplings in the form of a finger; roasted duck let loose; beef rashers beaten up in the country people's fashion'

On the door of a Moscow hotel room: 'If this is your first visit to the USSR, you are welcome to it'

At a Budapest zoo: 'Please do not feed the animals. If you have any suitable food, give it to the guard on duty'

And my favourite, from the brochure of a car-rental firm in Tokyo: 'When passenger of foot heave in sight, tootle the horn. Trumpet him melodiously at first, but if he still obstacles your passage then tootle him with vigor'.

Obviously, foreign holidaymakers in Britain are denied this kind of fun at our expense due to the overwhelming lack, apart from the odd desultory line of French or Spanish, of signs in any language but English. And yet there is no shortage of anecdotal evidence to suggest that Brits trying to speak the local lingo overseas make chumps of themselves every bit as much as foreigners misfiring in English. I love the word 'chump', by the way. It's very P. G. Wodehouse, and very English. Can anyone but an Englishman really be described, whatever the circumstances, as a chump? Can a Frenchman, or a Romanian, or a Kenyan, or even a Scot, be a chump? I think not. A fool, an idiot, a pillock, definitely. But chumps have to be English.

As for that anecdotal evidence, my old school friend Chris Taylor tells a nice story about a family holiday in France when he was in his teens. His father was driving, and Chris and his two sisters were trying to teach their dad some basic French. At the very least, they said, he ought to be able to ask for a full tank of petrol in French, the next time they stopped at a service station, which in those days were manned by pump attendants.

Mr Taylor agreed that this small bit of dialogue ought not to be beyond him, and for the next twenty miles he was intensively coached to say 'Plein d'essence, s'il vous plaît.' Over and over he rehearsed, refining every nuance of pronunciation, until finally a petrol station appeared. He pulled up beside the pump, and a few moments later the attendant loped out from the small shop, not quite with a beret on his head and string of onions around his neck but nevertheless, as Chris tells it now, looking like a cartoon Frenchman. Mr Taylor wound down his window. The attendant stood, waiting for his instructions. The children on the back seat stiffened, waiting for their dad to utter the first complete French sentence of his life. But at the very last second he lost his nerve, or half of it anyway. 'Fill her up, s'il vous plaît,' he said.

More often than not it is France that presents these linguistic booby traps. Another old friend, Johnny – although not the Johnny who missed a flight at Manchester Airport and ended up racing through the streets of Cairo on a camel, trying to catch up with his family – has a story about his father wandering round the streets of Boulogne in the early 1980s, trying to find the train station. Unlike Chris's dad, Johnny's dad felt confident that he knew a few words of French, and duly stopped a series of passers-by, asking them to direct him to 'la guerre'. Crucially, he confused the word for station – 'gare' – with the word for war – 'guerre' – and one can only imagine that the good folk of Boulogne assumed that they had a seriously befuddled Englishman on their hands, asking them, some decades after the Allied liberation, to point him towards the war.

As for my favourite story of an Englishman's linguistic inadequacy in France, it is told in full, unexpurgated detail in a book of mine called *The Pheasants' Revolt*, but let me at least repeat it in a nutshell here. And on the subject of nutshells, I might as well add another story I've related in a previous book, which shows that an Englishmen doesn't even have to step abroad to get his words wrong. When my father-in-law Bob was a mining engineer, he was once present at an interminable pitch, by an extremely verbose salesman, to the weary foreman of a South Yorkshire colliery. When the salesman finally came to the end of his monologue, he said, 'Reet, let me just put all that in a nutcase', to which the foreman tartly replied, 'Ah'm bloody nutcase, standing 'ere listening to thee.'

That favourite story of an Englishman all at sea with the French language concerns an acquaintance, to whom I'll give the pseudonym Dobber, not least because I once told this tale at a dinner at which Dobber and his wife were present, and Mrs D was none too impressed with me for so publicly poking fun at him. Anyway, here goes again. He was staying some years ago in a provincial pension and something he'd eaten had disagreed terribly with him, taking him back and forth to the loo all night. But on the umpteenth visit, to his utter horror, the flush malfunctioned, and the water cascaded out of the bowl on to the toilet floor, carrying with it – I'll put this as delicately as I can – Dobber's evacuations. Clearing up the very considerable mess was beyond him, so at first light he went to fetch *la patronne*, and made her understand that she should follow him back to his room.

In they went and Dobber, understandably mortified at the scene about to confront her, walked to the toilet door. He knew he ought to say something but could not even begin to articulate an apology in French, and the *patronne* spoke no English. So as he opened the door he produced the only two French words that seemed vaguely fitting. 'Voilà, madame!' he said.

I love that story for all kinds of reasons, but in the context of this book, it beautifully encapsulates – if beauty and diarrhoea can ever truly belong in the same anecdote – the challenges perennially facing the British on holiday. Problems on the loo and problems with the lingo; how many of us can honestly claim that we've never been there?

And let's just dwell awhile on that word 'lingo'. Does any other nationality have a slang word, smacking a little of imperialism and slightly pejorative, collectively meaning foreign languages? I doubt it, just as I doubt whether any other nationality revels quite so much as we do in the proper nouns that carry no ambiguity in their native land but mean something rude in English. Austria may well be the best place in the world for the phenomenon of chuckling British visitors taking photographs of signs, and once again I plead guilty myself. On my eventful InterRailing trip with Mark Sutcliffe in 1982, we were as thrilled as you can imagine two twenty-year-old Brits might be to walk round a corner in Innsbruck and there to be confronted with a large sign over a sporting-goods shop bearing the name of the owner, Robert Wanker. Did we take it in turns to pose outside Robert Wanker making suggestive gestures? Hell, yes.

And speaking of Hell, towards the end of March 2010 a priceless story about the Austrian town of Fucking, near Salzburg, appeared in the British press. Had it been published just a couple of days later, on the first day of the following month, I might have suspected its veracity, but apparently it was perfectly true that the

European Union had just given the thumbs-up for a new beer called Fucking Hell (the word 'Hell', when used in connection with beer, meaning light). The EU's Trade Marks and Designs Registration Office rejected an argument that the brand name Fucking Hell was 'upsetting and derogatory', and issued a frankly hilarous bit of bureaucracy-speak, insisting that the 'word combination contains no semantic indication that could refer to a certain person or group of persons. Nor does it incite a particular act. It cannot even be understood as an instruction that the reader should go to "hell". Neither can it be considered as reprehensible to use existing place names in a targeted manner, merely because this may have an ambiguous meaning in other languages.'

And with that solemn judgement the delicious prospect arose of a customer standing at the bar of a British pub, quite legitimately saying 'Half a Fucking shandy and a bag of dry roasted peanuts, please.' Maybe, even as you read this, Fucking Hell is already a fixture in the UK's pubs and bars. Whatever, it was not a development that the mayor of Fucking, Franz Meindl, welcomed back in the spring of 2010. A beer called Fucking Hell was actually the last thing his town needed, he said, after years of the signs bearing its unfortunate name disappearing from the streets. 'Twelve of the 13 signs have been stolen,' he told the *Independent*. 'We've taken to fixing them with concrete, welding and rivets.' Fucking typical, you might say. As of course is the theft of the signs in the first place. Typical, that is, of British holidaymakers not content with just a photograph to amuse their mates at home.

To paraphrase Queen Victoria, we are easily amused. Especially, I might add, in Austria, where even the cadences of speech are enough to tickle us. In April 2007 Jane, the children and I stayed at a lovely hotel in the village of St Christoph in the Austrian Alps called the Hospiz (a little disconcertingly close to 'hospice' but we overlooked that), where every night the owner, Florian Werner, toured the tables in the restaurant, asking if his guests were happy. We were impressed with his devotion to duty, and with his command of languages – he slipped effortlessly from German to French to English – but we couldn't help noticing that in English, Austrian hospitality and solicitousness came across as slightly challenging. 'Your dinner vos good!? The vine vos nice!?'

I think this is one of the reasons why so many Brits cannot quite overcome their suspicion that the Teutonic races are innately aggressive. Even if we can forgive the Germans in particular their predilection for invading other European countries, on the basis that it all happened rather a long time ago, there remains the problem that even when they're being perfectly friendly, they sound as though they're issuing you with an arrest warrant. Every week during the skiing season the Hospiz holds what it calls a Kuchenschmankerl party, when guests are encouraged to tour the kitchens. As we filed in, Herr Werner was standing to attention at the door popping a prawn into everyone's mouth, a curious hybrid of larkiness and formality. And when my son Joe, wearing a rather natty jumper, reached him, Herr Werner looked down and exclaimed 'Jesus Christ, zat's a nice pullover!' It was a wonderful example of a compliment that would doubtless have sounded fine in German, but jarred in English. I hardly need add that once we'd all left the Kuchenschmankerl party, and Joe told us what Herr Werner had said to him, we laughed until the tears trickled down our cheeks.

Whether it is our slight tendency to xenophobia or our fabled British sense of humour that makes us laugh at other languages and peoples without very much prompting, I'm not quite sure; I suppose it's a combination of the two. But we are not immune to this piss-taking ourselves. After all, there might only be one thing that the world scoffs at us for, but it is a big, important thing, and scoff is precisely the right word.

26

Escargots, España and El Quim

Food. Only the sun has given the British on holiday so much pleasure and yet so much trouble as food, although at least in the twenty-first century the inveterate British suspicion of such 'foreign' foodstuffs as garlic, as so eloquently expressed by the dyspeptic eighteenth-century Scotsman Tobias Smollett, has subsided. Mind you, I don't doubt that I still have some compatriots who travel to Spain and even France with cases crammed with Heinz baked beans and Fray Bentos pies. I myself, much as it pains me to admit it now, went to France for the first time in the summer of 1979 with a rucksack full of Golden Wonder's recently invented and much-acclaimed Pot Noodle.

These days, to travel overseas and not embrace the local eating culture seems to me downright irresponsible, but then again I've never been to those parts of the world where bulls' testicles and fish eyes are considered delicacies. That might bring me down off my high horse, which come to think of it might enable someone else to cook it. I should think you can get more than a few rump steaks out of a high horse.

In Europe, though, and especially in France, Italy and Spain, there's almost no excuse for not looking for the best of the local cuisine. We Brits understandably cling to the belief that the good Chinese restaurants in the UK are the ones with Chinese people eating in them, and yet east of Dover this rule often gets scrapped, if not actually turned on its head, with many holidaymakers actively seeking out the restaurants with a little Union Jack in the window, meaning that there will be a laminated menu in English with a blurry photograph of each dish and almost certainly a party from Milton Keynes in the corner. That's not my idea of a holiday experience, but sometimes you get suckered into it. Jane and I, on the first night of that weekend in Barcelona when I was robbed, rather naively followed the advice of our *Time Out* guidebook, and went to a restaurant in an old mansion designed by Antoni Gaudi, the father of the fantastical Modernisme style of architecture, which actually isn't my cup of English breakfast tea at all, although you've got to see at least one Gaudi building when you're in Barcelona. It's decreed by law.

Anyway, the place we went to was called Casa Calvet, and as soon as we arrived I knew we'd made a mistake. Because when a restaurant is in your guidebook, it is very likely in everyone else's as well. The place was full of tourists. And then we were shown into a section off the main dining-room, with a kind of burnished wooden wall like an old railway car, which was very charming and all that, but the only other couple in there were English, a couple in their sixties talking to each other in an almost reverential whisper, and resolutely avoiding eye contact with us, even though our table was no more than five feet away. We could have been in Horsham; I hated it.

I duly asked the waiter if we could move into the main dining-area – 'nothing personal,' Jane trilled cheerfully to the English couple as we went, but still they didn't demonstrate the slightest bit of friendliness, and in any case, it *was* personal – and there sat with a preppy American family on one side of us and a garrulous French trio on the other. This was a marginal improvement, but in Barcelona I wanted to be surrounded by Catalans. I paid the very hefty bill, resolving never again to make a guidebook the main source of advice of where to dine on a foreign holiday.

Happily, we got it right the next day, wandering round the frankly awe-inspiring food market near the Ramblas, the Boqueria, and on an impulse finding a couple of seats at one of the frantically busy counter-cafés in there, a place called El Quim, which incidentally meant that it also ticked the 'rude word in English' box – always a bonus. At El Quim we shared a plate of garlicky king prawns and another dish of baby squid stir-fried in garlic butter and heaped on top of two fried eggs, which had been cooked on a hot plate so sizzlingly hot that they puffed up in seconds. The waiter then slapped the plate down in front of us with a basket of bread and instructions – entertainingly conducted in mime – to mix the squid with the egg. I can barely describe how delicious it was, indeed I would include our mid-afternoon lunch at El Quim, along with my *poulet-frites* at a French motorway service station in 1979, among my ten most memorable meals of all time. For the record, and since nobody is ever likely to make me a respondent to a magazine questionnaire, and since this is my book and I'll do what I want to, here in no particular order, and feel free to skip them, are the other eight.

Lunch at Club 55, near St Tropez; again this was just Jane and me, unencumbered by our children, bless their cotton socks, digging in for a hedonistic three-hour lunch in one of the French Riviera's classic eating and drinking venues, on Pampelonne

Beach and supposedly created in 1955 when the film director Roger Vadim, while making *Et Dieu Crea La Femme* with the nubile Brigitte Bardot, asked the owners of a shack selling coffee and sandwiches if they could cater for his crew. It's still a movie stars' hangout, but the only celebrity we spotted was Richard Branson, who very coolly arrived directly from the sea, like Ursula Andress in *Dr No*, but without the cleavage.

Breakfast at the Mandarin Oriental, Columbus Circle, New York; it was my birthday, during October half-term 2006, and we'd taken the kids to Manhattan for the first time. We were staying in a friend's apartment, and wanted to give the children a posh hotel-breakfast experience, but they were quite young and I warned them beforehand to be on their best behaviour, not to attract undue attention. Moments later, Eleanor knocked over her cup of hot chocolate and in rocking back to avoid the cascade of steaming liquid, I overbalanced on my chair and fell flat on my back, kicking half the crockery and cutlery off the table as I went over. As an exercise in drawing attention, I couldn't have done a better job if I'd streaked around the room singing 'New York, New York'. But as a family we remember it with great affection and, albeit at my expense, mirth.

Dinner at Dar El Djed in Tunis; an Ottoman mansion in the heart of the medina, with an intricately beautiful interior of mosaic floors and carved doorways, sensational food, and a sweet custom of splashing rose water on your hands as you depart.

Lunch at the Seafood Restaurant, Padstow; Rick Stein's flagship is one of my favourite restaurants in the world, and I won't listen to anyone who considers it overpriced or overrated. We used to go once for dinner during our summer holidays in Cornwall, but memorably took the kids for lunch one year when, reckoning that we might be better off at a time of year when we had zero expectations of good weather, instead of that perennial glimmer of hope in the August drizzle that 'it seems to be getting brighter on the horizon', we spent February half-term in Cornwall. Anyway, as a starter we slowly motored through one of those huge platters of 'fruits de mer', which the kids loved. They were very animated throughout the meal, in fact, and Jane and I braced ourselves when a couple who'd been sitting at a neighbouring table got up to leave and made their way over to us. 'Excuse me,' the woman said, 'but we'd just like to say how marvellous your children have been. They've been so chatty, and have enjoyed their food so much, it's been a real pleasure for us to watch you.' Well! We very nearly burst with pride.

Dinner on a boat just off Tortola in the British Virgin Islands; a fantastic meal catered by the girlfriend of the young skipper, as our yacht bobbed on a moonlit Caribbean bay. And all made even more memorable when one of my companions, Julie, a wonderful and indomitable Scottish woman in late-ish middle age, unveiled her prodigious but by us hitherto unrecognized talent for singing, and serenaded us with a version of 'Moon River' that Ella Fitzgerald herself might have envied.

Lunch in Bari, Puglia; Jane and me on another of our occasional escapes from childcare responsibilities, stopping off in Bari, a bustling port on the heel of Italy, on our way to the airport, and coming across what looked like a makeshift restaurant in an alley, with people's washing festooned overhead and a couple of Vespas parked among the tables. Several of the tables had been joined together to make one long one, at which were seated eighteen fishermen, almost certainly just off the morning boat, and all but singing Italian fishing shanties. Had Marcello Mastroianni or possibly Gina Lollobrigida appeared to take our order, we wouldn't have been the slightest bit surprised. Well, maybe only slightly surprised. And the grub, of course, was simple yet magnificent.

Lunch on the terrace of a mountain restaurant, Serre Chevalier,

France; this was one of those long indulgent lunches that you take slightly for granted before you have children, though we treasured this one, because we stopped for coffee at 10.45 a.m. intending to ski on until lunch, but coffee led to the day's first bottle of wine which slid imperceptibly into the next bottle, until we realized that the sun had moved half-way round the sky, and it was almost evening.

Jane and I don't remember the food, but the occasion remains dear to our hearts, not least because my old university friend Mike Hodgson told us a long story we still cherish, about his travails as a ten-year-old pupil on a French exchange trip. On which subject, I'd like to add a favourite recent story of a French exchange, concerning our friends Jane and James, and their thirteen-year-old son Jack, who was despatched to a home near Grenoble for a week. After a couple of days, they still hadn't heard from Jack, although they took this to be a sign that everything was fine, and knew already that the French mum was a nurturing type because before Jack left they'd received an e-mail asking 'What does it eat for its breakfast?' Wisely, they had ascribed this to Madame's slightly shaky English, rather than any inclination to regard the teenage *Anglais* as inanimate or inhuman.

Dinner in a tent in Arvidsjaur, close to the Arctic Circle in Sweden; I went on my own one February, in search of the northern lights and also to play one of the understandably few golf courses in the world made from snow, which I did, with a reindeer caddie. The dinner was hosted by the town's mayor, who was excited that a British journalist was visiting, and arranged for me to be taken on a sledge pulled by reindeer across a frozen lake to a tent made from reindeer skin where we ate a dinner of reindeer meat cooked and cured eight different ways, accompanied by a ferocious alcoholic drink of vivid yellow that was almost certainly fermented reindeer piss.

But whatever it was, the point is that I very much doubt whether I'm alone in identifying the ten most memorable meals of my life as holiday meals. For all the many enjoyable mealtime occasions I've had in the UK, dinner, lunch and tea parties, birthdays, Christmases and New Year's Eves tend to merge into one, whereas holiday meals stay distinct in the mind for one or more of all kinds of reasons; the location, the companionship, the unexpectedness, the weather, and of course, the food.

Sometimes, it should be said, all these factors can fall into place except the food. In August 2009, while holidaying in the Languedoc, we met up with our dear friends Alison and Chris and their kids, who were staying a couple of hours away from us. About equidistant between our villa and theirs was a little seaside town called Mèze, and that's where we met, spending an entertaining afternoon on the beach – the afternoon, indeed, of the pasty Yorkshire family's 'I'm not looking for t' bloody water!' exchange – before finding a likely-looking harbourside restaurant for an early dinner. There, Chris and I, fearless gourmands that we considered ourselves to be, ordered 'escargots de mer'. What kind of crustaceans these were I'm still not sure, but the really disconcerting thing was that they were served cold to the point of being semi-frozen.

I summoned the waitress. 'These are cold, almost frozen,' I said in my best French. She looked at me with the pitying smile that pleasant French people reserve for the British (the rest of them register contempt) and said 'C'est normal', meaning 'I don't know what kind of *escargots de mer* you eat where you come from, pal, but if you're going to eat them here, you really ought to fall in with the rest of us'. Either that or it was a huge practical joke, and the kitchen staff were all peeping through the swing doors to watch 'les deux idiots Anglais' tuck into shellfish that they'd been effortlessly fooled into thinking were actually meant to be frozen almost solid. Whatever the truth of the matter, the *escargots de mer* looked and tasted like those grey rubber stoppers for wine bottles, or like those grey rubber stoppers might taste after an hour in the freezer. 'C'était bon?' asked the waitress, collecting the plates. 'Oui, c'était tres bon,' I said, neither my French nor my gastronomic confidence being up to essaying, 'Actually, they were fucking revolting and I rather suspect you were having us on, love.'

A disappointing meal in France or Italy especially is so much more of a letdown than a disappointing meal in Britain, which I suppose is the flip side to a marvellous meal being that much more marvellous. But of course we no longer just eat in restaurants on foreign holidays; for four decades or so, ever since the self-catering trend began, we shop for food as well, and for me this is where the real pleasure of a holiday lies. In fact Jane and I have decided that we suffer from a quantifiable syndrome: market envy.

I love foreign markets. I love the look and smell and glorious unfamiliarity of them, and I have hung out in some of the world's best: in Tunis and Marrakech, San Francisco and New York, Paris and Barcelona. At their best, or to be frank, even at their most mediocre, they are enough to make a British consumer weep with frustration at the pathetic fare we are served here. I don't just mean those dismal small-town markets where the fruit and veg stall stands between a stall selling knock-off batteries and another offering ten pairs of socks for a fiver, I mean even our nice English farmers' markets. I've put in the hours at Borough Market in London, the shrine where British so-called foodies go to genuflect, but by comparison with an average Saturday morning in the Boqueria in Barcelona, for example, we're mere novices at buying and selling food. Any one of the half-dozen or so fish counters at the Boqueria is 100 times more impressive than any fishmonger's spread in Britain, and you know how remarkably fresh it all is not least because most of it is still twitching.

Mind you, on this subject I should quote our old friend Dr Jane Wilson-Howarth, who advises the readers of *Bugs, Bites and Bowels* to beware a delicacy in the Philippines called 'jumping salad', containing shrimps so fresh they are still moving. 'This', she points out, 'can give you capillariasis, a worm infestation that debilitates locals who cannot seek a cure'. She helpfully adds that 'shellfish are efficient concentrators of faecal bacteria (including cholera), so should only be eaten if you can be sure they were caught far from sewage outfall'. In other words, unless you have a Spanish or Italian or for that matter Filipino phrasebook enabling you to say to a foreign fishmonger, 'Excuse me, can you guarantee that this prawn was caught far from sewage outfall?' you should probably steer clear.

All of which brings me back to the default setting of the British on holiday, which is suspicion and sometimes downright fear of that 'foreign muck', with a commensurate yearning for all that is familiar. That suspicion has eased slightly in recent decades with the proliferation of foreign restaurants in the UK. For example, if you lived in the provinces in 1970s, or probably 1980, possibly even 1990, the chances were that you would have sampled Greek food only if you'd been lucky enough to go to Greece, or maybe London. The same applied, if not so much to French, Italian, Indian and Chinese, then certainly to Spanish, Mexican, Turkish, North African and Middle Eastern food. Our tastes are more cosmopolitan now, but still we seek the comforts of home.

In his book *Welcome to Everytown: A Journey into the English Mind*, Julian Baggini recalls his visit to Cala d'Or in Mallorca, where there is a pub called the Tartan Arms, offering quiz nights every night except when it's bingo night or race night. 'I ordered a pint of John Smith's and sat at the bar,' Baggini wrote. 'I had come all the way to Spain to hole up in a corner of Britain.' And that's the point. A cliché greatly beloved of Brits on holiday in Britain is this: if the weather were better here, why would anyone bother going abroad? I could offer plenty of reasons, but for more of us than we perhaps care to admit, that conundrum is solved by places like the Tartan Arms.

27

Cruising, crooning and carved elephants

Another reliable way of escaping the uncertainty of the British weather but indulging yourself with familiar comforts is to take a holiday with a British, or British-based, cruise line. Cruises have been popular with the British ever since dear old Thomas Cook started offering trips up the Nile in 1869. Yet I confess that there is no easy way to persuade me to take a cruise, short of dragging me kicking and screaming up the gangplank, and fortunately Jane feels the same. In fairness, though, most of the people we know who have taken cruises have come back full of enthusiasm, even those who went as sceptics.

I don't know why I remain so opposed to the idea. Maybe I've simply sat in too many bars in too many ports around the world, watching cruise ships disgorging hundreds of passengers on to the quayside. It is never a pretty sight: acres of Hawaiian shirt, acres of wobbling, mottled flesh, and that's just Chuck and Cindy from Topeka, Kansas.

As for the cruising Brits, a disproportionate number of them seem to come from the north of England. Not that there's anything wrong with that; so do I. But Jane and I were once in Sorrento on the lovely Amalfi coast when a cruise ship anchored in the harbour, and within about an hour the streets were crammed with people who sounded like extras on *Emmerdale*. In fact as we walked along one of the shopping streets just off the main Piazza Tasso we passed a couple of women who were marvelling that it was 'just like t' Shambles in York'. Which to them, I might add, was unequivocally a good thing. The Brits like to be reminded of home, which might also be why we're so bad at haggling even in those countries where it is expected of us: haggling with a wizened old man selling pots in the souk in Marrakech simply doesn't play to British sensibilities. It's certainly not how they do things down the Shambles in York.

As evidence for this, let me cite our friends Jane and James again, or at least Jane's brother Bill. In July 2010 they were all on holiday together in Kalkan in Turkey, as coincidentally were we, and we met up one evening to be told about Bill's frankly feeble attempt at haggling over a shirt. It was on sale for 27 Turkish lire, so he, knowing he was expected to haggle, hesitantly suggested 20. The shopkeeper, clearly knowing a rubbish haggler when he saw one, countered with 30 lire, three more than the price on the tag. 'OK, let's make it 27,' said Bill, not wanting the embarrassment to go on any longer, a peculiarly British neurosis.

Still, at least those day-trippers from the cruise ships have conquered another British neurosis; the fear of looking too much like a tourist. I think that's one of the reasons I can't ever seeing myself doing it; I would feel, every time I stepped ashore, as if I had 'another sucker from the cruise ship' tattooed on my forehead, in the appropriate language. And that of course is my problem, nobody else's.

Occasionally, though, I have spoken to people who have confirmed all my prejudices about cruising. One of them was a woman called Natasha, a fellow northerner, who was once forced to take a cruise with her fiancé and most of his extended family, in lavish celebration of his parents' thirty-fifth wedding anniversary. Hearing her story made my toes curl. It was a ten-day cruise of the Mediterranean and Natasha described it – without too much hyperbole, I'm sure – as 'a living hell'. For one thing, she had a vomiting bug for twenty-four hours, although at least it got her out of playing bingo with her fiancé's wheelchair-bound grandmother. Actually, though, bingo was the least of grandma's enthusiasms. Before the cruise the old girl had been seriously ill and it seemed unlikely that she would survive, let alone get to cross off two fat ladies on her bingo card. But she did make it, albeit in a worryingly fragile state. The family were worried that grandma might actually snuff it on board, yet as soon as they wheeled her into the casino she miraculously seemed to find a new lease of life. Apparently it was a truly remarkable spectacle. Grandma, who spent most of her time slumped under a rug, would sit at the roulette table practically leaping out of her wheelchair to place her chips. Later, they discovered that the ship's crew pumped the casino with extra oxygen to stop tired punters heading off to bed. It was just what grandma needed.

Another cruise story, toe-curling for different reasons, was told to me by the Scottish singer-songwriter Jackie Leven, whose agent, in 2002, booked him a gig as the main entertainment on a two-week cruise of the Norwegian fjords, with the Norwegian company Hurtigruten. Jackie had serious misgivings about this; his repertoire is strictly limited to his own rather poignant material and he's not the man to cover even an Elvis Costello song, let alone Dean Martin's 'Amore'. Jane McDonald he most definitely isn't. But the money was good and two weeks on a cruise ship at someone else's expense didn't seem like such a terrible idea.

The ship duly set off from Bergen, and the entertainments officer, a friendly Norwegian woman, asked Jackie to perform on that first night in the main bar. He sang three of his songs and was just about to embark on a fourth, when a big Englishman in his late sixties walked purposefully towards the stage. 'Can I have a word?' the English guy said.

'Sure,' said Jackie.

'You see that table over there,' said the man, jerking an agricultural thumb towards a large group of mostly glowering Lancastrians. 'Well, they're all my friends, and we've all saved up for years to come on this cruise. You see that woman on the left. Well, that's my wife. And I've come up here to tell you that you're depressing the living shit out of us. Now, we're going to be in this bar most nights. And if we hear one more song from you, I'm going to fuckin' lamp yer. Is that fuckin' understood?'

Jackie said wryly that he would pass this information on to the entertainments officer, whereupon the man moved a few inches closer. 'One more fuckin' note, and I'll fuckin' lamp yer,' he said. 'And in particular, don't ever, ever sing "My Way".'

There had never been much chance of that, but Jackie sensibly stopped his set right there, and sought out the entertainments officer. She listened sympathetically.

'I think all you can do', she said, 'is not play. It is one of these things. We will pay you what we agreed, but I suggest that you just relax and enjoy the cruise.'

Jackie said that he was uncomfortable with this solution; he didn't like the idea of being paid when he was not fulfilling the contract. So in the circumstances, wouldn't it be better for everyone if he left the ship at Trondheim, the next port?

'No,' said the ents officer. 'You must stay and I'll tell you why.

We very often get English groups like this, and always they get drunk, fall out and stop speaking to each other. Then the weather gets bad, and many of them leave the cruise at Hammerfest. I think this will happen again.'

Unfortunately, it didn't. The glowering Lancastrians got drunk and fell out but they didn't leave, and Jackie didn't play. 'Fortunately,' he told me, 'I'd just discovered the novels of Carl Hiaasen, so I worked my way through all of them, and shared a dinner table with a really charming bunch of German twitchers, who only wanted to talk about the wildlife they'd seen that day. I kept passing the English guy and his friends on board, but they didn't say anything; there was just this kind of menacing low-level rumble.'

Finally the cruise got back to Bergen, and they started to disembark. But as they walked down the gangplank, Jackie found himself just behind his nemesis, and couldn't resist crooning 'Regrets, I've had a few, but then again, too few to mention . . .'

The man spun round. 'I fuckin' told you,' he growled, but Jackie interrupted him. 'No, this time I'm telling you,' he said, evenly. 'You had your say and I did as you asked, but we're off the ship now, I'm no longer an employee and you're no longer a passenger, so I'm not beholden to you any longer. And if I see you again, I'll be the one fucking lamping you. Is that understood?'

It was a classic case of the bully bullied. The man fell instantly silent, his aggression disappearing as if he had been injected with some kind of meekness serum. And that was that, a funny but also dispiriting story. The way Jackie tells it, most of the passengers were either British or German and there was an extraordinarily stark contrast between them: the Brits, on the whole, were boorish, argumentative and more interested in getting drunk than seeing dolphins, a type the entertainments officer clearly recognized from past experience, whereas the Germans were educated, cultured and genteel.

Needless to add, I don't present this as a portrait of two nations. I think we all know that the Germans have been better at picking arguments than almost anyone else over the past 100 years or so. And the British on holiday can give anyone a run for their money on the culture and gentility front; indeed, I have another friend, also a musician, who has worked on a British-run cruise which was themed on the operettas of Gilbert and Sullivan. By day, over two rollicking weeks on the high seas, academics gave lectures on the lives and times of W. S. Gilbert, Arthur Sullivan, and other prominent Victorians. And by night a theatrical company performed *The Mikado*, *Pirates of Penzance* and *HMS Pinafore*. The audience, almost all British and almost all attired in period dress, were encouraged to join in with the songs, which they did with word-perfect enthusiasm. The irate Lancastrian warning the Lord High Executioner of Titipu that if he sang one more word he'd get fuckin' lamped, was of course conspiciously absent. Suffice to say that blithe generalizations cannot be made about British passengers on cruise ships (except that they're always from the north of England), any more than they can be made about the British in general on their holidays.

On the other hand, what a joyless world it would be without sweeping generalizations and casual stereotyping, and I do think the British, for reasons already outlined in this book, are more temperamentally disposed than many other nationalities to take holidays on which eating, drinking, entertainment and childcare choices are presented on a platter, perhaps garnished with a couple of slices of orange. This is why Billy Butlin, Fred Pontin and later Center Parcs had so much success in the UK, and it also explains the popularity of companies such as Mark Warner that have applied the cruise-ship ethos to land.

The protoype of the all-inclusive resort, however, was the brainchild of a Jew from Antwerp, a counterblast to those of us who enjoy the sweeping generalization that Belgium is a singularly boring and unproductive country. In 1950 Gérard Blitz, an international water polo player, founded the first Club Méditerranée in Mallorca, having been inspired by a stay at the Club Olympique in Corsica, the very place where Vladimir Raitz, just months earlier, had got his idea for package holidays to the sun. Club Méditerranée was a mouthful, but Club Med, as it quickly and necessarily became, was a wonderful name, evocative of sunshine and fun; the resorts soon proliferated and other entrepreneurs, enjoying Richard Branson's old dictum that it is better to follow a pioneer than to be a pioneer, adapted the idea.

In 1970, for example, the Italian-born Charles Forte, who had rather brilliantly parlayed the experience of working in his family's café in Weston-super-Mare into a vast hotel and catering empire, founded a Club Med-style resort in Sardinia and with characteristic humility called it the Forte Village. It's a beautiful place. In recent years we have had two hugely enjoyable family holidays there, but in terms of acquiring a deep and meaningful experience of Sardinia, we might just as well have eaten a plate of sardines.

On both occasions, we saw nothing of the island except what flashed past our taxi window between the airport in Cagliari and the Forte Village some forty-five minutes away, and in truth that wasn't particularly inspiring, embracing a few industrial lagoons and the kind of colossal factory plant in which Mediterranean countries seem to specialize when you're on your way to your holiday destination. Once we were inside the bougainvillea-covered walls of the Forte Village, we didn't step beyond them until it was time to go home: for a week we did nothing except swim, sunbathe, sleep, read, play tennis, football and water sports, and of course eat and drink copiously, once we had made the tough decision concerning which of the umpteen restaurants we were going to patronize that day. It was fantastic, but essentially we could have been anywhere under the Mediterranean or for that matter the Caribbean sun, a fact which bothered neither us nor our fellow guests, who on our first holiday there were overwhelmingly British.

The nationality of the Forte Village clientele varies from month to month. We first went during May half-term back in the UK, but returned the following year at the height of summer to find the number of British equalled if not surpassed by Italians and Russians. I don't suppose it bothered them any more than it did us that they went home having made only the most fleeting acquaintance with Sardinia the island.

For all we had in common with our foreign neighbours on the sunbeds, though, the Brits were easy to spot. I don't mean that they were paler or pastier than anyone else, although plenty were. What I mean is that we British on holiday, while not one homogenous bunch, sometimes wear our nationality like a badge.

I noticed it especially on the beach, which was patrolled, like so many other beaches in the Med, by those African guys relentlessly and unsuccessfully trying to sell watches, hats, balls and sunglasses, or even fake Gucci handbags and small carved elephants. I spent an enthralling hour one morning, studying the responses they got, as they stopped, ever hopeful, at each sunbed. The Italians waved them away with an almost imperceptible shake of the head, the Russians ignored them completely, as did the French. The Germans issued a sharp 'No' or 'Non' or 'Nein', and so did the Dutch and Scandinavians. But the Brits, practically without exception, said 'No, thank you.' Not 'Non grazie' – that would have been too much to expect – but still, it made me feel distinctly proud to be British, and my pride was compounded by affection when, back in the main swimming pool, I watched one of the exercise classes, run by a wiry young Italian woman in a leopardskin-effect bikini who spoke hardly any English, but whose five or six punters were all middle-class, middle-aged and not at all wiry British mums.

She was putting them through their paces in the water, while next to her on the side of the pool a speaker blared out a rap song that was obviously intended to energize them, but the lyrics, to say the least, were unfortunate. 'SHUT, SHUT, SHUT THE FUCK UP … SHUT, SHUT, SHUT THE FUCK UP … SHUT, SHUT, SHUT THE FUCK UP', went the song, at full throbbing volume, and as I watched these women trying to suppress giggles, and trying to raise one leg to the horizontal, neither with very much success, I reflected that, really, I wouldn't want to be part of any other tribe.

Epilogue

What now, in the second decade of the twenty-first century, for the great British holiday? In many ways its future is reassuringly rooted in its past: the British seaside, so popular from the late nineteenth century right up until the package-holiday boom of the 1960s and 1970s, is enjoying something of a revival. Those resorts that looked so shabby and melancholy when they were forsaken in favour of Greece and the Costa del Sol are being scrubbed up again, acquiring arts festivals and Michelin-starred restaurants. Nothing can be done about the horribly unpredictable British climate, of course, but even so, all the available evidence shows that we are favouring our own country for our holidays in numbers that haven't been known for decades. In 2009, visits abroad by UK residents fell at the fastest rate since the 1970s. That year, according to the Office for National Statistics, we made 58.6 million trips overseas, which sounds like a lot, yet there were 69 million the year before, and that was down from 2007.

It's debatable whether anxieties about carbon footprints are greatly influencing this decline; it's surely much more to do with a crisis of economics than a crisis of conscience. Nevertheless, sustainable tourism, or eco-tourism, is a significantly growing market. And for those with time and money, the world is their sustainably fished oyster. In November 2010 it cost £1745 a head, excluding flights, for a five-week scuba-diving trip to the Seychelles, not for your own indulgence but to join a scientific research team, collecting data on coral and counting whale sharks, turtles, octopus and lobster. Or for £900 excluding flights you can, at the time of writing, go to Peru and help build shelters for street children deliberately 'lost' by their parents, who can no longer afford to care for them. Or for £425, excluding flights, you can spend a week at a wildlife rescue centre in Tha Ling, Thailand, helping to walk, bathe, feed and water elephants.

Many such trips are offered by small independent tour operators, more than 300 of which have signed up with a central marketing operation called responsibletravel.com, which brings us back to the internet, for if any one phenomenon has changed the way we British choose our holidays, it is the remarkable world wide web (invented, like the jet engine, by one of our own, Sir Tim Berners-Lee). These days, there is no kind of bespoke holiday that you can't find for yourself at the click of a mouse, and as an antidote to all the jolly family holidays I have written about in this book, let me mention just a few of the websites for people wanting, or compelled, to holiday on their own. A website called JustYou puts solo travellers together in groups of up to thirty; the splendidly named www.thelmaandlouise.com helps lone women find female travelling companions; another website called i-to-i even offers single people a companionship and eco-tourism combo, putting together trips for like-minded 'voluntourists' to teach English in the Himalayas.

I suppose it's possible that, as with the drift from CDs back to vinyl, holidaymakers will in the future take their needs back to high-street travel agents. Possible, but highly unlikely. There will always be a place for specialist tour operators, of course, but the internet tends to be the place to find them, and will become increasingly influential in determining the form of the great British holiday, especially when you consider that by the 2020s every sentient British adult will have grown up with computers. Even the over-sixties (of which I will be one) will be fully computer-literate.

Will I, however, ever be able to sit at my keyboard arranging a holiday in space? In 2011 space tourism is still one of the great imponderables, with just about all of us currently priced right out of the market. As I write, only the Russian Space Agency offers commercial flights beyond the earth's atmosphere, and the cost of a trip aboard a Soyuz spacecraft is reportedly in the region of $25 million. Inevitably, this price will tumble; maybe last-minute.com will one day offer a week of planetary orbiting for £499 per person, inclusive of flight, obviously, plus bed and freeze-dried breakfast. And just as inevitably, British vision and expertise will find a way of getting in on the act. Just as we pioneered many of the world's great sports – football, cricket, rugby, golf, tennis – so we Brits, from Thomas Cook to Richard Branson, have effected many of the great improvements in the holiday experience, and I don't see why space travel should be any different. Maybe an offshoot of Ryanair – Ryannoair – will run trips to the moon from Stansted, sounding their triumphant trumpets when they touch down on time at the Sea of Tranquility. And maybe, it has to be said, not. The single incontestable truth is that nobody really knows what the British will do for their holidays a century from now, but I like to think that the families heading off for a fortnight in 2111 will have fathers repeatedly patting their pockets to check that the passports are there, children repeatedly asking 'Are we there yet?', and a three-mile line of traffic stuck behind a caravan being towed by an elderly man in an ancient Triumph Dolomite, remarking to his wife that the road seems miraculously clear.

Acknowledgements

In writing this book I relied on a great number of sources, from other books and newspaper articles, to the anecdotes and reminiscences of relatives and friends. I also had some invaluable help with research from Tom Kennedy and Jim Mariner. I thank them, and also my mates in the travel industry, Stephen Bent and Frank Kenyon-Slaney, for passing on a few juicy trade secrets.

Further thanks must go to Jane and James Clayton, Stuart Fletcher, Ian Broome, Becky Rumsey, Sally Oosthoek, Jonny Lea, Jackie Leven, Ali Shurden, Rosie Alexander, Ali Couch, Wally Vellacott and the staff of the Treglos Hotel, Mark Johnson, Kim and Will Staniland, Mike King, Anne and Bob Sanderson, and Deborah Joseph. If I have misquoted them, misunderstood them, or in any unwitting way denigrated them, I offer my heartfelt apologies. If I have failed to mention others, I'm sorry. Any errors of omission or fact in this book, or lapses of taste, are all mine.

As for the various journalists and authors whose work I have plundered, I think they are all credited in the text. If not, I apologise.

My editor at Simon & Schuster, Mike Jones, has been highly supportive throughout the writing process, and a particular thank-you too to Rory Scarfe, plus everyone else at Simon & Schuster involved with this project. My splendid former literary agent, Camilla Hornby, chose while I was writing the book - coincidentally, I hope - to leave the publishing scene behind for a rural idyll in Somerset; I wish her all the luck in the world. I also thank my new agent, Andrew Gordon, for his unfailingly wise counsel.

Finally, and as always, I thank my beloved wife Jane, and children Eleanor, Joseph and Jacob, for their love and support, and in this instance for permitting me to embarrass them with stories of our family holidays.

Brian Viner, Herefordshire
December 2010